POWER

FOR DAILY LIVING

365 DAILY DEVOTIONS

Dr. Jack Graham

POWER
FOR DAILY
LIVING

Dr. Jack Graham

POWER
POINT.

With Jack Graham

P.O. Box 262627
Plano, TX 75026
1-800-414-7693 (1-800-414-POWER)
jgraham@powerpoint.org
jackgraham.org

Published by DUNHAM BOOKS
Copyright © 2006 by Dr. Jack Graham and
PowerPoint® Ministries
Published 2006

ISBN-13: 978-0-9787116-4-1
ISBN-10: 0-9787116-4-5

Unless otherwise indicated, Scripture verses
quoted are taken with permission from the
English Standard Version.

Cover design by: Michael Holter Creative

For more information:
DUNHAM BOOKS
15455 Dallas Parkway, Sixth Floor
Addison, TX 75001
dunhambooks.com

FOREWORD

Hebrews 4:12 tells us, "For the word of God is *living and active*, sharper than any two-edged sword, piercing to the division of soul and of spirit, of joints and of marrow, and discerning the thoughts and intentions of the heart" (italics added).

The Word of God is alive! Its truth is able to energize, encourage, and empower you. Yet with the breakneck speed of life, it is hard to have a consistent time in the Word each day...and as a result, I find Christians struggling, drained, and sapped of spiritual energy instead of feeling energized and excited!

If this describes you today, then this devotional book is for you.

On each page you'll find a short passage of Scripture and a clear, concise application of the truth contained in that particular passage. And because God's Word is alive, I would encourage you to approach each day's Bible reading like you would any other relationship—expectantly, enthusiastically, and energetically!

Then I would challenge you not only to read the daily passage, but to make it a focus of your heart and mind throughout the day. Meditate on it. Take time to think carefully about the truth we discuss that day. Ask God to speak to your heart...and to help you apply that truth to your life.

If you will consistently do this, you'll begin to see things in God's Word that you've never seen before...God will reveal things to you in a brand new light....and you will begin to experience life with the power, energy, and excitement that God intends for you to have!

Jack Graham
Plano, Texas

Day 1

I press on toward the goal for the prize of the upward call of God in Christ Jesus.

—Philippians 3:14

The day you and I, as believers, come face to face with Jesus in heaven will be glorious. There is great hope in what's to come if you know Jesus personally. In fact, we are to pray for His coming every day and should live as though His return will come at any second.

Friend, it's so important to remember that we are just passing through this life. As the Scripture says, life "is…a vapor that appears for a little time and then vanishes away."

You may be going through a difficult situation in life right now. Maybe you're struggling with divorce…the loss of a loved one…or perhaps you're desperate to regain control of your finances.

Whatever it is, it is my prayer that you will stay strong in Christ. And remember that you have the hope of spending eternity with Jesus—without pain and full of joy—if you are a believer in Him.

Until the day you meet Jesus in heaven, push forward in sharing Him with others and following Him passionately in every aspect of your life!

LIFE "IS…A VAPOR THAT APPEARS FOR A LITTLE TIME AND THEN VANISHES AWAY." SO LIVE A LIFE THAT'S PASSIONATE FOR CHRIST!

Day 2

Give thanks in all circumstances; for this is the will of God in Christ Jesus for you.

—1 Thessalonians 5:18

It's very easy to complain about what we don't have...or how bad things are in our lives...instead of being thankful for what we do have.

Let me ask you, how many times a day do you thank God for the blessings in your life or the assurance of eternity you have with Him?

And—by contrast—how many times do you complain about what's wrong in your life and what you wish you had?

Do the math! I think—if you're honest—the results will surprise you.

God gives us specific directions on how we are to live:

First, live with an expectant attitude. Are you living as if Jesus could return today? Live every moment anticipating His arrival.

Second, live with a grateful heart. Every day, carry with you an attitude of gratitude and praise.

Third, live with a sober, serious mind. Remember that there are people in your life who still don't know Jesus. Live your life in such a way that they will want to know Him.

Finally, live with a confident hope. If you're a believer, live your life knowing that your future is secure!

OUR LIVES SHOULD BE MARKED BY A GRATEFUL SPIRIT, NO MATTER WHAT OUR SITUATION MAY BE.

Day 3

Now faith is the assurance of things hoped for, the conviction of things not seen. For by it the people of old received their commendation. By faith we understand that the universe was created by the word of God, so that what is seen was not made out of things that are visible.

—Hebrews 11:1-3

I truly believe that faith is a must-have when walking daily with the Lord. The Bible says that "without faith it is impossible to please Him, for he who comes to God must believe that He is, and that He is a rewarder of those who diligently seek Him" (Hebrews 11:6).

Ask yourself right now…

Do I worry about how I'm going to pay next month's bills? Or do I trust that God will take care of me?

Do I stress over difficult situations…trying to work them out on my own? Or do I have faith that God will work all things together for my good?

Do I rely on my own judgment and planning? Or do I have faith that God will provide the wisdom I need to proceed in making decisions?

True faith can only come from a personal relationship with Jesus. And that relationship can only be deepened by spending time each day in His Word.

Faith is like a muscle: the more you exercise it, the stronger it becomes. Faith isn't feelings or emotions. Faith is believing that God will do what He says He will do as stated in His Word.

GOD REQUIRES YOU TO TRUST HIM. SO HONOR HIM TODAY BY SPENDING TIME IN HIS WORD AND THEN TRUSTING WHAT HE SAYS.

Day 4

By faith Abel offered to God a more acceptable sacrifice than Cain, through which he was commended as righteous, God commending him by accepting his gifts. And through his faith, though he died, he still speaks.

—Hebrews 11:4

The Bible is full of stories about faithful followers of the Lord. Most of these men and women were very plain and ordinary people.

But because of their extraordinary faith, God blessed and used them—like He did Abel.

The biggest lesson we can learn from the sacrifice of Abel is that he brought his best before the Lord, and he did so by faith. It's important to remember that good works will never be the answer...nor will religion.

But faith—acting on our trust in what God says is true—is the key.

My friend, the Lord deserves your very best. Are you giving everything over to Him in your personal life—marriage, family, friendships? Are you offering it all up to Him by faith?

Lay your life on the altar as a sacrifice before God...by faith...so that you can be used by Him today.

YOUR FAITH CAN DEMONSTRATE TO OTHERS THE WAY TO JESUS, THE WORSHIP OF JESUS, AND THE WITNESS OF HIS GRACE AND POWER IN YOUR LIFE.

Day 5

By faith Enoch was taken up so that he should not see death, and he was not found, because God had taken him. Now before he was taken he was commended as having pleased God.

—Hebrews 11:5

Enoch walked with God for the sake of his children. And I believe it is vital for more mothers and fathers to be like him today and follow God wholeheartedly in front of their spouses and children.

Enoch walked with the Lord 300 years. That's hard for me to grasp sometimes! But more importantly, he did it in front of his family and in spite of a sinful generation.

We are living in perverted days as well, and things aren't getting any better. Our children are at risk and our families are threatened on so many sides.

So I want to challenge you to make a powerful impact on those around you by demonstrating your faith in God. How? By walking in truth—without compromise—regardless of what your family, friends, co-workers, or neighbors might think.

Get alone with God each day, pray that He would fill you with the Holy Spirit, and be strong and steadfast in His Word. If you walk with God by faith, steadfast in your commitment every day, then you'll experience His great blessings both now and for eternity!

YOU CAN MAKE A POWERFUL IMPACT ON THOSE AROUND YOU BY LIVING OUT THE TRUTH EXPRESSED IN GOD'S WORD...BY FAITH.

Day 6

By faith Noah, being warned by God concerning events as yet unseen, in reverent fear constructed an ark for the saving of his household. By this he condemned the world and became an heir of the righteousness that comes by faith.

—**Hebrews 11:7**

In James 2:17, God's Word says, "…faith by itself, if it does not have works, is dead."

Noah showed that his faith was alive and real because he believed what God said and acted on it. Friend, you and I should do the same thing in our own lives!

The Bible also says in Romans 10:17 that "faith comes by hearing, and hearing by the word of God." Noah listened for God and then obeyed Him when he was called out.

If you're reading this today and you hear a still, small voice speaking to you, then don't shut it out! That quiet voice is the Holy Spirit of God calling you to Him. No…you can't see Him, but you can know that He is there by faith.

You can rise above our sinking culture just as Noah rose above his. And if you step out of your comfort zone and place your faith in Jesus Christ, then you can have the forgiveness of sins and the promise of eternal life that God gives through the death, burial and resurrection of Jesus.

My friend, your sin isn't too much to forgive!

SHOW THAT YOUR FAITH IS REAL BY BELIEVING IN WHAT GOD SAYS AND ACTING ON IT!

Day 7

By faith Abraham obeyed when he was called to go out to a place that he was to receive as an inheritance. And he went out, not knowing where he was going.

—Hebrews 11:8

The faith Abraham displayed is one of the greatest in all of Scripture...and we can learn so much from how he trusted God even in incredibly difficult circumstances.

As the Bible says in Hebrews 11:8, "By faith Abraham obeyed when he was called to go out...and he went out, not knowing where he was going."

You know, God just may be calling you right now to do something great for His Kingdom.

Let me ask you: Are you willing to step out, to leave that which is familiar to you to follow His direction? Abraham left everything he knew...his friends and his hometown...to follow the call of God on his life.

God may be calling you into the unknown. The question is, are you willing to go?

It can certainly be frightening to abandon what you know to follow the Lord in obedience. But if your faith is real and genuine...like Abraham's...and you trust God completely with your life...then any road you travel down will ultimately be a blessing.

You have a choice to make: Are you ready to follow God by faith no matter the cost?

IF YOU TRUST GOD COMPLETELY WITH YOUR LIFE, ANY ROAD YOU TRAVEL DOWN WILL ULTIMATELY BE A BLESSING.

Day 8

By faith he went to live in the land of promise, as in a foreign land, living in tents with Isaac and Jacob, heirs with him of the same promise.

—Hebrews 11:9

It's true that young people today are being pressured more and more by their friends and by society.

And if you're a parent, I strongly encourage you to model Christ to your children first...before anything else. If you build your home on the foundation of the Word of God, then you will raise up your children with an unshakable commitment to Christ...a commitment that not only will make them successful adults, but one that will attract others to Him.

If you want to pass along your faith to your children, then

- work to build a strong, healthy Christian marriage;
- devote yourself to being a godly parent;
- train your children in Christian discipleship.

Then continue to make disciples of your children by giving them

- unconditional love, encouragement, and praise;
- a genuine godly example to follow;
- godly leadership, discipline, and wisdom.

Parents, the ball really is in your court. God has called you to pass along your faith to your family. Coach your children to be players who follow the Lord by faith...and attract others to Him through their witness and example!

IF YOU BUILD YOUR HOME ON THE FOUNDATION OF THE WORD OF GOD, THEN YOU WILL RAISE UP YOUR CHILDREN WITH AN UNSHAKABLE COMMITMENT TO CHRIST.

Day 9

By faith Moses, when he was born, was hidden for three months by his parents, because they saw that the child was beautiful, and they were not afraid of the king's edict. By faith Moses, when he was grown up, refused to be called the son of Pharaoh's daughter, choosing rather to be mistreated with the people of God than to enjoy the fleeting pleasures of sin. He considered the reproach of Christ greater wealth than the treasures of Egypt, for he was looking to the reward. By faith he left Egypt, not being afraid of the anger of the king, for he endured as seeing him who is invisible.

—Hebrews 11:23-27

If you want to develop an overcoming faith, it's important to remember what God says in 1 John 5:4, "For everyone who has been born of God overcomes the world. And this is the victory that has overcome the world—our faith."

Moses was a man of great faith. And one of the things that made his faith strongest was his willingness to make a break from the world...an example each of us should follow today.

When Pharaoh tried to oblige Moses by telling him to stay in Egypt to worship God, Moses adamantly refused. He knew Egypt was a land of bondage and that his people could never freely worship God there.

This is the same trick the devil tries to play on you and me today. He wants us to play the religious game...to look godly, but to really deny the power of God. To not really trust in Him.

You and I must learn to separate ourselves from the world...and to overcome the world through our trust in God and His Word. Only then will we develop a faith that will help us weather any storm we face.

LEARNING TO MAKE A BREAK WITH THE WORLD WILL HELP MAKE YOUR FAITH STRONG.

Day 10

By faith the walls of Jericho fell down after they had been encircled for seven days. By faith Rahab the prostitute did not perish with those who were disobedient, because she had given a friendly welcome to the spies.

—Hebrews 11:30-31

So many great men and women are mentioned in the Bible, not because of personal greatness, but because their faith pleased God. And as a result, God used their faith to miraculously change their lives and the lives of those around them.

You may be in a situation today that seems impossible. Perhaps your life is literally spinning out of control. Let me assure you…if you are a believer in the Lord Jesus Christ, then your faith can make the impossible…possible.

In the book of Luke, Jesus said, "If you have faith as a mustard seed, you can say to this mulberry tree, 'Be pulled up by the roots and be planted in the sea,' and it would obey you."

But to have this kind of faith, let me remind you to do these three things:

- First, surrender your life completely to the Lord and worship Him in the way you live your life.
- Second, be completely obedient to what He calls you to do.
- Third, never stop believing and trusting in Him.

Faith is not just hoping that God will come through as He promised…it is knowing that He will, no matter how bleak your situation might look.

GOD CAN USE YOUR FAITH IN HIM TO CHANGE YOUR LIFE AND THE LIVES OF THOSE AROUND YOU.

Day 11

And what more shall I say? For time would fail me to tell of Gideon, Barak, Samson, Jephthah, of David and Samuel and the prophets—who through faith conquered kingdoms, enforced justice, obtained promises, stopped the mouths of lions, quenched the power of fire, escaped the edge of the sword, were made strong out of weakness, became mighty in war, put foreign armies to flight.

—Hebrews 11:32-34

The men and women in Hebrews 11 displayed a great faith and commitment to the Lord. They were from all different walks of life, most of them ordinary people just like you and me. But they all had one thing in common: their trust in and commitment to the Lord.

You know, it doesn't really matter what kind of car you drive or where you live. God isn't limited by how much you do or don't have. He wants to use you right where you are!

Many believers in Christ claim to have faith in Him, but they don't follow through in their actions. They see obstacles or face trials, and take off running in the other direction!

But I want to challenge you today, if you are a follower of Christ, to respond by faith to what the Lord is calling you to do. To live the life He is calling you to live through His Word…by faith!

As long as you are open to letting Him use you…as long as you trust Him and are unmoved in your commitment to Him…He'll do something extraordinary with your life.

GOD WANTS TO USE YOU RIGHT WHERE YOU ARE!

Day 12

Therefore, since we are surrounded by so great a cloud of witnesses, let us also lay aside every weight, and sin which clings so closely, and let us run with endurance the race that is set before us.

—Hebrews 12:1

The Christian life is not a 100-yard dash. It's a marathon. It shouldn't be lived in spurts and jumps and stops and starts, but like a great marathon racer running hard all the way to the finish line.

Let me ask you today, do you think that because you're a Christian, life should somehow be easier? That because you walked the aisle as a child God owes you a comfortable and easy life?

Believe it or not, many believers today think this way! Though few of them would honestly admit it.

Friend, the Christian life demands discipline! It demands hard work. And it demands endurance. The Bible tells us we're in a war, where the spiritual bullets are real and the casualties are high.

It's my prayer today that you will renew your commitment to live for Christ today…and every day. And that you will ask Him to help you build the endurance that's required to finish the race of life in victory!

THE CHRISTIAN LIFE SHOULD BE LIVED LIKE A MARATHON RACER…RUNNING HARD ALL THE WAY TO THE FINISH LINE.

Day 13

Indeed, all who desire to live a godly life in Christ Jesus will be persecuted.

—2 Timothy 3:12

Christianity has become comfortable for too many people today. It's easy to be a "Sunday morning Christian" and live like the world the rest of the week.

While most believers in America don't face physical persecution for their faith, what this verse affirms is that Christianity is not easy. If you stand for Christ, you will be spiritually attacked and your faith will be tested.

If you are a true believer, you may not be accepted in every circle because you won't compromise your beliefs...and you may not get invited to hang out with your co-workers because they know what you stand for.

But if your faith is genuine, then the persecution and spiritual attacks you face are just part of living for Jesus. Just remember that a true Christian is someone who

- has made a choice to follow Jesus Christ;
- picks up his or her cross daily and follows the Lord no matter the cost.

Have you made the decision to follow Christ? If so, I want to challenge you today to stand firm in your faith and let Him continually transform your attitude and actions so that the world will see in you a true Christian.

IF YOUR FAITH IS GENUINE, THE PERSECUTION AND SPIRITUAL ATTACKS YOU FACE ARE JUST PART OF LIVING FOR JESUS.

Day 14

For I delivered to you as of first importance what I also received: that Christ died for our sins in accordance with the Scriptures, that he was buried, that he was raised on the third day in accordance with the Scriptures.

—1 Corinthians 15:3-4

The Gospel message is so simple…yet incredibly powerful. If you are a believer, you can stand on the fact that the Gospel is the truth that saved you from your sins. And you can live each day with a genuine peace because you can be confident you will live with God for eternity!

But maybe today, you're still confused. Perhaps you've heard many different versions of so-called truth before, and you're still not sure which version is true.

Let me help you out: No other philosophy, no other belief, no other theory will restore your soul or give you joy and peace like the Gospel of Jesus Christ. Nothing in this world can give you abundant and eternal life like a relationship with Jesus Christ!

John 3:16 says, "For God so loved the world that He gave His only Son, that whoever believes in Him should not perish but have eternal life." It's not complicated…it's just the simple truth.

NOTHING IN LIFE WILL RESTORE YOUR SOUL OR GIVE YOU PEACE LIKE THE GOSPEL OF JESUS CHRIST.

Day 15

Because, if you confess with your mouth that Jesus is Lord and believe in your heart that God raised him from the dead, you will be saved. For with the heart one believes and is justified, and with the mouth one confesses and is saved.

—Romans 10:9-10

I'm confident there are many people today who don't exactly know the true meaning of salvation.

Maybe you were raised in church and you have heard the term *salvation* your entire life. Or perhaps you have never set foot inside a church building before. Either way, maybe you are uncertain about what salvation really is.

God's Word is very transparent regarding salvation. Jesus came to "seek and to save the lost" (Luke 19:10).

You see, every human being is born into sin and is separated from God. We all are in need of salvation through Jesus Christ. It doesn't matter what you've done in the past. And Jesus simply wants you to come to Him and place your faith in Him for your salvation.

It really is very simple—confess with your mouth, believe in your heart, and you will be saved!

JESUS CAME TO "SEEK AND TO SAVE THE LOST."

Day 16

No temptation has overtaken you that is not common to man.

—1 Corinthians 10:13

There's no place you and I can hide from temptation. But we can certainly fight it, and as a result, triumph over it with Christ's help.

Whenever you feel like the temptation you face is too much to handle, just remember that Christ was tempted just as you are! He understands what you are going through and has provided you a way of escape.

Remember, you need to always be aware that Satan is watching to trip you up. His goal is to get you to give in to temptation. So be on the alert! Jesus said to His disciples in Mark 14:38, "Watch and pray, that you may not enter into temptation. The spirit indeed is willing, but the flesh is weak."

When temptation tries to entice you with your physical appetites, trip you up through your personal ambitions, or test your spiritual allegiance, run to God's Word for strength...stand on His truth...and rest in His promises. God has provided you that way of escape!

YOU CAN TRIUMPH OVER TEMPTATION WITH CHRIST'S HELP.

Day 17

He said to them, "Because of your little faith. For truly, I say to you, if you have faith like a grain of mustard seed, you will say to this mountain, 'Move from here to there,' and it will move, and nothing will be impossible for you."

—Matthew 17:20

Faith is not something that merely needs to be learned, it needs to be lived. Over and over in the Bible, we meet men and women who faced impossible situations with an incredible faith. And they came through their trials victorious.

The Bible specifically says, "Without faith, it is impossible to please God...." I don't know about you, but I want to please and delight God! And without learning and living faith, that is impossible!

Faith is also a vital part of living the Christian life because you and I will go through trials and experiences that don't make sense to us. There will always be questions that are left unanswered. A.W. Tozer once said, "Let faith support us where reason fails...." And I believe this is so true.

Hebrews 11:1 says, "Faith is the assurance of things hoped for, the conviction of things not seen." Faith gives you something to stand on...it gives you hope in the midst of hopelessness...and it gives you evidence of God's presence in your life!

FAITH IS NOT JUST SOMETHING THAT NEEDS TO BE LEARNED...IT MUST BE LIVED.

Day 18

Then he began to invoke a curse on himself and to swear, "I do not know the man." And immediately the rooster crowed. And Peter remembered the saying of Jesus, "Before the rooster crows, you will deny me three times." And he went out and wept bitterly.

—Matthew 26:74-75

Simon Peter was a man of incredible potential who had determined to leave everything else behind to follow Christ. But He failed at a crucial moment by denying the Lord.

There are many things we can learn from Peter's life, like how to avoid pride, prayerlessness, and following the crowd.

Peter went from walking in the counsel of the ungodly to standing in the paths of sinners to finally sitting in the seat of the scornful. While it is vital for believers to get out in the world and witness to others, we need to guard ourselves against becoming worldly.

The good news is there is hope if you have failed spiritually! There is forgiveness and mercy from the Lord. Simon Peter was forgiven and commissioned again to go and be a powerful preacher for Christ.

Do you need to be restored because of some kind of failure today? If so, ask God to restore you. When you come back to Him, you will find forgiveness and a new beginning. Failure as a believer is never final!

THERE IS ALWAYS FORGIVENESS AND MERCY FROM THE LORD IF YOU HAVE FAILED SPIRITUALLY.

Day 19

"I have said these things to you, that in me you may have peace. In the
world you will have tribulation. But take heart; I have overcome the world."
—John 16:33

Everyone faces trials, even believers in Christ. In fact, there's a
very real price to pay when we live sold-out lives for Jesus.

But the great thing is that as followers of Christ, we really can
have joy even in the midst of life's stresses and trials!

It's important to remember that in the midst of life's
tribulations, you can trust God. He is always faithful. As 1 Peter
4:19 says, "Therefore let those who suffer according to the will of
God commit their souls to Him in doing good, as to a faithful
Creator."

Nothing can ultimately harm you as a child of God if you are
fearless and faithful to Him!

Today, I want to challenge you. The next time you face a trial in
your life, remember that Christ went through trials just like
you...and came out victorious! As a follower of Christ, you can have
the same victory that Jesus did.

NOTHING CAN ULTIMATELY HARM YOU AS A CHILD OF GOD.

Day 20

That the God of our Lord Jesus Christ, the Father of glory, may give you a spirit of wisdom and of revelation in the knowledge of him, having the eyes of your hearts enlightened, that you may know what is the hope to which he has called you, what are the riches of his glorious inheritance in the saints, and what is the immeasurable greatness of his power toward us who believe, according to the working of his great might that he worked in Christ when he raised him from the dead and seated him at his right hand in the heavenly places, far above all rule and authority and power and dominion, and above every name that is named, not only in this age but also in the one to come.

—Ephesians 1:17-21

While I believe true followers of Christ desire to live a life that pleases Him, many people really don't understand how to live a life of spiritual authority and power in the Lord.

Scripture tells us that we have legitimate spiritual authority as believers in Jesus Christ. Unfortunately, though, many believers live as though this world is a playground, rather than a battleground. And as a result, they end up falling into Satan's traps.

Friend, each of us needs to understand that Satan is real and active in our world today! His greatest desire is to see your spiritual defeat.

But as a believer in Jesus, you are on the winning team. You have spiritual authority because Christ has dominion over the devil. Notice that in our verses today, you and I have been given the "exceeding greatness of His power," a power far above any other power.

So the next time Satan tries to destroy your worth, your joy, or your peace…when he tries to remind you of all your past sins and failures…remind him of the power you have in Christ.

Remember, the power of the cross, the power of your confession, and the power of your commitment to Jesus Christ is what gives you spiritual authority in this life.

YOU HAVE SPIRITUAL AUTHORITY OVER SATAN AS A BELIEVER IN JESUS CHRIST.

Day 21

"How can a man be in the right before God?"

—Job 9:2

This question posed by Job is the most important question a person could ever ask.

None of us is born righteous. No one! And there's no religion or human effort that could ever make us right with God. This is why we must look to God's grace for our salvation…period.

The apostle Paul tells us in Romans 3:23-26, "For all have sinned and fall short of the glory of God, and are justified by His grace as a gift, through the redemption that is in Christ Jesus, whom God put forward as a propitiation by his blood, to be received by faith. This was to show God's righteousness, because in his divine forbearance he had passed over former sins. It was to show his righteousness at the present time, so that He might be just and the justifier of the one who has faith in Jesus."

God's transfer of righteousness into our hearts does not come through rules and regulations, but through justification, an act in which God declares the believing sinner righteous through faith in Jesus Christ.

And if you have placed your faith in Jesus Christ, God will never declare you unrighteous again!

This is the good news of the Bible. God loves you and has chosen to forgive you of your sins through the shed blood of Jesus Christ. You are indeed righteous before God!

AS A BELIEVER, GOD HAS DECLARED YOU RIGHTEOUS THROUGH FAITH IN JESUS CHRIST.

Day 22

I do not understand my own actions. For I do not do what I want, but I do the very thing I hate.

—Romans 7:15

Every Christian—at least those of us who are really honest with ourselves—admits there is something going on inside us...a war between the desire to do right and the inclination to do wrong.

How many times have you found yourself wishing you would stop worrying, or lusting, or lying, but find you just can't break the habit?

God's Word tells us we will never be able to win the battle going on inside us on our own.

You've probably heard the old analogy that compares these conflicting desires—that of our flesh and that of God's Spirit—to two dogs...how whichever one you feed the most will win.

Today, I want to ask you, which "dog" in your life are you feeding the most? Is it the Spirit or your flesh? Because I can promise you on the authority of Scripture and personal experience that whichever one you feed the most will win.

It is my prayer that you will feed the Spirit by loving and obeying Christ more...and starve the sin in your life...so that through His power, you will win that battle raging inside you today.

THERE IS A BATTLE BETWEEN YOUR FLESH AND THE SPIRIT, AND WHICHEVER "DOG" YOU FEED THE MOST WILL WIN!

Day 23

What then shall we say was gained by Abraham, our forefather according to the flesh? For if Abraham was justified by works, he has something to boast about, but not before God. For what does the Scripture say? "Abraham believed God, and it was counted to him as righteousness."

—Romans 4:1-3

The great principle that Paul is trying to illustrate here is that salvation is by faith alone. Not faith including good deeds, church attendance, or moral character. Faith in Jesus Christ is all you need for salvation!

We cannot save ourselves because our sin prohibits us from reaching God's holy standards. Abraham was a good and moral man, but he was only saved through his faith.

Consider this acrostic for FAITH:

F is for *facts*. You must understand the facts of God's Word.

A is for *affirmation*. There must be an affirmation of those facts in your mind.

I is for *internalization*. You internalize God's Word in your heart.

T is for *trust*. This means to simply trust God every day in every way.

H is for *hope*. Because of faith, you have a hope in Jesus Christ and eternal life with Him.

The fact is you and I can live trying to gain God's favor. But we can never perform enough to earn His acceptance and approval. Like Abraham, we must believe in God to be declared righteous.

FAITH IN JESUS CHRIST IS ALL YOU NEED FOR SALVATION!

Day 24

"But you will receive power when the Holy Spirit has come upon you, and you will be my witnesses in Jerusalem and in all Judea and Samaria, and to the end of the earth."

—Acts 1:8

The first-century Christians were bold in seeking to capture their city, country, and world for Jesus Christ.

But sadly, the church today has become increasingly distracted from what God has called us to do—which is to share the message of salvation in Christ with the world. People desperately need the hope that is only found in Jesus, and it is our job to tell them!

If revival is going to come about in our world, then it needs to first begin in your heart and mine. We must become like the early Christians who had a boldness in the face of fierce resistance. Through that boldness the Gospel spread like wild fire...and it was done without technology, computers, and e-mail!

How did they do that, you may ask? They did it through the power of the Holy Spirit!

Wouldn't you like to see a spiritual awakening in our nation and world? It can as you and I are empowered by the Spirit of God to boldly proclaim the Gospel wherever God might place us. Emboldened with His power, you can make a difference in this generation for Jesus.

IF REVIVAL IS GOING TO COME ABOUT IN OUR WORLD, IT NEEDS TO BEGIN IN YOUR HEART AND MINE THROUGH THE POWER OF GOD'S SPIRIT.

Day 25

And when they had prayed, the place in which they were gathered together was shaken, and they were all filled with the Holy Spirit and continued to speak the word of God with boldness.

—Acts 4:31

Unlike many people today, those in the first-century church didn't rely upon emotions to experience God's power. Rather, they knew how imperative it was to stay connected with God through prayer.

In the same way, you and I need to stay connected to God through prayer so that we can allow Him the opportunity to move in our hearts...and to be a witness for Him.

Maybe today you're in a situation where there seems to be no way out. Maybe you're in an impossible predicament that doesn't seem to have an answer.

Whether your marriage is in trouble or your finances are crumbling, there is power, comfort, and wisdom in God through prayer. And as you take your requests to God, people will see the work of His power and peace in your life.

As Paul tells us in Philippians 4:6-7, "Do not be anxious about anything, but in everything by prayer and supplication with thanksgiving, let your requests be made known to God. And the peace of God, which surpasses all understanding, will guard your hearts and minds in Christ Jesus."

If you want to experience the power and peace of God in your own life, then you must have a consistent, daily prayer life. Ask the Lord today to help you make this a priority!

WE NEED TO STAY CONNECTED TO GOD THROUGH PRAYER IF WE ARE TO EXPERIENCE HIS POWER AND PEACE IN OUR LIVES.

Day 26

And when they had brought them, they set them before the council. And the high priest questioned them, saying, "We strictly charged you not to teach in this name, yet here you have filled Jerusalem with your teaching, and you intend to bring this man's blood upon us." But Peter and the apostles answered, "We must obey God rather than men."

—Acts 5:27-29

As you study the book of Acts, the impact of the early church on the city of Jerusalem is apparent. Believers were under serious persecution and pressure during this time, but despite the rejection of the Gospel by many, they were consistent in sharing their faith.

There is much you and I can learn from their example.

Peter and the early apostles had a deep commitment to capture their own city and surrounding cities for Christ. They passionately spread the Gospel...and the Holy Spirit moved in a powerful way.

And in the process, lives were changed for eternity.

Today I'd like to ask you, are you willing to share your faith despite how uncomfortable it might make you? Is there someone in your life...a co-worker...your neighbor...your hairstylist...who needs to know the love and forgiveness that Jesus Christ offers?

I encourage you to share your story of grace with someone you know today. You never know, it might just open the door to a life being changed for eternity!

ARE YOU WILLING TO SHARE THE LOVE OF CHRIST WITH SOMEONE YOU KNOW TODAY?

Day 27

Then Philip opened his mouth, and beginning with this Scripture he told him the good news about Jesus.

—Acts 8:35

The Bible tells us that in the early days of the Christian church, seven men were chosen to help the twelve disciples attend to routine matters of the church. One of these men was Philip. And God used him in a mighty way to lead others to Christ.

In the same way, God still empowers His people today. You don't have to be a preacher or missionary to be a powerful witness for Christ. God has empowered you through His Holy Spirit to be a powerful witness no matter what you do for a living.

Some people are hesitant to share their faith because they don't see themselves as a Bible scholar, a theologian, or even a persuasive salesperson. But the fact is God can use anyone who's willing and available to share the message of hope and truth found in Jesus Christ.

Are you open to letting God use you today?

If you're a follower of Jesus Christ, you have a testimony as to how Christ has changed your life. What this world needs right now is Jesus…and you're just the person to be used by God to share that life-changing message!

GOD HAS EMPOWERED YOU THROUGH HIS HOLY SPIRIT TO BE A POWERFUL WITNESS TO OTHERS.

Day 28

And when he had come to Jerusalem, he attempted to join the disciples. And they were all afraid of him, for they did not believe that he was a disciple. But Barnabas took him and brought him to the apostles and declared to them how on the road he had seen the Lord, who spoke to him, and how at Damascus he had preached boldly in the name of Jesus.

—Acts 9:26-27

Barnabas was a man known for the way he encouraged and built up other people. He was the ultimate people person!

If you and I are going to be the kind of people God wants us to be, we must be "people persons" as well. This includes building relationships with people both inside and outside the family of God.

In 2 Corinthians 1:3, Paul says, "Blessed be the God and Father of our Lord Jesus Christ, the Father of mercies and God of all comfort."

As believers, shouldn't we want to pattern our lives after our Lord's? To do so, you and I must work to respond to others generously, receive others gladly, rejoice with people greatly, and renew people graciously.

People need affirmation from an unbreakable band of believers who will encourage, support, and point them toward Christ…someone like Barnabas, a man who sought ways to refresh God's people.

Is your life a river of encouragement, acceptance, and love to those who come in contact with you? Or is it a desert?

I challenge you today to be that river of refreshment to those around you. Look for people who you can build up and encourage, and know that God will equip you to be the people person He wants you to be.

IF YOU ARE TO BE THE KIND OF MAN OR WOMAN GOD WANTS YOU TO BE, YOU MUST BECOME A TRUE PEOPLE PERSON!

Day 29

So Peter was kept in prison, but earnest prayer for him was made to God by the church. Now when Herod was about to bring him out, on that very night, Peter was sleeping between two soldiers, bound with two chains, and sentries before the door were guarding the prison. And behold, an angel of the Lord stood next to him, and a light shone in the cell. He struck Peter on the side and woke him, saying, "Get up quickly." And the chains fell off his hands. And the angel said to him, "Dress yourself and put on your sandals." And he did so. And he said to him, "Wrap your cloak around you and follow me."

—Acts 12:5-8

Like Peter, perhaps today you feel like you're in a "prison" of illness, loneliness, or depression. Perhaps you feel as though you're walking down a dead-end path. Or perhaps you feel you are chained to your past and it seems as though there is no way out.

I want you to know that God can make a way when there seems to be no way out. And the way He works is through His Word…and through prayer.

More than ever, you and I have to spend more time in prayer— for our own strength and courage, for our family and friends, for our ministers, and for our government. Because prayer can dramatically change situations!

Even now, you may still be asking yourself, "Where is my life going? What's my purpose here? Why do I seem to lack direction in my life?"

Well, let me ask you…have you truly focused on praying about your situation?

When you're trying to dig your way through the muck and mess of life, remember that prayer will get you through it. It's the only way you will ever know the provision, perfect joy, peace, and power through the Lord Jesus Christ!

THROUGH PRAYER, GOD CAN MAKE A WAY WHEN THERE SEEMS TO BE NO WAY OUT.

Day 30

And we are writing these things so that our joy may be complete.

—1 John 1:4

When the Apostle John wrote this letter so long ago, he was very concerned that we experience the reality of Jesus Christ in our lives and the joy that He gives.

He was concerned because he knew from experience the many tricks and lies the devil uses to steal our joy. As he wrote in John 10:10, "The thief comes to steal and kill and destroy. I have come that they may have life and have it abundantly."

One of the lies the devil tells us is that joy equals happiness. And our culture tells us that "being happy" is one of the loftiest achievements in life. But really, happiness is dependent on our circumstances...and circumstances change so much that it's impossible to depend on them to ever make us happy!

True joy...that inner happiness...only comes from knowing Jesus Christ.

So today I want to ask you, are you experiencing the joy that comes from an intimate relationship with the Lord? Or are you letting the circumstances of life steal that joy?

I'm confident that the more you focus on Jesus (Hebrews 12:2)—and not all the negative stuff going on around you—the deeper and more real your joy in Christ will be!

TRUE JOY ONLY COMES FROM KNOWING JESUS CHRIST.

Day 31

If we confess our sins, he is faithful and just to forgive us our sins and to cleanse us from all unrighteousness.

—1 John 1:9

Every person who has lived or ever will live has a problem that must be dealt with. It's called sin. Yet many people today, even some preachers, shy away from the subject altogether. They don't want to step on any toes or make anyone feel bad.

But the truth is the Bible tells us that "all have sinned and fall short of the glory of God" (Romans 3:23).

The presence of sin in our lives is the one thing that keeps us from a fulfilled life here on earth. And it's the one thing that will keep many people from enjoying an eternity spent with God.

But thankfully, John tells us that God can forgive your sins because of what Jesus did for you on the cross and through His resurrection, which ultimately defeated death.

If you've accepted Jesus as your Savior, let me remind you that the blood Jesus shed on the cross can cover any sin. Don't ever let Satan trick you into believing that you are too far gone to come back to the Lord.

Because of His death and resurrection, your sins can be forgiven! So take them to Christ today and be cleansed.

THE BLOOD OF JESUS CHRIST CAN COVER ANY SIN.

Day 32

And by this we know that we have come to know him, if we keep his commandments.

—1 John 2:3

I want to ask you today, are you truly committed to Christ? Does He have 100% of your life?

You know, our commitment to Christ is similar to our commitment to our spouse. No one would honestly say to their husband or wife, "You know, honey, I love you so much that I'm going to commit to staying 98 percent faithful to you in our marriage."

But how many of us say the same thing to the Lord each day in how we live our lives?

So many Christians today pick and choose which commandments of the Lord they want to obey. But true commitment to the Lord is complete and total or it's none at all!

Today, I want to challenge you to show the world your commitment to Christ by obeying God in your thought life...in the way you react to your spouse and children...in your business affairs...in your finances...in every part of your life.

Second Corinthians 5:17 says, "Therefore, if anyone is in Christ, he is a new creation. The old has passed away; behold, the new has come." I challenge you to live fully committed to Christ in that newness of life today!

TRUE COMMITMENT TO THE LORD IS COMPLETE AND TOTAL OR IT'S NONE AT ALL.

Day 33

"By this all people will know that you are my disciples, if you have love for one another."

—John 13:35

Love is what identifies you and me as believers in Jesus Christ. And the reason you and I can—or should—love others is because God loved us first. As John wrote in 1 John 4:19, "We love because he first loved us." This is where any discussion of love must begin!

God didn't create us to live in isolation, but in a relationship with Him. To know and experience His love. So He made His amazing love known to you and me through what His Son did for us on the cross.

Isn't it amazing that God wanted a relationship with you so much that He sent Jesus to die for you? That He reached out to you in love, not because you earned or deserved it?

That means there's nothing you can do in life to cause God to love you more than He loves you right now. And there's nothing you can do to make Him love you any less!

He loves you perfectly...and He loves you eternally. You are secure in His love! And it is that unconditional and all-encompassing love that should drive you and me to love others today and every day.

YOU ARE FREE TO LOVE OTHERS BECAUSE YOU ARE SECURE IN GOD'S LIMITLESS LOVE.

Day 34

At the same time, it is a new commandment that I am writing to you, which is true in him and in you, because the darkness is passing away and the true light is already shining. Whoever says he is in the light and hates his brother is still in darkness.

—1 John 2:8-9

Yesterday, we talked about how we, as followers of Christ, can love others because God first loved us.

Today, I want to talk to you about how God empowers you and me to love others. That's what the verses above are talking about...how we move from the darkness of indifference towards others, to being able to show them love and grace.

Did you know that God never commands us to do anything He won't enable us to do? It would be unfair for God to expect something of us that we couldn't do. So what does God do? He fills us with His love, which gives us a greater capacity to love others.

God has commanded you and me to love others. In fact, Jesus tells us in Luke 10:27, "You shall love the LORD your God with all your heart and with all your soul and with all your strength and with all your mind, and your neighbor as yourself."

This is the bottom line according to Jesus! Your neighbor is anyone who is in need. And because we can see others through eyes of God's love, our hearts should beat for people a different way.

So if you find yourself indifferent to people today, ask God to help you take His love which fills your life and have it overflow to others.

GOD GIVES US THE POWER TO MOVE FROM INDIFFERENCE TO A GENUINE LOVE FOR OTHERS.

Day 35

Now I would remind you, brothers, of the gospel I preached to you, which you received, in which you stand, and by which you are being saved, if you hold fast to the word I preached to you—unless you believed in vain. For I delivered to you as of first importance what I also received: that Christ died for our sins in accordance with the Scriptures, that he was buried, that he was raised on the third day in accordance with the Scriptures.

—1 Corinthians 15:1-4

Doesn't it seem that bad news is all around us? It's not only the top story on the news or the main headline in the paper…it seems to fill our day.

But as believers, we know the best news is that our Lord Jesus was resurrected from the grave. This is the event that conquered sin…that conquered death…and that made it possible for you and me to have a personal relationship with God!

Perhaps, today, this is the first time you've ever heard or understood this Good News.

If so, I want to tell you something: Jesus died on the cross for you. He wore a crown of thorns and was nailed to a tree because He loves you. And He wants to have a personal relationship with you today.

If you haven't already, I pray you will accept Jesus as your Savior today. And if you have placed your faith in Christ, I challenge you to share that Good News with someone this week.

SHARE THE GOOD NEWS WITH SOMEONE WHO NEEDS TO HEAR IT!

Day 36

And Jesus said, "Father, forgive them, for they know not what they do." And they cast lots to divide his garments.

—Luke 23:34

As we all know, words are powerful…especially dying words. And it's important each of us remembers the words of Jesus right before His earthly life ended.

Some of the last words Jesus uttered while hanging from the cross were words of forgiveness.

Today I want to ask you, if Christ could pray a prayer of forgiveness for those who were putting Him to death, can you pray a prayer of forgiveness for those in your life who mistreat you?

Despite what you may be going through today, can you look past your own "junk" and extend forgiveness to others?

Jesus' dying words on the cross are a powerful example of how you and I ought to treat those who mistreat us. Are you willing to follow His perfect example in every area of your life today? Will you extend forgiveness to those who don't deserve it?

I challenge you to pick up your cross today…and live out the life of forgiveness Christ has given you!

CAN YOU FOLLOW CHRIST'S EXAMPLE AND FORGIVE THOSE WHO MISTREAT YOU?

Day 37

When Jesus saw his mother and the disciple whom he loved standing nearby, he said to his mother, "Woman, behold, your son!"

—John 19:26

Yesterday, we talked about Jesus' dying words on the cross...how He showed forgiveness for those who tortured and killed Him.

And today, I'd like us to reflect on some other words that Jesus spoke during His final hours...when He spoke words of comfort and compassion, like those in the verse above.

Isn't it amazing that in His moment of dying Jesus thought of others? He didn't care about Himself. In the midst of His excruciating pain...in spite of His horrible humiliation...He still reached out and cared for others.

And the application for you and me is clear, isn't it?

In the midst of whatever you may be facing today...a mound of bills...a pile of laundry...or a load of frustration...could you speak a word of compassion to someone who needs it?

Who knows, your words might be the very things that shine the light of Jesus Christ into the darkness of someone's life...and bring them to a saving knowledge of Him!

IN THE MIDST OF YOUR PERSONAL STRUGGLES, REACH OUT WITH COMPASSION FOR OTHERS.

Day 38

When Jesus had received the sour wine, he said, "It is finished," and he bowed his head and gave up his spirit.

—John 19:30

We've all celebrated victory with cries of joy. It's exciting to be a part of a victory shout!

Well, let me assure you that even though these last words of Jesus on the cross are not a shout of victory, they are words of victory. They don't describe someone who is finished...but someone who has finished the assignment that God had given Him.

Jesus was not finished...the plan of salvation was finished! And the devil himself was finished.

Jesus had won the battle of the ages. And because His assignment has been successfully completed, you and I can live in His victory today.

As a believer, you are forgiven of your sins...you can share His confidence...and you can be empowered in your life because you have power over all the works of the enemy!

Jesus Christ is victorious! "It is finished!"

BECAUSE OF JESUS' VICTORY ON THE CROSS, YOU CAN LIVE IN VICTORY TODAY!

Day 39

Jesus said to her, "Mary." She turned and said to him in Aramaic, "Rabboni!" (which means Teacher). Jesus said to her, "Do not cling to me, for I have not yet ascended to the Father; but go to my brothers and say to them, 'I am ascending to my Father and your Father, to my God and your God.'"

—John 20:16-17

What an amazing scene. Mary Magdalene had thought Jesus was dead. Instead she comes face to face with the resurrected Lord!

The hope that Mary experienced is hope that comes from Jesus Christ...it's not just wishful thinking. It is a powerful reality that changes all of life. HOPE...

Helps you. It helps you cope with the darkness of disappointment.

Opens to you the possibility of restoration after defeat. Because Jesus came back from the grave, you can be restored and renewed, no matter how defeated you may feel.

Provides you an answer when you doubt. Today, you may be wondering if all this is really true. If so, I advise you to sincerely search for God with all your heart by reading the Bible and listening to His Word being preached. Because He will show Himself strong on your behalf.

Enables you to conquer death. Through your trust in Christ, you will live forever with Him.

Because Jesus Christ lives, you can be forgiven of your sins, you can live a fulfilling life, and you can have eternal HOPE!

YOU CAN HAVE HOPE TODAY BECAUSE OF CHRIST'S RESURRECTION!

Day 40

See what kind of love the Father has given to us, that we should be called children of God; and so we are. The reason why the world does not know us is that it did not know him. Beloved, we are God's children now, and what we will be has not yet appeared; but we know that when he appears we shall be like him, because we shall see him as he is. And everyone who thus hopes in him purifies himself as he is pure.

—1 John 3:1-3

As a believer, you are God's child. And in a day and age when people yearn so deeply for some form of security in our world, this is a message of comfort and hope for all of us.

As a son or daughter of God, you have security in knowing you have a heavenly Father who is faithful. You can depend on Him because He will never fail you!

Perhaps you, like many people, grew up without knowing any security from your earthly parents. Today, I want to repeat that you have a heavenly Father who is faithful and unflinching in His love for you!

As His child, there is nothing—NOTHING—you can do to make God love you any more than He already loves you because He loves you perfectly! And there's nothing you can do to cause God to love you any less.

Remember what Romans 8:38 and 39 say: "For I am sure that neither death nor life, nor angels nor rulers, nor things present nor things to come, nor powers, nor height nor depth, nor anything else in all creation, will be able to separate us from the love of God in Christ Jesus our Lord."

I hope these words from our Lord encourage your heart today. And thát you will understand that you are eternally secure in Jesus Christ!

AS A BELIEVER, YOU ARE ETERNALLY SECURE IN THE LOVE OF GOD THROUGH JESUS CHRIST.

Day 41

"You are the salt of the earth, but if salt has lost its taste, how shall its saltiness be restored? It is no longer good for anything except to be thrown out and trampled under people's feet. You are the light of the world. A city set on a hill cannot be hidden."

—Matthew 5:13-14

As you read these verses, there is a powerful truth that many Christians miss. That truth is simply this: As a follower of Christ, you are influential.

So let me ask you, what does that Christian influence look like in your life? Or to put it even more plainly, are you a good or bad influence on those around you?

As we think about salt and light, it's important to realize what each of them do. They penetrate. Salt penetrates the substance and flavor of meat...and light penetrates darkness. They both influence what they touch.

Our world is full of darkness, and is in desperate need of the light of Jesus Christ. And our world is full of decay and is in urgent need of the salt of the Gospel. And the only way our world will know that light and salt is through believers like you!

As a believer, are you penetrating your particular area of influence for the Lord Jesus Christ? Are you showing Christ off in how you think...how you speak...how you react to stress...and how you serve others?

Are you being salt and light to a decaying and dark world? You are influencing the world around you...for good or for ill.

ASK GOD TO MAKE YOU A GOOD INFLUENCE ON THOSE AROUND YOU.

Day 42

Share in suffering as a good soldier of Christ Jesus. No soldier gets entangled in civilian pursuits, since his aim is to please the one who enlisted him.

—2 Timothy 2:3-4

I want to ask you a very simple question: As a believer, are you a volunteer in God's army...or are you watching while others are in the battle?

As a pastor, I see the need all the time for more reinforcements. And it's because so many Christians are watching from the sidelines instead of being in the game!

I know there are a lot of pastors today who would skirt around this issue, but let me tell it to you straight: Sitting on the sidelines while your brothers and sisters in Christ are warring is a sin. And it's time we call it that!

Friend, as a child of God, you've been given the tools, the resources, and the gifts you need to make a difference for the Kingdom.

So I want to challenge you today...if you aren't plugged into your local church...if you aren't serving the Lord with your talents and abilities...then gear up and start being a soldier for Christ!

Get in the battle!

LIVE EVERY DAY TO BE IN THE BATTLE, FOLLOWING OUR COMMANDER IN CHIEF, JESUS CHRIST.

Day 43

Yet if anyone suffers as a Christian, let him not be ashamed, but let him glorify God in that name.

—1 Peter 4:16

What do you think a Christian is? Now, I know there are many ideas, definitions, and descriptions of what people think a Christian really is.

As a matter of fact, if you took a survey of random people on the street, you'd probably get as many answers to that question as the number of people you ask! Everyone has an idea of what defines a Christian.

Ironically, though, did you know that the word *Christian* is only used three times in the Bible? That's right.

One time it's used is in today's verse. And 1 Peter 4:16 gives us a keen insight in to what it means to be a Christian: It's someone who is willing to pay the price in order to follow Christ.

So let me ask you this question: Are you willing to make whatever sacrifice to follow Him?

It is my prayer that you would be willing to pay the price to follow Jesus Christ in every part of your life…so that you are a true reflection of someone whose life has been changed by Him.

Live the life of a true Christian by paying whatever price is necessary to follow Christ.

ARE YOU WILLING TO MAKE THE SACRIFICE TO FOLLOW CHRIST IN EVERY AREA OF YOUR LIFE?

Day 44

Passing alongside the Sea of Galilee, he saw Simon and Andrew the brother of Simon casting a net into the sea, for they were fishermen. And Jesus said to them, "Follow me, and I will make you become fishers of men." And immediately they left their nets and followed him.

—Mark 1:16-18

You know, there are far too many Christians who think, "I'll just live a good and upright life…and win people to Christ through how I influence them."

That's just like a fisherman who tries to influence fish to jump into his boat instead of using a pole! It doesn't work!

It doesn't work because—let's face it—none of us can live a perfect life. And besides, people don't need your life. They need the life of the Lord Jesus Christ!

Remember, to be an effective fisher of men, not only do you have to live a life that's different…you have to tell people why you have the hope that you have! The two go hand in hand.

Just living a good life won't cut it, no matter what you were taught growing up.

Today, I want to challenge you to take the net to where the fish are. Break out of the harbor and the safety of the shoreline and get out there where the fish are! Because it's true…fish aren't swimming their way to churches anymore!

Live a good and upright life…and tell people the reason for the hope that is in you!

MAKE A HALLMARK OF YOUR LIFE AS A CHRISTIAN TO BE A FISHER OF MEN!

Day 45

Therefore let us not pass judgment on one another any longer, but rather decide never to put a stumbling block or hindrance in the way of a brother.

—Romans 14:13

As believers in the Lord Jesus Christ, you and I have been given a tremendous gift: the forgiveness of our sins.

And as a result, you and I are people who are deeply indebted…it's an indebtedness that should directly impact our lives. This means we have a responsibility not to do anything that would cause a weaker brother or sister to stumble into sin.

Now, it's important you realize that I'm not endorsing any form of legalism. But you need to look carefully at your life and make sure you're not doing or saying anything that could cause a brother or sister in Christ to stumble…to fail in their Christian walk.

I know this isn't the easiest question to answer, but it's vital that your life not be a stumbling block to others.

I want to challenge you today to eliminate anything from your life that might make another brother or sister stumble. Because as a follower of Christ, you have the responsibility…you owe the debt… to only "pursue what makes for peace and for mutual upbuilding" (Romans 14:19).

PAY ATTENTION TO THE DEBT YOU OWE TO NOT CAUSE YOUR WEAKER BROTHER OR SISTER STUMBLE.

Day 46

Therefore, we are ambassadors for Christ, God making his appeal through us. We implore you on behalf of Christ, be reconciled to God.

—2 Corinthians 5:20

As Christians, the Bible calls us children of God…it tells us we are salt and light…that we're soldiers…spiritual athletes…pilgrims…and we're priests.

And as the verse above tells us, every Christian is also an ambassador of the kingdom of God! We have been born of the kingdom of heaven and we are citizens of heaven.

Remember, as a follower of Christ, you are a special agent of God living in hostile territory…in a war zone. And God has given you a particular assignment in this war zone: to be an ambassador…a reconciler.

He has given you the ministry of peace and reconciliation. He has duly authorized you. He has absolutely appointed YOU. You are His change agent!

Are you doing everything possible in your life to help others reconcile—or make peace—with God? Once you see your life as a mission of reconciliation with God, it will change the way you look at this world.

It will change your life…your perspective…and your attitude. Friend, live like an ambassador of Christ!

LIVE EVERY DAY AS AN AMBASSADOR FOR CHRIST…HELPING OTHERS MAKE PEACE WITH GOD.

Day 47

"But you will receive power when the Holy Spirit has come upon you, and you will be my witnesses in Jerusalem and in all Judea and Samaria, and to the end of the earth."

—Acts 1:8

Being a witness…sharing Jesus Christ in the power of the Holy Spirit…is the supreme service of every child of God. It is not only a mark of spiritual maturity, but it is also a means of developing that spiritual and Christian maturity.

In Mark 1:17, Jesus said, "Follow me, and I will make you become fishers of men." If you're following, you should be fishing!

But the sad truth today is that many Christians don't make a habit of sharing their faith with others. This sin of silence is, I believe, the most habitual sin of the average believer. The cruelest lie of all is to know the Gospel…to know the Lord Jesus…and never share it!

Friend, sharing your faith is your first responsibility as a believer. You should be motivated by the incredible love of God…which changed your life…and the fact that people need to be saved.

Today, are you fulfilling your responsibility to "fish for men"? If not, I challenge you to start making this a priority in your life. Because I can promise you that someone you know today needs to hear the Good News of Jesus Christ and how He changed your life!

IF YOU'RE FOLLOWING CHRIST, YOU SHOULD BE FISHING FOR MEN!

Day 48

"If I then, your Lord and Teacher, have washed your feet, you also ought to wash one another's feet."

—John 13:14

Jesus gave us the command to wash one another's feet. Some have suggested that this is an ordinance of the church that ought to be practiced customarily.

Yet when you examine the text you realize that Jesus is giving us an example here and not an ordinance. He is giving us a demonstration of what a servant of God is like…and what a servant of God does.

Jesus is instructing us to submit our lives to one another and serve one another like He served us. He wants you and me to love like He loved.

In John 13:34, Jesus said, "A new commandment I give to you, that you love one another: just as I have loved you, you also are to love one another."

Jesus showed us a new kind of love! It was a love that had never been expressed or experienced before. It was and is a love of service and sacrifice for others. And He wants us to show that same love to those around us!

Who is someone you could serve unselfishly? Whoever it is that God brings to mind, I urge you to go out of your way today to show them the love of Christ…to be the servant Jesus wants you to be.

JESUS WANTS YOU TO LOVE LIKE HE LOVED.

Day 49

I am the vine; you are the branches. Whoever abides in me and I in him, he it is that bears much fruit, for apart from me you can do nothing.

—John 15:5

The Christian life really is very simple…it's not the complicated thing we often try to make it.

Now, I'm not saying there aren't deep and profound things we can discover about Christ and being His child as we walk with Him day by day. But really, Jesus reduced the Christian life down to one simple word in the verse above: abide.

He said, "If you abide in Me just like a branch stays connected to a vine…if you abide in Me, and I in you…you will bear much fruit."

I'm convinced that there are many Christians who are running around trying to live the Christian life who would profit a great deal if they could just learn this simple lesson. To learn that we need to have both union and communion with the Lord if we are to bear fruit.

When you learn how to abide in Christ, you'll find that every other thing in the Christian life will take care of itself.

All you need to do is to be available. All you need to do is say, "Lord, here I am in communion with You; I am in union with You, and You can do with me what You will."

That is the Christian life in its simplest, yet most profound form!

ARE YOU MAKING EVERY AREA OF YOUR LIFE AVAILABLE TO CHRIST?

Day 50

As each has received a gift, use it to serve one another, as good stewards of God's varied grace.

—1 Peter 4:10

I know the word *steward* may sound like one of those words you only hear in church. But really, a steward is just someone who's been entrusted with something valuable. And as believers in the Lord Jesus Christ, God has given you and me something very precious to take care of.

Those things include our lives and bodies...our influence...our children...our time...the spiritual gifts God has given us...and our possessions.

But I want to focus today on the responsibility we have to be good stewards of the Gospel of Jesus Christ. This includes guarding the purity of the Gospel in a culture that sees all truth as relative.

Jude 3 and 4 tell us, "contend for the faith...for certain people have crept in unnoticed...who pervert the grace of our God into sensuality and deny our only Master and Lord, Jesus Christ."

But being a good steward of the Gospel also means giving it away as well.

Paul tells us in Romans 1:14 and 15, "I am under obligation both to Greeks and to barbarians, both to the wise and to the foolish. So I am eager to preach the gospel to you also who are in Rome."

So today, I want to challenge you...as a believer in Jesus...to both guard and to give away the Gospel of Jesus Christ. If you will, you will indeed be a good steward of His Gospel!

AS A BELIEVER IN CHRIST, YOU HAVE THE RESPONSIBILITY TO BE A GOOD STEWARD OF THE GOSPEL.

Day 51

But Naomi said, "Turn back, my daughters; why will you go with me? Have I yet sons in my womb that they may become your husbands? Turn back, my daughters; go your way, for I am too old to have a husband. If I should say I have hope, even if I should have a husband this night and should bear sons, would you therefore wait till they were grown? Would you therefore refrain from marrying? No, my daughters, for it is exceedingly bitter to me for your sake that the hand of the LORD has gone out against me."

—Ruth 1:11-13

When we first meet Naomi in the first chapter of Ruth, she is an optimist…an enjoyable person who lived up to the meaning of her name, "pleasant."

But as Scripture tells us, life was harsh for Naomi. It was cruel as her husband and sons all died…and it was supposed to have been a short stop down in Moab but lasted many years.

As a result, Naomi became a broken and bitter woman. Her countenance changed. And the joy she once knew was gone.

When life gets hard, it's easy to become bitter like Naomi did…to feel that life is unjust and unfair. And sometimes it's tempting to blame God for the terrible turn that life has taken.

Yet there was the seed of faith in Naomi's life when she said, "I'm going back to Bethlehem." And her faith was renewed soon thereafter.

You know, my friend, Jesus came because life can be cruel. Life can be harsh. And life can be bitter. We all deal with pain, sorrow, and grief in this world. And yet, there is hope in Jesus Christ.

No matter what you may be going through today, I pray you will let Jesus turn your hurt into the hope found only in Him. Because your renewal…like Naomi's…could soon come!

NO MATTER WHAT YOU MAY BE GOING THROUGH, THERE IS GREAT HOPE IN JESUS CHRIST!

Day 52

But Ruth said, "Do not urge me to leave you or to return from following you. For where you go I will go, and where you lodge I will lodge. Your people shall be my people, and your God my God. Where you die I will die, and there will I be buried. May the LORD do so to me and more also if anything but death parts me from you."

—Ruth 1:16-17

The scene we witness above is one of the great confessions of faith in all of the Bible and in all of history.

Here, on the road to Bethlehem, Ruth accepted God's grace. He had brought her to the road to Bethlehem…and she was persuaded in her faith, even though her own mother-in-law said, "Turn back."

Orpah, Ruth's sister-in-law, came to the crossroads with her and cried and wept and was full of emotion. And she turned on her heels and went back into Moab and died without God.

Ruth came to that same crossroads at Bethlehem, and she clung to her commitment. And as a result, her entire life was changed forever.

You know, that's what commitment to Christ really is. It's not fence-straddling. It's cross-bearing! Jesus said, "It's not always going to be easy. If you're going to follow Me, take up your cross…don't take the easy way…take up your cross and follow after Me."

Friend, today I challenge you to make your commitment to God total and final! Get rid of the escape clauses, the fine print, and the footnotes on the contract of your commitment to Him.

Be like Ruth and make that all-out commitment…and your life, too, will be changed forever!

A COMMITMENT TO CHRIST IS NOT FENCE-STRADDLING…IT'S CROSS-BEARING!

Day 53

Then Boaz said to his young man who was in charge of the reapers, "Whose young woman is this?" And the servant who was in charge of the reapers answered, "She is the young Moabite woman, who came back with Naomi from the country of Moab. She said, 'Please let me glean and gather among the sheaves after the reapers.' So she came, and she has continued from early morning until now, except for a short rest."

—Ruth 2:5-7

Ruth is an example for you and me because she was faithful where she was…to what God had assigned her to do. She went to the field and worked, and she worked hard. According to verse 7 above, she arrived early and stayed late!

You see, Ruth didn't have ulterior motives. She didn't know about the future…about Boaz being her future husband. She didn't know she would become the great-grandmother of David and a direct ancestor of the Lord Jesus Christ.

She didn't have a clue about any of that! Ruth simply did what she was assigned to do that day, letting God lead her as she faithfully obeyed and served Him.

And that is how God leads you and me. We're called to "bloom where we're planted." We should work hard doing what we're called to do…right now! Because God will not lead us one step further than the measure of our current obedience to Him.

That's the story of Ruth's life. She met success in a common hour by simply doing what God had directed her in her heart to do.

Are you doing the will of God in your life right now? Are you blooming where God has planted you today?

Faithfully serve and obey God each day and entrust your future to Him.

GOD WILL NOT LEAD US ONE STEP FURTHER THAN THE MEASURE OF OUR CURRENT OBEDIENCE TO HIM.

Day 54

Then Naomi her mother-in-law said to her, "My daughter, should I not seek rest for you, that it may be well with you?"

—Ruth 3:1

In today's verse, Naomi provides an example for what you and I should do when life is hard. You see, in the midst of her state of depression, she did something that helped get her out from under the dark cloud of bitterness she was living in:

Naomi stopped thinking about herself and started thinking about someone else.

I don't know where you may find yourself today, but if you're down...I have a word for you: If you can get outside of yourself and start serving others, you will find any depression you have will begin to lift.

If you're discouraged today, I encourage you to get interested in someone else! Get involved in your church. Adopt a family or find a child that you can share a gift with.

And certainly it's important to share your faith. Nothing will lift your spirits and enliven your heart like sharing the Good News with someone who needs to hear it!

When you're discouraged or depressed, the best thing you can do is to get your mind on the Lord Jesus Christ...to worship Him, to look to Him, to speak to Him, to open your Bible, and to ask the Spirit of God to mend your broken heart.

And then for someone else to bless. When you do, watch God begin to restore and replenish and refresh your despondent spirit.

DO SOMETHING POSITIVE ON BEHALF OF OTHERS TODAY.

Day 55

> Now this was the custom in former times in Israel concerning redeeming and exchanging: to confirm a transaction, the one drew off his sandal and gave it to the other, and this was the manner of attesting in Israel. So when the redeemer said to Boaz, "Buy it for yourself," he drew off his sandal.
>
> —Ruth 4:7-8

In today's passage, we witness an interesting custom from the days of the Old Testament.

According to the custom at the time, when a married man died childless, it was the responsibility of that man's brother or another close relative (a "near kinsmen") to marry his wife (or "redeem" her) and purchase the land that he would have enjoyed.

Boaz was a near kinsman who wanted to redeem Ruth. But according to Jewish law, there was a nearer kinsman, someone who was closer to Ruth. So Boaz had to make sure that this man signed off in order for him to marry Ruth.

So according to custom, when the nearer kinsman agreed to allow Boaz to redeem Ruth, the nearer kinsman took off his sandal and gave it to Boaz. And Boaz slipped on that sandal as a sign of his willingness to stand in the nearer kinsman's shoes...to redeem and purchase what was rightfully the nearer kinsman's.

What we see in this ancient custom is a vivid illustration of what Jesus Christ did for you and me on the cross! We, the near kinsman, cannot save ourselves, so we take off our shoe and give it to Christ.

Praise God for the salvation we have as believers: Jesus standing in our shoes and us standing in His!

SALVATION IS JESUS STANDING IN YOUR SHOES AND YOU STANDING IN HIS.

Day 56

Her children rise up and call her blessed; her husband also, and he praises her: "Many women have done excellently, but you surpass them all."

—Proverbs 31:28-29

You know, there are a lot of things I could say about my mom. While she is in heaven today, I can still remember my mother's eyes. They were bright and beautiful and they danced when she looked at you.

I also remember by mother's smile...her laughter. Her laughter could light up a room!

But what I really remember most about my mom was her hands...the tenderness and the love of those hands. She was a mom who would put her arms around me, and love me and encourage me like no one else could.

Dr. Ed Wheat gives us a formula for a successful marriage, but it's also a formula on how to be a successful mother and parent. It's called the BEST formula:

B stands for *bless.* Bless your children with praise, admiration, and affirmation, both publicly and privately.

E stands for *edify.* Build your children up spiritually, emotionally, and personally.

S stands for *share.* Communicate...share with your children and allow them to share with you.

T stands for *touch.* Express your love to your kids by hugging them and showing them the tenderness I mentioned above.

I hope you will take time today to be the BEST parent you can be...and help your children become all they can be.

TAKE TIME TO EXPRESS YOUR LOVE TO YOUR KIDS BY SHOWING THEM LOVING AFFECTION!

Day 57

At this time Moses was born; and he was beautiful in God's sight. And he was brought up for three months in his father's house, and when he was exposed, Pharaoh's daughter adopted him and brought him up as her own son. And Moses was instructed in all the wisdom of the Egyptians, and he was mighty in his words and deeds.

—Acts 7:20-22

Most of us know the story of Moses…how he was born as a slave into a Hebrew family, but raised as a prince in the palace of Pharaoh.

We also know how God orchestrated events so that Moses' biological mother, Jochebed, after placing him in a basket in the Nile, was able to become a part of Pharaoh's household and raise Moses as his "nanny."

And in those formative years, this little babe grew under the tutelage and the direction of his own mother. And there he learned in her lap what he would need as the leader of the nation of Israel, and as one of the greatest men the world has every seen or known.

What did Jochebed do in directing Moses that we can reproduce in our own generation as we pass along our faith?

For one thing, she taught Moses to discover his own true identity…who he was and what he could become. And that is the assignment and responsibility of every parent today.

And moms, you in particular can help your child discover his or her own self-worth. God created your child in His own image, with a desire for him or her to become His child forever.

Not all children are like Moses, but each one is unique and under the providential care of God. And it's up to us to teach them this every day of their lives!

TEACHING OUR CHILDREN THEIR SELF-WORTH AS A CHILD OF GOD IS THE RESPONSIBILITY OF EVERY CHRISTIAN PARENT.

Day 58

Older women likewise are to be reverent in behavior, not slanderers or slaves to much wine. They are to teach what is good, and so train the young women to love their husbands and children, to be self-controlled, pure, working at home, kind, and submissive to their own husbands, that the word of God may not be reviled.

—Titus 2:3-5

The first priority of a wife, a mother, and of all women is to live for Jesus Christ. The second priority…if you're married and you have a family…is to take care of the needs of your family.

The Christian wife and mother's primary mission is to make the home a royal residence for the Lord of glory and for the family of faith. That is your mission in life! Caring for the home means loving your husband, developing your children, and managing your household affairs.

Now, there is nothing in Scripture that forbids a woman from working outside the home, but it is absolutely clear in the Bible that the mother's priority is in the home.

I certainly understand when single moms are required to work just to make ends meet. And I understand sometimes it becomes a financial necessity for a mother to work. But make sure before you leave that home to go to work, wife and mother, that it is God calling you to do it and not the world calling you to do it.

The highest calling in life is your calling as a wife and a mother. Don't accept a lesser calling if God doesn't call you from that exalted place! Don't let the world squeeze you into its mold.

THE CHRISTIAN WIFE AND MOTHER'S PRIMARY MISSION IS TO MAKE THE HOME A ROYAL RESIDENCE FOR THE LORD OF GLORY AND FOR THE FAMILY OF FAITH.

Day 59

> Then Mordecai told them to reply to Esther, "Do not think to yourself that in the king's palace you will escape any more than all the other Jews. For if you keep silent at this time, relief and deliverance will rise for the Jews from another place, but you and your father's house will perish. And who knows whether you have not come to the kingdom for such a time as this?"
>
> —Esther 4:13-14

Throughout history, we observe the influence of faithful and courageous women who have chosen to make a positive difference in the world…to stand for truth and righteousness, and to speak out against evil.

Some have served and labored in public places, others in obscure places, but all of them, by their choice to follow Christ, have changed the world.

One of these women is Esther. Her story demonstrates the power of one person's choice—in this case, one woman's choice—to make a significant difference in the lives of those around her.

You know, a woman's choice has become a part of the vernacular of our culture. Typically it refers to the so-called right of a woman to choose an abortion rather than to give birth to the life within her.

Yet in spite of those who may have abused the right of choice, there are many faithful women who have chosen the way of faith and the way of God.

Today, if you are a mother, I challenge you to embrace the opportunity you have to make a difference in the world and in your home by choosing to follow Jesus Christ. Because the rewards of your decision will last an eternity!

YOU HAVE THE OPPORTUNITY TO CHANGE THE WORLD WHEN YOU CHOOSE TO FOLLOW CHRIST!

Day 60

I sought the LORD, and he answered me and delivered me from all my fears. Those who look to him are radiant, and their faces shall never be ashamed.

—Psalm 34:4-5

According to the Scriptures, worship is the most important thing we're called to do as believers in Christ.

Yet, as A.W. Tozer once said, "Worship is the missing jewel in modern evangelicalism." And I believe this is so true. So many believers miss the joy of genuine worship. They just sort of go through the same old routine, week after week.

But one of the greatest reasons why we should make the worship of God a habit is because worship fortifies our faith. When your faith needs a boost, look up! Praise, worship, singing spiritual songs, and expressing adoration to God all strengthen your faith and draw you nearer to Him.

Remember what Psalm 22:3 tells us: God is "enthroned on the praises of Israel." Wherever genuine praise is, so is God!

Today, in spite of what kind of storm you may be facing at home or work, I challenge you to find one thing for which to praise the Lord.

I am confident that taking your focus off of your troubles and genuinely thanking God for what He has done in your life will strengthen your faith and brighten your outlook on life!

WHEN YOUR FAITH NEEDS A BOOST, LOOK UP IN PRAISE AND WORSHIP!

Day 61

I appeal to you therefore, brothers, by the mercies of God, to present your bodies as a living sacrifice, holy and acceptable to God, which is your spiritual worship.

—Romans 12:1

More than ever, I believe Christians today need to remember that worship is a verb.

It's not sitting and watching, it's something you do. It is participation. It is not mere emotion. It is not a feeling or a thought process, but rather the active response of your heart, your life, and even your body to God!

If you go to a worship service and watch everyone else worship, you haven't worshiped—you have become a religious consumer rather than a spiritual communer. You've become a spectator rather than a true worshipper.

Perhaps you grew up in a church where you sang hymns and participated at some level. But, maybe, just maybe, you have never had a genuine experience of encountering the presence of God in true worship.

If not, I challenge you to take time even today to tell God you desire to be a genuine worshipper. He will honor your prayer because He has made you to worship Him! You were created that you might know Him and make Him known.

As a believer in Jesus Christ, worshiping Him intimately and intensely should be the driving force in your life. That's why I want to call you to become a true worshiper of the Lord Jesus Christ today, whether in or out of church!

YOU WERE MADE TO WORSHIP GOD!

Day 62

Now when they saw the boldness of Peter and John, and perceived that they were uneducated, common men, they were astonished. And they recognized that they had been with Jesus.

—Acts 4:13

Peter and John were two men who had been with Jesus. For three years they had looked into His eyes and heard Him pray.

They'd listened intently as He taught lessons of the kingdom and what it meant to follow Him. They'd seen His tears in the Garden of Gethsemane. They even watched Him die. Then they saw Him in the glory of His resurrection!

Because they had been with Jesus, Peter and John acted like Jesus. In fact, their lives had been revolutionized so dramatically because of the time they spent with Jesus that when people observed them—even their enemies—they knew there was something distinct, something uniquely different about these men.

When the world looks at you as a believer in Christ, I wonder if they can say the same thing. Can a watching world tell when you have worshiped…when you have bowed in your own time of prayer? Do they see evidence you have been with Jesus?

When you interact with your friends, your family, and your business associates, I pray they will see that there is something different about you…that you have been with Jesus Christ.

CAN THE WORLD TELL YOU HAVE BEEN WITH JESUS?

Day 63

Six days before the Passover, Jesus therefore came to Bethany, where Lazarus was, whom Jesus had raised from the dead. So they gave a dinner for him there. Martha served, and Lazarus was one of those reclining with him at the table. Mary therefore took a pound of expensive ointment made from pure nard, and anointed the feet of Jesus and wiped his feet with her hair. The house was filled with the fragrance of the perfume.

—John 12:1-3

You know, there are few better examples of what a true worshipper looks like than Mary of Bethany. Her dedication and love for Christ is such an inspiration to me.

Mary was a living testimony to what Paul talks about in the verse we looked at earlier this week, Romans 12:1, which says to "present your bodies as a living sacrifice, holy and acceptable to God, which is your spiritual worship." Mary came with all that she had and with all that she was to worship Christ.

She was so focused on Him and centered on Him that she paid no attention to the many distractions around her. She absolutely and recklessly abandoned herself and she generously and extravagantly gave all of herself in worship to Christ!

Friend, that's how we're to worship Him each and every day.

As a believer, is there anything that's distracting you from worshiping the Lord? If so, I urge you to confess it to God and ask Him to help you refocus on what's truly important…becoming a true worshiper of Him!

FOCUS TODAY…AND EVERY DAY…ON GIVING ALL OF YOURSELF IN TRUE WORSHIP OF GOD.

Day 64

And they came to Jerusalem. And he entered the temple and began to drive out those who sold and those who bought in the temple, and he overturned the tables of the money-changers and the seats of those who sold pigeons. And he would not allow anyone to carry anything through the temple. And he was teaching them and saying to them, "Is it not written, 'My house shall be called a house of prayer for all the nations'? But you have made it a den of robbers."

—Mark 11:15-17

The verses above describe one event in Jesus' life that lets us know just how He feels about those who worship Him improperly. Jesus displayed His power that day to show us how He values genuine worship.

When God looks at your life, does He see genuine worship or does He see a counterfeit? Does He see something real or is it phony?

The bottom line is that each of us was made to worship God. And until we realize the true purpose in life, which is to worship Him and enjoy Him forever, we'll always be floundering. We'll always be frustrated because worship is the central purpose of life!

It is impossible to be a productive, positive Christian without participating in meaningful, genuine worship!

And I'm not just talking about corporate worship. Worship is something more than what we do, worship is a lifestyle. It is an attitude that we carry with us day by day. It is an activity and an attitude that reveals the inner heart and recognizes the value we place on God in our lives. That's what worship is!

So today, let me challenge you to make your life a life of worship…an exclamation of the glory of our God!

IT IS IMPOSSIBLE TO BE A FULFILLED CHRISTIAN WITHOUT GENUINELY WORSHIPING GOD.

Day 65

My soul makes its boast in the LORD; let the humble hear and be glad. Oh, magnify the LORD with me, and let us exalt his name together! I sought the LORD, and he answered me and delivered me from all my fears.

—Psalm 34:2-4

Have you ever wondered why the Scripture instructs us to praise God? Three reasons can be found in the verses above from Psalm 34.

First of all, praising the Lord encourages others. I think you'd be amazed at how people, Christian and non-Christian alike, respond to something as positive as honest and sincere praise to God when something good or bad happens to you.

Second, praising God naturally brings fellowship. There is a closeness…a bond…that is created when you're praising God together.

And last, praising the Lord gives you power for your day-to-day life. I don't know what you may be facing today, be it a temptation you can't let go of or a sin you can't escape. Whatever it is, praise will bring you out of it!

My friend, God responds to your honest, genuine praise of Him. So I urge you to make praise a habit no matter what you may be going through!

MAKE PRAISE A PRIORITY REGARDLESS OF YOUR CIRCUMSTANCES.

Day 66

Do not be conformed to this world, but be transformed by the renewal of your mind, that by testing you may discern what is the will of God, what is good and acceptable and perfect.

—Romans 12:2

When I was a kid, I made a pine box derby car. And you know, it was easy to keep up some speed as long as I was rolling down a hill!

But gradually I'd start to slow down, and eventually I'd stall and stop. Then I had to push the car up the hill and have somebody shove me down the hill again.

I think a lot of Christians are like that. As long as somebody pushes us…as long as we're at the top of the hill…we're flying high! But what we need today is the constant, continual commitment to the Word of God that will propel us forward in our walk even when we are at the bottom of the hill.

We're so bombarded and brainwashed and softened up by our culture that we're drunk on pleasure and happiness. But God says not to be conformed like that. Don't be manipulated like that. Don't be molded into the image of things around you!

It is my prayer that you will be committed to being conformed to the image of Jesus Christ in your life today by making a constant, continual commitment to the study of God's Word!

IF WE ARE TO THINK LIKE CHRIST, WE MUST HAVE A CONSTANT COMMITMENT TO THE WORD OF GOD.

Day 67

Having gifts that differ according to the grace given to us, let us use them: if prophecy, in proportion to our faith; if service, in our serving; the one who teaches, in his teaching; the one who exhorts, in his exhortation; the one who contributes, in generosity; the one who leads, with zeal; the one who does acts of mercy, with cheerfulness.

—Romans 12:6-8

Perhaps the best illustration in Scripture of the Church is that of a body. And just as there are various instruments and members of the body...all functioning in unity and yet in diversity...each member of the body is important and provides a crucial function. As it is said, "Everybody is somebody in His body."

While we aren't all equal in giftedness, we're all equally needed with our gifts that God has given to us.

And you already have your gift. It's not something that you get somewhere down the road of life. It's something you discover! God determines the gift, and He'll enable you to discover it.

The moment you were saved...the moment you were born into the family of God...the Spirit of God did not come in empty handed. He came into your life with birthday gifts...His gifts of the Spirit!

Which means you have special gifts to serve the Body of Christ. Have you discovered your gifts? And are you using your gifts from the Spirit to make an impact for the Kingdom today?

If not, begin by asking God to reveal the giftedness He has given you...and then begin to use that gift to bless others.

YOUR SPIRITUAL GIFTS ARE NEEDED TO MAKE AN IMPACT FOR THE KINGDOM OF GOD!

Day 68

Let love be genuine. Abhor what is evil; hold fast to what is good. Love one another with brotherly affection. Outdo one another in showing honor.

—Romans 12:9-10

If there's anything the Church of Jesus Christ needs today, it's a good dose of reality! Real Christians who are authentic...who are real saints in a real world.

With all the criticism and skepticism regarding churches and ministries today, it's time the world take notice of some Christians who are committed to Jesus Christ in truth, obedience, integrity, and honesty!

In the verses above, Paul tells us how we can be authentic Christians. And the first thing he mentions is that we are to love sincerely.

Part of taking up our cross every day means we take up that kind of love. If we're going to be real, we must honestly and sincerely exercise the ministries of love.

So I want to ask you, what does your love look like today? Is it truthful? Tenacious? Tender? Thoughtful? Does the way you demonstrate love tell others that you're a follower of Christ?

May your life today reflect John 13:35, "By this all people will know that you are my disciples, if you have love for one another."

SEEK TO LOVE TENACIOUSLY IN TRUTH, TENDERNESS, AND THOUGHTFULNESS.

Day 69

Do not be slothful in zeal, be fervent in spirit, serve the Lord. Rejoice in hope, be patient in tribulation, be constant in prayer.

—Romans 12:11-12

Authentic Christians don't lag behind when it comes to service for the Lord Jesus Christ. They lead the way, taking care of God's business!

I believe there ought to be a sense of urgency, a sense of intensity, and a passion for spiritual ministry. And certainly there is no room for laziness and there is no room for lukewarmness when it comes to serving the Lord Jesus Christ.

Ecclesiastes 9:10 says, "Whatever your hand finds to do, do it with all your might." If it's worthy to do, then it's worthy to do with all of your might.

Ephesians 5:16 says that we are to make "the best use of the time, because the days are evil." Friend, we're to turn it up a notch or two in these evil days, and redouble and triple our efforts. Not our self-efforts, but our spiritually energized efforts in the work of the Lord Jesus Christ!

So are you working hard in the service of Jesus Christ? Or are you hardly working?

Don't be like so many Christians who are rusting out instead of wearing out in serving the Lord Jesus Christ!

DETERMINE TO SERVE GOD WITH ALL OF YOUR MIGHT.

Day 70

And I will make of you a great nation, and I will bless you and make your name great, so that you will be a blessing. I will bless those who bless you, and him who dishonors you I will curse, and in you all the families of the earth shall be blessed.

—Genesis 12:2-3

I'd like to talk briefly about how we as Christians are to respond to the blessings God has bestowed upon our country.

This response can be summarized in the acrostic of the word PATRIOT:

P stands for *pray*. We're to pray for our nation, our leaders, and for those whose minds and hearts are blinded and seduced by the god of this age.

A stands for *accept*. You and I are to accept the responsibilities of citizenship, which includes paying taxes and voting.

T stands for the word *treat*. Each of us is to treat our freedom with care because it was bought with a price.

R stands for *resist*. Resist the temptation to trade spiritual values for material values. Remember that God is interested in your character more than your money!

I stands for *identify*. We're to identify places where we can make a positive difference in our community.

O stands for *overcome*. You and I should overcome acts of evil with acts of grace, kindness, and goodness.

T stands for *thank*. We need to thank God regularly for our salvation and for the privilege of living life in this God-blessed nation.

It is my prayer that the Lord would help you become a patriot for the Lord Jesus Christ today!

THANK GOD FOR THE PRIVILEGE OF LIVING IN THIS GOD-BLESSED NATION!

Day 71

"For God so loved the world, that he gave his only Son, that whoever believes in him should not perish but have eternal life."

—John 3:16

Jesus is the one life that changed the history of the world. And His is the one life that dramatically rescued all of humanity. It is His story that empowers you and me to live life and give of ourselves in service to others.

And I don't think there's ever been a better time to proclaim the truth of who Jesus really is!

Isn't it wonderful that in the midst of such cultural confusion about Christ, we as believers can stand on the biblical truth of who Jesus is…and what He did for us in coming to earth as a man?

Yes, He was a man…a perfect, sinless man. But He was also God…who loved us so much that He laid His life down so that we might be saved.

Most believers have heard John 3:16 since their days as baby Christians. But it's my prayer that God would give you a new perspective and fresh insight about just how much He loves you today!

THERE'S NEVER BEEN A BETTER TIME TO PROCLAIM THE TRUTH OF WHO JESUS REALLY IS.

Day 72

But from there you will seek the LORD your God and you will find him, if you search after him with all your heart and with all your soul.

—Deuteronomy 4:29

There are two kinds of seekers of truth in our culture today: Those who don't know and want to find the truth…and those who don't know but really don't want to find the truth.

Which kind of seeker are you? Do you really want to know the truth?

If you have a genuine desire to find God…to follow Him… and really know who He is…God will show Himself to you! If you respond to even the tiniest pinprick of light, God will reveal more light when you genuinely want to know the truth.

I truly believe, according to the Scripture, that if a person really wants to know God… genuinely wants to know Jesus…God will move heaven and earth if necessary to bring that person to the knowledge of the truth.

If you will sincerely and honestly look for the light, God says you will discover it. It's that simple.

So today, if you're looking for a light in the midst of your darkness, what is your response to the light of Jesus Christ? Because I can assure you, once you've found Jesus, your search for truth is complete.

Turn your darkness to light by fully trusting in Christ today.

IF YOU SEEK THE LIGHT FOUND IN JESUS CHRIST, YOU WILL FIND IT!

Day 73

Worthy are you, our Lord and God, to receive glory and honor and power, for you created all things, and by your will they existed and were created.

—Revelation 4:11

Friend, life is all about Jesus. If He's not the center and circumference of your life, you have missed the point of life!

Now, by what right can Jesus claim to be so worthy?

First, because Jesus is your Maker. Jesus is the One who is the Source and the Sustainer of the universe. He made it all...including you! Therefore He is worthy to be the focus of your life.

Second, Jesus is your Victor. Revelation 5:5 says, "...the Lion of the tribe of Judah, the Root of David, has conquered, so that he can open the scroll and its seven seals."

Jesus is absolutely victorious over your sin...over your sadness...over any darkness that may be in your life right now. Christ is the Victor! Therefore He is worthy.

Third, Jesus is your Savior. Revelation 5:9 says, "And they sang a new song, saying, 'Worthy are you to take the scroll and to open its seals, for you were slain, and by your blood you ransomed people for God from every tribe and language and people and nation.'"

Jesus is your Maker, your Victor, and your Savior. Which means you and I owe Him our worship...and our lives!

JESUS IS WORTHY OF YOUR ALL!

Day 74

For all have sinned and fall short of the glory of God.

—Romans 3:23

Today, I'd like to ask you how you have dealt with the sin in your life.

Have you jumped on the religious ladder? Are you trying to be a good person and do the right things hoping that somehow God's scorecard will add up in your favor?

Or maybe you're one of those people who has denied the existence of sin in your life at all. You've just sort of numbed yourself to the fact that you're a sinner...or you think it's an archaic idea that no longer merits consideration.

Friend, neither of these things will solve the problem of your sin! Because trying to be perfect is impossible...and denying that there isn't sin in your life isn't rational.

And neither of these approaches to sin will solve the problem with a holy God.

So really there is only one option to deal with your problem of sin: The grace of the Lord Jesus Christ. Only the blood that Jesus shed on the cross will ultimately pay the penalty for your sin.

If you are reading this as a child of God, take time right now to thank God for His grace in providing a solution to your sin. However, if you can't say you are a child of God, then I challenge you to stop right now and accept God's free gift of Christ's shed blood for your sin. Just tell God you accept His gift and let Him cleanse you from ALL your sin!

THANK GOD FOR THE GIFT OF CHRIST'S DEATH TO PAY THE PENALTY FOR YOUR SIN!

Day 75

For the eyes of the LORD run to and fro throughout the whole earth, to give strong support to those whose heart is blameless toward him.

—2 Chronicles 16:9

God is looking for men and women who are willing to steadfastly give their whole hearts to Him. In fact, putting Christ first and living radically for Him is a prerequisite if we are to become successful in the Christian life!

But some people don't like the idea of being a radical. They don't want to be seen as a Jesus freak or a fool. They don't want to be seen as extremist or someone who's intolerant. As a result, they settle for something less than maxing out for Christ.

But did you know that maximum commitment is really the normal Christian life? This is the way the Christian life should be lived!

First century believers embraced the call to maximum commitment. They picked up their cross and followed Jesus. They went into the world and made disciples regardless of the cost.

What does maximum commitment look like for you and me today? It's a simple thing, really. It's disciplining ourselves… training under the authority of God's Word…and then living in daily devotion to what we're learning. It's then practicing what we learn in our daily lives.

I challenge you today to heed the call to maximum commitment to Christ!

BEING A DISCIPLE OF JESUS CHRIST MEANS MAXIMUM COMMITMENT TO HIM.

Day 76

But sexual immorality and all impurity or covetousness must not even be named among you, as is proper among saints. Let there be no filthiness nor foolish talk nor crude joking, which are out of place, but instead let there be thanksgiving.

—Ephesians 5:3-4

It's impossible to be a man or woman of honor unless you heed the call to moral purity and make a commitment to stay sexually pure.

While you might not be engaged in adultery or in overt acts of sexual immorality, many times we often settle for something less than holiness when it comes to purity of mind, purity of heart, and purity of body.

Let me give you a blueprint to holiness in your life which is found in the acronym PURE:

Prepare for spiritual attack. First Corinthians 10:12 says, "Therefore let anyone who thinks that he stands take heed lest he fall."

Unfasten defiling associations. Biblical separation is positive. It's not just *not* doing something or isolating yourself from the world. It means you turn from sin and turn to God.

Remember the consequences of fatal attractions. Yes, as believers, Christ has taken our sin. But our God is a God of holiness and purity and righteousness.

Engage in positive spiritual activities. If you really want to defeat the power of sin in your life, then you need to engage in positive spiritual activities like Bible reading, prayer, and fellowship with other believers.

Make a commitment to live a sexually pure life today by using the blueprint above to be PURE.

IT'S IMPOSSIBLE TO BE A PERSON OF HONOR UNLESS YOU MAKE A COMMITMENT TO SEXUAL PURITY.

Day 77

Wives, submit to your own husbands, as to the Lord. For the husband is the head of the wife even as Christ is the head of the church, his body, and is himself its Savior. Now as the church submits to Christ, so also wives should submit in everything to their husbands. Husbands, love your wives, as Christ loved the church and gave himself up for her, that he might sanctify her, having cleansed her by the washing of water with the word, so that he might present the church to himself in splendor, without spot or wrinkle or any such thing, that she might be holy and without blemish.

—Ephesians 5:22-27

I truly believe that one of the primary reasons for the breakdown of the home today is that husbands and wives don't understand or practice their roles and responsibilities. They have bought into the confusion of our culture and as a result their marriages suffer.

The verses above give us a clear definition of the roles God has designed for husbands and wives. And in a world in which equality is promoted as the highest ideal it's not popular. But remember that equality does not mean "sameness."

We are heirs together of the grace of God as men and women, and we are absolutely equal in value in God's eyes. But He has assigned specific and strategic roles and responsibility within the marriage relationship. And we are to live and to practice these roles.

But here's what I want you to notice: The bulk of the responsibility rests squarely on the shoulders of men! Men, we are called to love our wives as Christ has loved the church. And if we do, our wives will respond to our sacrificial and steadfast love…because that's the way God has created them. But, men, it must start with us.

So husbands, love your wife. And wives, respond to the love of your husband. That's how you practice a covenant marriage!

PRACTICE THE SPECIFIC AND STRATEGIC ROLE GOD HAS GIVEN YOU IN YOUR MARRIAGE RELATIONSHIP.

Day 78

This is the message we have heard from him and proclaim to you, that God is light, and in him is no darkness at all. If we say we have fellowship with him while we walk in darkness, we lie and do not practice the truth.

—1 John 1:5-6

As followers of the Lord Jesus Christ, you and I have moved by Him from darkness to light. And now we are to live as children of light…not children of darkness.

How do we know if we are walking in that light? If we are following Jesus, because He is that light! In fact, if you want to put the Christian faith in one sentence you could put it this way: God became one with us in order that we might become one with Him.

So how do you live and walk in the light? It starts with what you are doing right now, and that's to spend time meditating on His Word. I hope you will take seriously the need to dig into God's Word each and every day. Only through His Word can you know how to walk in the light. The Psalmist says, "Your word is a lamp to my feet and a light to my path"(Psalm 119:105).

It also means a commitment to intimacy with God through prayer. Allow God to speak to you through His Word and through prayer. As you do, you find that you will have sweet fellowship with Him and walk in the light as He is in the light.

Commit today to walk in the light through meditating on God's Word and a life of prayer!

WALK IN THE LIGHT AS GOD IS IN THE LIGHT.

Day 79

Go therefore and make disciples of all nations, baptizing them in the name of the Father and of the Son and of the Holy Spirit.

—Matthew 28:19

You and I are called to take our Lord and His message of salvation to others. But we're not only called, we're commanded to do this. And as soldiers under authority, our Commander-in-Chief has given us clear instructions!

Matthew 28:19 is often called the Great Commission. It's never called the great suggestion, because it's not an option. Rather, it's a clear command of our Commander-in-Chief. And all of us, therefore, are called and commissioned to share the faith we have in Jesus Christ.

Friend, you don't have to be a polished speaker or a winning debater or a trained theologian in order to share your faith. God expects you and I to share our faith in a relational and natural way.

For example, let's suppose you were cured of a fatal disease. Wouldn't you want to tell everyone you knew who had this same disease about the doctor and the medicine that cured you? Of course, you would! You'd be so thrilled, so excited about what had happened to you that you couldn't possibly keep it to yourself. To keep it to yourself at that point would be one of the most selfish acts in the world.

As believers, all of us have been cured of the fatal disease called sin! And the doctor who cured us is Jesus.

And Jesus, by the power of His blood, which cleanses us from every sin, has changed our hearts. And because we have been transformed by the love and grace of God, we can and should tell others!

AS A BELIEVER, YOU NEED TO SHARE THE GOOD NEWS THAT YOU'VE BEEN CURED OF A FATAL DISEASE CALLED SIN.

Day 80

Blessed is the man who walks not in the counsel of the wicked.

—Psalm 1:1

What does a man or woman of God look like? For one thing, they are distinctively different in the way they think. A man or woman of God is not to be influenced by the counsel of those who are godless. In fact, we are to be separated from their thinking.

Friend, beware of the mindbenders! There's huge pressure today to be softened up to accept the world's values…to be brainwashed by the god of this age.

But our lives are not to be directed by the wisdom of this world! They're to be directed by the wisdom that comes from above. The true man or woman of God gets their counsel from heaven.

Proverbs 23:7 says, "…as he thinketh in his heart, so is he…" (KJV). The heart is the center of reflection. It's who you are down deep on the inside when you commune with God. Don't allow that to be influenced by the world's values and thinking.

Remember that what you think about, what you hear, and what you allow to enter the gates of your mind will ultimately determine the path your life takes!

A MAN OR WOMAN OF GOD IS SEPARATED FROM GODLESS THINKING.

Day 81

Blessed is the man who walks not in the counsel of the wicked, nor stands in the way of sinners.

—Psalm 1:1

A man or woman of God is to be distinctively different in the way they live life. They are to be separated from lawless living.

As it says in the verse above, those blessed of God do not stand in the way of sinners. While we have contact with those who don't know Christ, we're not to have communion with those who don't know Him.

What do I mean by that? Simple. While we're called to be friends with unbelievers (like Jesus was), we're not to share the lifestyle and values of those who do not share our faith.

That's why the Bible says we are to marry in the faith. It says not to be unequally yoked together with unbelievers, because how can you share life and love together if you don't share Christ together?

The man or woman of God shouldn't participate in the lifestyle of the lost. They refuse to walk where sinners congregate.

You show me the kind of company you keep, and I'll show you the kind of person you are or soon will become! Proverbs 13:20 says, "Whoever walks with the wise becomes wise, but the companion of fools will suffer harm."

That's why we are to reject the company of lawless living and love the fellowship of God's people!

A MAN OR WOMAN OF GOD IS SEPARATED FROM LAWLESS LIVING.

Day 82

Blessed is the man who walks not in the counsel of the wicked, nor stands in the way of sinners, nor sits in the seat of scoffers.

—Psalm 1:1

As we have seen in the last few days, we are to be careful about the company we keep. But not only is a man or woman of God to be different in the way they think and live, they are to be distinctively different in the way they speak. They are to be separated from careless speaking.

Notice the progression in Psalm1:1 above. We go from walking to standing to sitting.

Walking in the counsel of the wicked is listening to the counsel of the ungodly. Standing in the way of sinners is living a lifestyle like the spiritually lost. Finally, sitting in the seat of scoffers is laughing at or mocking the things of God.

Those who listen to the counsel of the ungodly generally end up sitting in the seat of scoffers. And the seat of scoffers (those who mock the things of God) is the chief seat in Satan's kingdom.

As believers, we're to avoid those who mock the Word of God and separate ourselves from those who would destroy and defile our faith.

A MAN OR WOMAN OF GOD IS SEPARATED FROM CARELESS SPEAKING.

Day 83

Blessed is the man who walks not in the counsel of the wicked, nor stands in the way of sinners, nor sits in the seat of scoffers; but his delight is in the law of the LORD, and on his law he meditates day and night.

—Psalm 1:1-2

A true man or woman of God is separated from the world in their thoughts, their actions, and in the way they speak. But a man or woman of God also saturates his or her life with the Word of God.

For the Christian, the Word of God is not an obligation. It's an opportunity to spend time with God and to learn His truth for living the life that will bring the greatest blessing to you!

Don't you want to spend time with those you love? If you love God the way you ought to love God, you'll want to spend time with Him.

The way to spend time with God...the way to fellowship with God...is by spending time in His Word. That's why the man or woman of God appreciates the Word of God, longs to hear the Word of God, and loves to read the Word of God.

But not only should you and I appreciate the Word of God, we need to meditate on the Word of God. Now, I'm not talking about the new age type of meditation you hear so much about today. As believers, we shouldn't put our minds in neutral and open them up to just anything. Biblical meditation is to concentrate upon the Scripture.

Friend, we need to saturate our lives with the Word if we are to become true men and women of God!

A TRUE MAN OR WOMAN OF GOD SATURATES HIS OR HER LIFE WITH THE SCRIPTURE.

Day 84

Your words were found, and I ate them, and your words became to me
a joy and the delight of my heart, for I am called by your name, O LORD,
God of hosts.

—Jeremiah 15:16

Medical science has proven that meditation is actually healthy for you. And for us as believers, that is quieting ourselves before the Lord and His Word.

In a day in which we're running here and there, knocking ourselves out in our fast-paced life, it's important that we, as men and women of God, take time to meditate upon the Word of God! After all, as our Scripture today reminds us, the words of God will bring joy and delight to your heart.

What will meditating upon the Scripture do for you?

1. It will quieten your heart.
2. It will develop your mind.
3. It will still your body.
4. It will fortify the will and quicken your spirit.

My friend, God wants to speak to you! He wants to meet with you. The King of kings and the Lord of lords wants to give you His counsel. And I tell you, there's not a subject imaginable that isn't dealt with in the Word of God.

As you look back on your week, have you taken the time to really meditate and quiet your spirit before the Lord? Because I can assure you that God's Word will indeed bring joy and delight to your heart!

MEDITATING ON GOD'S WORD WILL BRING JOY AND DELIGHT TO YOUR HEART.

Day 85

And these words that I command you today shall be on your heart. You shall teach them diligently to your children, and shall talk of them when you sit in your house, and when you walk by the way, and when you lie down, and when you rise.

—Deuteronomy 6:6-7

You know, it's not poverty, crime, drugs, abuse, or unemployment that are really the biggest problems for our culture today. The biggest problem is families with dads who are missing in action.

Many fathers are physically present with their kids, but they are spiritually absent. They haven't assumed the responsibility God has given them as fathers to lead their families spiritually.

My friend James Merritt has given an acrostic that describes the four main responsibilities of a dad:

D stands for *direction,* or giving guidance.
A stands for *availability,* to be there.
D stands for *discipline,* firm and fair discipline.
S stands for *spirituality,* to be a spiritual man.

Dads, our children don't need substitutes! They want you to be the champion of their faith, to stand firm and strong as a courageous parent to help them fight the raging secularism attacking them from every side.

It's my prayer that every dad reading this will commit to being the spiritual leader in their family today!

GOD HAS CALLED DADS TO BE THE SPIRITUAL LEADERS OF THEIR FAMILIES.

Day 86

So we do not lose heart. Though our outer nature is wasting away, our inner nature is being renewed day by day.

—2 Corinthians 4:16

You know, this old world is a desert! It's a dry and barren place. But the true man or woman of God has roots that sink down deep into the hidden spiritual springs that satisfy and supply the longings of his or her heart.

Our relationship with God through Jesus Christ releases the rivers of God's Spirit so that we are refreshed and revitalized daily.

And friend, that's what God is trying to do with your life! God wants to renew and refresh you spiritually each day.

But the question is this: Are you planting yourself by "streams of water" (Psalm 1:3) by spending time with God each day? There are tremendous benefits to situating yourself by the refreshing, life-giving waters of Jesus Christ: stability, vitality, productivity, consistency, and maturity.

Don't be a man or woman who's lost his way, but one who has discovered "the way, and the truth, and the life" (John 14:6) that is in Jesus Christ!

A TRUE MAN OR WOMAN OF GOD LIVES LIFE BY THE SPIRITUAL WATERS OF GOD AND HIS WORD.

Day 87

"Everyone then who hears these words of mine and does them will be like a wise man who built his house on the rock."

—Matthew 7:24

Yesterday we saw how a true man or woman of God is planted by the spiritual streams of God and His Word. What does this result in? Today's verse gives us a clue: They're grounded and settled. They have deep roots. They have depth of character and strength of will because they have roots.

I'm sure you know people who are all showcase and no warehouse. They talk a big game, but when the storms of life blow, their facade crumbles!

Friend, God wants you to be strong on the inside. He wants you to be strong and stable so that you can stand in the midst of the gales of life.

What are you doing today to deepen your roots in Jesus Christ? Do you find yourself sacrificing your time with God when the storms of life aren't blowing?

I'd like to challenge you today…wherever you are in your walk with Christ…to take some time each and every day to situate yourself near Him so that you'll be ready when life's storms come upon you.

Because being grounded in Jesus Christ is the only way you'll be able to stand strong when those times come!

A TRUE MAN OR WOMAN OF GOD IS GROUNDED IN JESUS CHRIST.

Day 88

"Whoever believes in me, as the Scripture has said, 'Out of his heart will flow rivers of living water.'"

—John 7:38

One of the benefits of situating ourselves near the waters of Jesus Christ is stability. Today we'll look at another benefit: vitality.

A true man or woman of God is energized. And it doesn't come by standing up on your own two feet. It comes through the Holy Spirit.

I know there are times in my life when I'm exhausted, both mentally and physically.

And it's in these times that I've experienced renewed energy and vitality from the Holy Spirit to continue the work or task that God has called me to do. And He can do the same for you!

If you find yourself weary today, it's my prayer that you will invite God's Spirit to revitalize you inside and out...and that you will experience the vitality that only He can bring!

A TRUE MAN OR WOMAN OF GOD IS ENERGIZED BY THE HOLY SPIRIT.

Day 89

But the fruit of the Spirit is love, joy, peace, patience, kindness, goodness, faithfulness, gentleness, self-control; against such things there is no law.

—Galatians 5:22-23

As believers, we're to be productive in our Christian lives. And as we are learning, God will enable and empower us if we will plant ourselves in Him and His Word.

The result? The fruit mentioned above…which is the fruit of the Spirit, or Christ-like character.

Remember in the Gospel of Mark, Jesus cursed a fig tree that produced nothing but leaves. He cursed it because it bore no fruit. And God is inspecting our lives for spiritual fruit.

I want to challenge you to be a reproducer…a reproducing believer in Christ. Because a healthy body reproduces!

And a healthy Christian will reproduce spiritual fruit: the fruit of character and the fruit of bringing people to Christ.

A TRUE MAN OR WOMAN OF GOD PRODUCES SPIRITUAL FRUIT.

Day 90

He is like a tree planted by streams of water that yields its fruit in its season, and its leaf does not wither. In all that he does, he prospers.

—Psalm 1:3

Over the past few days we've been examining what a true man or woman of God looks like. We've seen there are awesome benefits to planting yourself by the life-giving water of Jesus Christ, including stability, vitality, and productivity.

Today I want you to see that a true man or woman of God exhibits consistency and maturity.

"Its leaf does not wither" speaks to consistency. It means you won't burn out! Your leaves will not dry up...your fruit will not wither...you will be forever green.

There's nothing more pleasant and powerful than a strong, stable, solid man or woman of God....someone who lives the life they profess.

But he or she does even more than that. We see that everything the man or woman of God does prospers or matures. This means there is a maturity in your family life...your business life...your social life...your personal life...and in your witnessing life.

As you look at your life today, does it exhibit the qualities of stability, vitality, productivity, consistency, and maturity? It is my prayer that God will help you continue to grow in each of these important areas of life!

A TRUE MAN OR WOMAN OF GOD EXHIBITS CONSISTENCY AND MATURITY.

Day 91

My son, do not forget my teaching, but let your heart keep my commandments, for length of days and years of life and peace they will add to you.

—Proverbs 3:1-2

There are all kinds of money managers, advisors, and counselors in our world today.

There are also attorneys, financial planners, bankers, stock brokers, venture capitalists, and CPAs who offer sound financial advice. And there's much to be gained from listening to the counsel of these professionals.

But what if I could introduce you to one of the wisest and wealthiest men who has ever lived to give you counsel about your finances? That would be incredible, wouldn't it?

Well, that man is Solomon. And his counsel is known as the Old Testament book of Proverbs.

The book of Proverbs is a collection of wise sayings. It's a series of short sentences that are long in meaning. Every one of them applies to your life today—including your financial life. And as our passage tells us, obeying these truths will bring about tremendous benefits.

So over the next few days, we're going to taking a look at the book of Proverbs.

And we are going to see what God's Word says about money. I'm confident your outlook on your finances will be altered and challenged!

HEEDING THE WISDOM OF GOD'S WORD BRINGS TREMENDOUS BENEFITS.

Day 92

The blessing of the LORD makes rich, and he adds no sorrow with it.

—Proverbs 10:22

Money is a gift from God. But many people have a poor relationship with it—including many Christians.

Believers should have different attitudes about money than the culture at large. Because the Bible tells us there are things more important than money. For example, Proverbs 22:1 says, "A good name is to be chosen rather than great riches…."

Proverbs also tells us that wisdom (3:13-18), character (23:23), intelligence (20:15), and human relationships (15:17) are more important than money. Even Jesus concluded in Mark 8:36, "For what does it profit a man to gain the whole world and forfeit his life?"

In commercial office buildings, there are firewalls that protect the structure and its inhabitants from fire. When you're online, there are firewalls that protect your computer from viruses.

And in order to protect your family from the dangers of money, you need to build a financial firewall around your life. You do this by earning your money honestly, managing your money wisely, and giving your money generously.

Take careful stock today of how you are valuing and handling your money. Are you earning it honestly? Are you managing it wisely? And are your giving it generously?

AS A CHILD OF GOD, YOU SHOULD VALUE MONEY DIFFERENTLY THAN OUR CULTURE DOES.

Day 93

Wealth gained hastily will dwindle, but whoever gathers little by little will increase it.

—Proverbs 13:11

Most likely, I don't have to tell you that there's intense pressure to be successful in our world today.

And as a result, there's also incredible pressure to compromise our character in order to attain the world's definition of success. This compromise shows itself through dishonesty, greed, and a number of other wrong attitudes regarding money.

As a believer, the bottom line is that you must decide that your character is more important than your financial status. And the first financial firewall each of us must build around our families and homes is the firewall of honesty. This requires that we make honest financial decisions 100% of the time!

This means you tell the truth at any cost. It means you always pay your debts. You put in a hard day's work every day. You're a fair employer. And you always pay your taxes.

It means you'll remember that money is only temporary...and the thing that will last is your character!

YOU MUST DECIDE THAT YOUR CHARACTER IS MORE IMPORTANT THAN YOUR FINANCIAL STATUS.

Day 94

Precious treasure and oil are in a wise man's dwelling, but a foolish man devours it.

—Proverbs 21:20

Making good choices regarding the legacy and future of your family is vitally important. And as it says in the verse above, it's foolish to spend everything you have! We are to save money, and not just spend it.

But the problem is that many families today haven't built the financial firewall of spending money wisely. Their expenses exceed their income…and as a result, they're bridging the gap with more and more debt!

But accumulating excessive debt isn't wise. And in the limited space I have here, I want to advise you to deal aggressively with paying your creditors.

If you have debt that's grinding you down…if you have debt that creates pressure in your family…if you have debt that keeps you from giving as God would have you give…it's time you began to take a hard look at your spending habits and go after paying off your debts.

Do your spending habits glorify God? If not, I challenge you to begin making God a partner in your finances today by applying the truths mentioned above!

BUILD A FINANCIAL FIREWALL AROUND YOUR FAMILY THROUGH WISE SPENDING HABITS.

Day 95

Honor the LORD with your wealth and with the firstfruits of all your produce; then your barns will be filled with plenty, and your vats will be bursting with wine.

—Proverbs 3:9-10

Scripture teaches us the importance of putting first things first. We're to give the first day of the week to the Lord. We're to give the first part of our day to Him. And we're to give the firstfruits of our labor—a tithe—to Him.

This is the principle that's clear in Scripture: We're to give God off the top of what we've been given and what we have earned. Why? To honor Him! The reason we give generously and live generously is to honor God.

I would advise you and strongly urge you—if you want God to be in the middle of your financial picture—to begin tithing 10% in obedience to Him.

Now, I realize you may be having a hard time financially right now. Perhaps you're between jobs or you're really struggling with debt or other financial problems in your life.

If so, I want to challenge you today to begin obeying God, putting Him first in every area of your life. This includes what I mentioned in the devotional a few days ago...earning your money honestly, managing your money wisely, and giving your money generously. Then, trust Him for the rest!

Be patient...persevere...and know that at the right time, in the right place, God will bless you in the right way because you have honored Him with your firstfruits...and He knows He can trust you with what He gives you!

THE REASON WE GIVE GENEROUSLY AND LIVE GENEROUSLY IS TO HONOR GOD.

Day 96

Hear, my son, your father's instruction, and forsake not your mother's teaching, for they are a graceful garland for your head and pendants for your neck.

—Proverbs 1:8-9

Yesterday, we learned that wise families fear and respect the Lord. Today we'll see that wise families also understand the importance of and value obedience.

As parents, it's important to teach your kids to obey you, because as they learn to obey you, they will learn to obey God! And I think the verses above give two ways you are to do that...through instruction and teaching.

The word *instruction* is from a Hebrew word that includes the idea of counsel, warning, and correction. Dad, I believe this describes your role in the family...to be firm in instruction, to lay down reasonable rules and fair boundaries, and to give correction and fair discipline.

The word *teaching* in the verses above describes, I believe, the work of a mom in the home. It's a word that actually means coaxing or coaching. In other words, mom, your role is to teach your children...to push them forward to become all God desires for them.

It's like a mama bird with her nest full of little birds. When it's time for those baby birds to fly, the mama stirs up the nest, flaps her wings, and coaxes those little birds to elevate!

So parents, I want to ask you today, are you instructing and teaching your children? And as you do, are they learning to obey you? As they do, they will someday be ready to obey God.

WISE FAMILIES UNDERSTAND AND VALUE OBEDIENCE.

Day 97

My son, if sinners entice you, do not consent.

—Proverbs 1:10

If someone dumped a pile of smelly, dirty trash in your family room, you'd probably be incensed! Yet how many families allow the garbage of our culture into their homes every single day?

Did you know the average home today has three TVs, three radios, two CD players, one computer, two DVD players, and one video game system? That's a lot of the impurity and depravity of this world getting into our homes.

And that's how a lot of that depravity gets into the heads of our children!

The best parental control isn't the movie rating system or the television and video game rating system. The best parental control system is you, mom and dad!

Why? Because you're called to protect your children's purity.

The way you do this is by providing reasonable rules and boundaries regarding media consumption, computer use, dress…and your kids' friends.

First Peter 5:8 says, "Your adversary the devil prowls around like a roaring lion, seeking someone to devour." This includes your kids and mine!

So if you are going to fight the good fight of faith, you must protect the purity of your children…even if this means displeasing your kids at times. So take time today to look carefully at what you are allowing into your home and take whatever measures you need to so that your kids will be protected from the garbage of our culture.

WISE FAMILIES ACCEPT THE CHALLENGE TO LIVE MORALLY PURE LIVES.

Day 98

Do not withhold good from those to whom it is due, when it is in your power to do it.

—Proverbs 3:27

One of the most important things my parents taught me growing up was to love people and use things—not to use people and love things. That meant doing good to others when it was in my power to do so.

Parents, what are your children learning as they watch how you treat others? Are they seeing that love is an action, not just a feeling?

Our kids watch us as parents very carefully…and they know if we're applying this truth in how we live our lives. They know if we're caring and kind to people…and they know if we're rude. They know if we slander and gossip about others or if we build people up.

Our kids are smart enough to know if we truly care about others—and if we do good to people when it's in our power to do so!

Wise families learn that life is not just about "me." It's about caring for others as Jesus Christ cares for us. As Jesus said in Matthew 20:28, "…the Son of Man came not to be served but to serve, and to give his life as a ransom for many."

Teach your children to love those around them. And start by modeling that for your children today.

WISE FAMILIES LEARN HOW TO CARE ABOUT PEOPLE.

Day 99

Whoever walks with the wise becomes wise, but the companion of fools will suffer harm.

—Proverbs 13:20

Often when I read this verse I can't help but think of an old Texas proverb that states: "If you lay down with dogs, you're gonna come up with fleas!"

Who you hang around with will impact the person you are. And the people your kids hang with will influence the people they become.

If your kids spend time with those who are wise, they will become wise people. If they hang out with fools, their life's going to be a mess!

As parents, it's vital you impart this wisdom to your children. They need to understand that who they choose to hang out with will greatly determine who they'll become in the next five to ten years.

I'm so thankful my parents and grandparents instilled this principle in me as a young boy. And while I've made a few mistakes along the way, I'm grateful I was always connected to a church and was always involved with Christian friends.

Choosing wise friends will help save your kids from experiencing a lot of hurt and heartache along the way. And it will help set the stage for their success in life! So help your kids choose their friends wisely.

WISE FAMILIES CHOOSE GODLY FRIENDS.

Day 100

As soon as I heard these words I sat down and wept and mourned for days, and I continued fasting and praying before the God of heaven.

—Nehemiah 1:4

Numerous articles and studies, both Christian and secular, show me a disturbing trend. In just one of them, well-known pollster George Gallup, Jr. has concluded, "Fewer than 10% of Americans are deeply committed Christians."

What disturbs me about this statistic is that far more than 10% of Americans claim to follow Christ when asked about faith or about their beliefs. But studies go on to reveal how most people who claim to believe in Jesus are just as likely to engage in unethical behavior or fall prey to the latest religious fad.

Far too many Christians are not deeply committed to their faith. And if you find yourself struggling today, then I have a suggestion for you today. Make prayer a habit of your life!

Nehemiah had a deep and vibrant relationship with God. And that relationship was founded on prayer. In fact, as the book of Nehemiah opens up, we see Nehemiah petitioning God for days because his heart was troubled over his homeland of Judah. And as you read throughout the book of Nehemiah, prayer made all the difference in Nehemiah's life.

Without prayer, you will never stand apart from the world. And if you are to grow in your walk with God, you need to constantly be in communication with Him! So make prayer a priority in your life today!

A FERVENT PRAYER LIFE WILL DEEPEN YOUR RELATIONSHIP WITH THE LORD.

Day 101

Whoever makes haste with his feet misses his way.

—Proverbs 19:2

To be a faithful follower of Christ, you must be a patient person. Many times it's just our human nature to rush off and take swift action when we hear about a problem. But patience pays off—and few people in the Bible illustrate this better than Nehemiah.

In the first chapter of Nehemiah, Nehemiah heard that something was terribly wrong back in Jerusalem. But rather than rushing off to do something about it, he patiently prayed and sought the Lord as to what to do.

Nehemiah knew that he would not be successful without waiting on God.

Today's verse tells us that it's not only dangerous and unwise to rush into the unknown, but it's sometimes even sinful. Nehemiah prayed and prepared for four months! When was the last time you took four months to pray about and prepare for something?

God puts a premium on patience. We need to align our schedules with God's heavenly timetable. And the only way you will know God's schedule is if you talk to Him constantly...and wait on Him patiently.

Many of us want to give up if we don't get an immediate response. Patience is a hard lesson to learn in today's fast and furious society. But you can learn it! Imitate Nehemiah today, and seek the Lord fervently...and wait patiently for His answer!

GOD PUTS A PREMIUM ON PATIENCE.

Day 102

The king granted me what I asked, for the good hand of my God was upon me.

—Nehemiah 2:8

The door of opportunity swings on the hinges of prayer! All real success comes when God opens the door for us, but we must take our requests to Him in prayer.

Jesus tells us in Matthew 7:7, "Ask, and it will be given to you; seek, and you will find; knock, and it will be opened to you." The door will be opened, but the first step is prayer. And once Jesus opens that door, no one can shut it on you!

Nehemiah wanted to take action, but he waited for God to open the door. He learned a valuable lesson about leadership: In order to lead, you must first follow. Nehemiah followed God by asking Him to help him go back to Jerusalem to rebuild the city wall. And then God opened the door for him to lead the effort to do just that!

Remember, it won't do you any good to break down a door and rush through it if God does not open it. So commit your way to God today and then watch for the doors He opens.

GOD WILL OPEN DOORS THAT NO ONE CAN SHUT WHEN YOU SEEK HIS DIRECTION.

Day 103

I said to the king, "If it pleases the king, and if your servant has found favor in your sight, that you send me to Judah, to the city of my fathers' graves, that I may rebuild it."

—Nehemiah 2:5

Nehemiah had a very specific mission to accomplish. He wanted to go back home and rebuild the battered walls of Jerusalem. He had a passion for this work, and he sought the Lord in prayer for guidance and preparation.

As Christians…just like Nehemiah…we have a specific mission from the Lord. That mission is to reach others for Him. Following through on this mission is often difficult because it may require us to leave our everyday comfort zone—and what I've found is that most Christians are more interested in being comfortable than they are in reaching the spiritually lost!

But you and I should have a passion to reach nonbelievers with the Good News of Jesus Christ…just like Nehemiah had the passion to restore the walls of Jerusalem.

So pray for a passion to reach others today. Then be ready for opportunities to impact the world around you for Christ!

PRAY FOR A PASSION TO REACH OTHERS FOR CHRIST.

Day 104

The king said to me, "Why is your face sad, seeing you are not sick? This is nothing but sadness of the heart." Then I was very much afraid.

—Nehemiah 2:2

This verse reminds me of the parable Jesus told in Matthew 25:14-30. A wealthy king left three of his servants some money, and instructed them to invest it wisely. Two of them did just that, but the third did not.

When the king returned, he was very upset with this unfaithful servant and took away everything he had. Why didn't this servant invest his money? Because he was afraid!

Fear is an enemy for the child of God. A fearful attitude keeps us from being everything we are called to be.

Nehemiah was afraid as he approached the king to ask for permission to return to Jerusalem. But he overcame that fear and approached the king confidently because he knew God had opened the door.

I wonder how many times we fail to achieve wonderful things for the Lord because we give in to an attitude of fear. Are you ever afraid to do something you know you should do? Do you give into that fear?

God wants to give you an attitude of confidence, not fear. Pray today for His strength and His confidence to overcome your fears!

GOD WANTS TO GIVE US AN ATTITUDE OF CONFIDENCE, NOT FEAR.

Day 105

Now to him who is able to do far more abundantly than all that we ask or think, according to the power at work within us, to him be glory in the church and in Christ Jesus throughout all generations, forever and ever. Amen.

—Ephesians 3:20-21

I want to start today by telling you that God is able to do more for you than you could ever hope for or imagine. He can carry you through situations that seem impossible.

Just think about what God did for Nehemiah when he asked for permission to go back to Jerusalem! As we read in the first few chapters of the book of Nehemiah, God moved the king to allow Nehemiah to go and rebuild the walls of Jerusalem.

But to Nehemiah's surprise, not only did he receive a blessing from the king, he also received a military escort for protection as well! Isn't that just like God? If we are faithful enough to ask for His blessing…no matter how difficult the situation might seem…we receive it and so much more.

The problem comes when we think we can create our own success. And as a result, we mess things up…and then wonder why God isn't blessing us!

God wants to answer your prayers. He wants to bless you no matter how difficult or impossible your situation might seem. So ask for God's blessing today and don't forget to praise Him for His abundant answer!

GOD IS ABLE TO DO MORE FOR YOU THAN YOU COULD EVER IMAGINE.

Day 106

I told them of the hand of my God that had been upon me for good, and also of the words that the king had spoken to me. And they said, "Let us rise up and build."

—Nehemiah 2:18

Have you ever wasted or missed a great opportunity? Who hasn't? It's frustrating when we have a chance to do something great, but don't take advantage of that opportunity.

Nehemiah was granted permission to go back to Jerusalem and pursue his mission. What an exciting opportunity for a man who was afraid to ask, but did so nonetheless! It was a life-changing moment for him.

When God guides, God also provides. And because of that, you and I can proceed confidently when He gives us an opportunity. That doesn't mean the task will always be easy or predictable, but if it's from God, it's an opportunity not to be missed.

What are you going to do with your next opportunity for Christ? When God opens the door to the unknown and tells you to go, will you? Nehemiah went confidently because he knew his mission was from God.

Where is God leading you today? Pray that He will open up wonderful opportunities for you to serve Him and make Him known. And be assured that God will not lead you where He can't provide for you!

WHEN GOD GUIDES, HE PROVIDES.

Day 107

Then I arose in the night, I and a few men with me. And I told no one what my God had put into my heart to do for Jerusalem.

—Nehemiah 2:12

The world often defines a leader as someone who's in the spotlight...someone who gets all the attention. But God's idea of a leader involves far more than just being in the limelight.

Nehemiah was a true leader. While he led people to Jerusalem to rebuild the broken walls of the city, it was his actions and dedication for four months leading up to the journey that really made him a great leader.

And what we learn from Nehemiah is an extremely valuable lesson: An effective leader must prepare in private before he or she can lead in public.

Nehemiah knew this truth...and prayed in private for months to make sure his plans lined up with God's.

Great leaders know the practice of solitude. Even Jesus spent hours and hours alone with His Father on a regular basis.

Are you willing to spend time in solitude in order to be successful for the Lord? Pray today that He would burn in your heart the desire to spend time alone with Him in private so you can be used by Him in public.

GREAT LEADERS MUST PREPARE IN PRIVATE BEFORE THEY CAN LEAD IN PUBLIC.

Day 108

I told them of the hand of my God that had been upon me for good.

—Nehemiah 2:18

If you're anything like me, you've probably felt overwhelmed before. It's a sinking and discouraging feeling, isn't it?

Nehemiah surely felt overwhelmed by his task of rebuilding the walls of Jerusalem. He walked along the battered and broken down walls at night, probably feeling this task was much bigger than his ability to accomplish it. But through it all he never became discouraged because he knew God's hand was upon him.

We've all felt overwhelmed from time to time about the job in front of us. But when we feel this way, you and I must remember that we have a God who can do anything!

If a task seems bigger than what we can handle, that's okay because God is with us! If you're willing to make the sacrifice, there really is no limit to what God can do through you.

Sometimes paying the price means praying and seeking God while others are sleeping, like Nehemiah did. Sometimes it means simply pulling away from things that might distract us from our God-given task.

When God calls you to something, He also commits to help you do it. You can be assured that, like Nehemiah, God's hand will be upon you for good!

WHEN LIFE SEEMS OVERWHELMING, REMEMBER THAT GOD'S HAND IS UPON YOU FOR GOOD!

Day 109

Come, let us build the wall of Jerusalem, that we may no longer
suffer derision.

—Nehemiah 2:17

There are three kinds of people in this world: Those who don't
know what's happening, those who watch what is happening,
and those who make something happen!

Nehemiah was a man who made things happen. And that's the
kind of Christian I want to be! And I hope it's the kind of Christian
you want to be.

But often I find Christians stuck...unable to move forward.
Perhaps that's the way you feel today. If so, let me give you some
direction.

The first step to solving any problem is to identify it. Notice
that Nehemiah first inspected the walls of Jerusalem and then put
together a plan of action. Even though the people of Jerusalem had
been living and walking among the city's broken walls for decades,
they had failed to do anything about it!

It took a godly person with a vision and dedication to the Lord
to recognize the problem and then put together a plan of action.
And if you're feeling stuck, perhaps a new perspective would help.

Seek the insight of a trusted friend. Or try altering your normal,
everyday routine so you can look at things from a new angle. God
just may give you a new insight into an old problem, and a plan of
action to solve it!

**A NEW PERSPECTIVE ON AN OLD PROBLEM MAY JUST BE THE WAY TO
SOLVE IT!**

Day 110

I urge you, then, be imitators of me. That is why I sent you Timothy, my beloved and faithful child in the Lord, to remind you of my ways in Christ, as I teach them everywhere in every church.

—1 Corinthians 4:16-17

Jesus Christ has called His followers to be leaders and to set an example for others to follow. The motto for a believer should be, "Do what I do," not, "Do what I say."

This is exactly what Paul says in 1 Corinthians 4 when he tells the people of Corinth to follow his example. He didn't say this because he was self-centered or seeking attention. He knew that he was following Christ...and if others followed him, they too would be following Christ.

Paul didn't have any extraordinary qualifications. He wasn't rich, powerful, or well connected. He just made it his goal to glorify Christ through his words and actions in every circumstance in which he found himself.

In the same way, you don't have to be seminary educated or some powerful Christian to be an example for people to follow. Like Paul, you just need to make it your commitment to imitate and follow Christ in thought, word and deed.

Let me ask you a question today: If people imitated your life, would they imitate Christ? Paul could answer "yes" to this question. Can you?

IF PEOPLE IMITATED YOUR LIFE, WOULD THEY IMITATE CHRIST?

Day 111

They jeered at us and despised us and said, "What is this thing that you are doing?"

—Nehemiah 2:19

All leaders face resistance and take flak, especially those who make a decision to be a true Christian leader.

In the second chapter of the book which bears his name, Nehemiah was busy rebuilding the walls of Jerusalem—a task God had given him to do. But he was also receiving some unwelcome scrutiny from others. Nehemiah's enemies mocked and laughed at him as he tried to honor God.

What made Nehemiah different...what made Nehemiah successful...was his refusal to let the ridicule he received get him down. Instead, he responded in full confidence that God would give him success.

As a Christian, there will always be opposition when God calls you to do something. And it will often come from the evil one himself, Satan. That's why we need to have confidence as Nehemiah did that Christ will give us success no matter who or what opposes us!

No worthwhile task is ever easy, so pray today that you won't be discouraged or distracted away from what Jesus Christ is calling you to do in obedience to Him.

AS A CHRISTIAN, THERE WILL ALWAYS BE OPPOSITION WHEN GOD CALLS YOU TO DO SOMETHING.

Day 112

The sons of Hassenaah built the Fish Gate. They laid its beams and set its doors, its bolts, and its bars. And next to them Meremoth the son of Uriah, son of Hakkoz repaired. And next to them Meshullam the son of Berechiah, son of Meshezabel repaired. And next to them Zadok the son of Baana repaired.

—Nehemiah 3:3-4

The third chapter of Nehemiah gives us a key component to any successful endeavor that Christians attempt: cooperation.

Nehemiah organized many different people to help him rebuild the wall of Jerusalem. Even though these people were from different countries, backgrounds, and ethnic groups, they worked toward a common goal.

Instead of bickering with one another or questioning Nehemiah, they banded together behind a man who had a God-given mission. And God enabled them to accomplish the building of the wall of Jerusalem.

Cooperation is a key to spiritual growth for churches and families. Both must join together as a team, seeking the same goal and following the same leader. When this happens, there's no limit to what God can accomplish!

When it comes to your family and church, are you a team player? Or do you tend to question and bicker? If you're honest with yourself and find that you don't work well with others, admit it to God and ask Him to give you a spirit of cooperation. You'll be surprised how you and your family will grow spiritually…and the difference you will make in your church!

COOPERATION IS KEY TO SPIRITUAL GROWTH FOR CHURCHES AND FAMILIES.

Day 113

Then Eliashib the high priest rose up with his brothers the priests, and they built the Sheep Gate. They consecrated it and set its doors. They consecrated it as far as the Tower of the Hundred, as far as the Tower of Hananel.

—Nehemiah 3:1

Have you ever regretted not getting involved in something that turned out to be a really good thing? Maybe you hesitated because you were unsure of yourself or because you were afraid to take a risk.

Too many Christians operate that way—sitting back for whatever reason while others go out and join the exciting work of God. I don't ever want it to be said of me that something great happened for God's Kingdom, and I chose not to be involved!

Serving Christ means being willing to take part in the battle against evil. If we want to share in the excitement of victory, we have to be a part of the struggle!

The Christian life is not just a free ticket to heaven when you die. It's an exciting way of life each and every day! But you and I have to choose to get involved.

So let me challenge you with this: People all over the world are dying without the knowledge of Christ and the only way they will hear is through Christians like you and me. Choose today to participate in His work … and not just hold onto your ticket to heaven for later.

Be active for Christ every single day…starting today!

FIND WAYS TO ACTIVELY SERVE CHRIST TODAY.

Day 114

Now there are varieties of gifts, but the same Spirit; and there are varieties of service, but the same Lord; and there are varieties of activities, but it is the same God who empowers them all in everyone.

—1 Corinthians 12:4-6

God has blessed every Christian with spiritual gifts—talents and abilities given to us to accomplish His kingdom work.

First Corinthians tells us that God has bestowed certain gifts on certain people, and that He has a specific use for each gift within His Church. Nothing is wasted or unimportant in the work of Christ! Every gift you possess as a believer can be used for ministry.

God has bestowed a variety of gifts and He intends for us to use our diverse gifts to help achieve the same goal. This is hard for the world to grasp, because most people think that diversity breeds trouble and disagreement.

But this isn't the case in the body of Christ! God has given us these gifts "for the common good." That is how Christ accomplishes His work through His Church, by everyone cooperating and using their spiritual gifts.

What are your spiritual gifts? If you don't know, ask those who know you to help you identify them…and then start using them. If you know what your spiritual gifts are, then make sure you are using them to effectively minister in the church.

Offer your gifts to the Lord, and watch how He uses you to impact others!

USE YOUR SPIRITUAL GIFTS FOR THE COMMON GOOD.

Day 115

For God is not so unjust as to overlook your work and the love that you showed for his sake in serving the saints, as you still do.

—Hebrews 6:10

Have you ever done something good that no one seems to notice? Although it can be discouraging when you serve the Lord without notice or reward, rest assured that Christ sees and rewards every act of service for Him!

Jesus said that even giving someone who is thirsty a cup of cold water in His name does not go unnoticed in heaven. The smallest deed done on earth for God's glory is headline news in heaven!

Imagine how much good could be done if every follower of Christ used their gifts and abilities to serve others in the name of Jesus...no matter how small those acts of service might seem in the eyes of others.

With that in mind, make a commitment today to serve the Lord without worrying about who notices. When you serve God out of obedience and love alone, your reward in heaven will be much greater than anything here on earth!

THE SMALLEST DEED DONE FOR GOD ON EARTH IS HEADLINE NEWS IN HEAVEN.

Day 116

For land that has drunk the rain that often falls on it, and produces a crop useful to those for whose sake it is cultivated, receives a blessing from God. But if it bears thorns and thistles, it is worthless and near to being cursed, and its end is to be burned.

—Hebrews 6:7-8

It absolutely thrills me when I think that the God of heaven can actually use me! It blows my mind that I can be an instrument to accomplish His will…just like the land on which abundant rain falls.

Faithful Christians are the tools God uses to do great things that have eternal value. He uses His followers as witnesses to the entire earth to tell everyone about Him and His love. When you stop to think about it, you and I can truly alter the course of history and the world!

Unfortunately, some people are not being used by God because they are either unwilling or unfaithful.

It is said that Leon Trotsky, who was a key part of the Communist revolution in Russia, actually attended a Sunday school class one day during a visit to America. But the teacher of the class was absent that morning, and did not bother to get a substitute. So no one taught the Bible that morning, and as far as anyone knows, Trotsky never attended church again.

What if someone had been faithful enough to show up that Sunday morning? It may have helped to alter history!

All that God asks of us is to make ourselves available to Him. Tell the Lord today that you want to faithfully serve Him, to be like the land in today's verse that is a blessing to others and is blessed by God as a result.

ALL THAT GOD ASKS IS FOR YOU TO MAKE YOURSELF AVAILABLE TO HIM.

Day 117

"What are these feeble Jews doing? Will they restore it for themselves? Will they sacrifice? Will they finish up in a day? Will they revive the stones out of the heaps of rubbish, and burned ones at that?"

—Nehemiah 4:2

It's not unusual for someone who attempts to achieve great things for the Kingdom of God to be ridiculed and mocked for their efforts. Nehemiah certainly was.

Nehemiah and those who worked with him to rebuild the walls of Jerusalem were scorned and made fun of when they began their work. They were called feeble and weak, but they continued on, knowing that the Lord was greater than any opposition or ridicule they endured.

In the same way, you will be mocked and maligned when you take a stand for Christ in this world. Whether you are an adult or student, not joining in with the world will make you a target for criticism. The world will see you as feeble…weak… and not "with it."

Regardless, I challenge you to make the decision today to stand strong! Don't give in to their jeers and criticism. If you will stand strong, God will give you the strength you need to endure.

THE LORD IS GREATER THAN ANY OPPOSITION OR RIDICULE YOU WILL EVER ENDURE.

Day 118

So we built the wall. And all the wall was joined together to half its height, for the people had a mind to work.

—Nehemiah 4:6

Do you remember the old saying, "Sticks and stones may break my bones, but words will never hurt me"? I think we understand the point behind that saying, but it's absolutely untrue, isn't it? We all know how much words can hurt.

That is exactly what Satan wants to do to us—discourage and hurt us. And the way he does this is by telling us lies. With him, the truth doesn't matter. He's simply out to ruin your reputation and shake your confidence in Christ.

In Matthew 16:18, Jesus tells us that He will build His Church and that hell will not prevail against it. He also tells us that we can rebuild our lives and honor Him. But just when you start believing God, Satan will come and say, "You can't rebuild your life—it's too far gone."

This is exactly what Nehemiah was going through as he and the people of God were working to rebuild the walls of Jerusalem from rubbish. Satan sent people to tell him, "You can't possibly make this rubbish into a wall of defense."

But Nehemiah proved them wrong! And just like Nehemiah, so can you!

Don't let Satan steal the victory by believing him and doubting God. Ask God today to help you see the devil's lies for what they are so that you are believing God and doubting the devil.

LEARN TO IGNORE THE LIES OF SATAN AND TRUST THE WORD OF GOD.

Day 119

And lead us not into temptation, but deliver us from evil.

—Matthew 6:13

Too often we are complacent about our enemy, the devil. For some reason, many Christians today don't feel that he is a real threat…so they don't pray for deliverance from his attacks. That's a very dangerous risk, because the battle against the devil is only won on our knees!

Even Jesus in His model prayer made sure we understood the importance of praying for deliverance from the devil's attacks!

The Scripture says that if we love the Lord, then we should hate evil and iniquity. The church as a whole needs a holy anger toward sin and a passion for the work and glory of God. We should not let His name or His work be dishonored.

Nehemiah is a good example. When he was being taunted by his enemies as he rebuilt the walls of Jerusalem, he prayed, "Turn back their taunt on their own heads" (Nehemiah 4:4). This may not sound like your normal "Christian" prayer, but these evildoers were discrediting the name of God and needed to be silenced!

Nehemiah was praying for God to display His power and show the hecklers who was really in control. Nehemiah could pray this way because he knew that God was on the side of His people.

My challenge to you today is to take evil seriously. Pray for a renewed passion to fight against the sin and evil that are thrown your way. Do not underestimate your adversary, but fight the good fight by doing battle on your knees!

THE VICTORY OVER EVIL WILL COME ON YOUR KNEES.

Day 120

And I looked and arose and said to the nobles and to the officials and to the rest of the people, "Do not be afraid of them. Remember the Lord, who is great and awesome, and fight for your brothers, your sons, your daughters, your wives, and your homes."

—Nehemiah 4:14

In Nehemiah 4, the Bible gives us an account of a time when the children of Israel were debilitated by discouragement. They were halfway through completing the rebuilding of the wall of Jerusalem, and discouragement attacked them with full force.

Now, since discouragement is contagious, Nehemiah knew he'd better do something before it spread like a cancer throughout the entire camp.

In the verses above, Nehemiah gave the children of Israel the cure for their discouragement...a truth that will free you from discouragement every time.

Nehemiah knew he needed to take a time-out. So he got the Israelites together and said, "It's time to regain your perspective and remember your great and awesome God! Remember Him...look to Him...listen to Him!"

I can tell you there have been points in my life when I've been down and discouraged. And the cure has been to stop and remember all that God has done for me. In those moments, God Almighty has absolutely carried me through.

And He will carry you, too! He'll give you supernatural strength, even in the middle of a dark day...or the darkest night.

WHEN YOU'RE TEMPTED TO BE DISCOURAGED, REMEMBER HOW MUCH GOD LOVES YOU AND ALL HE HAS DONE FOR YOU!

Day 121

In Judah it was said, "The strength of those who bear the burdens is failing."

—Nehemiah 4:10

Fatigue…it's becoming epidemic in our culture today. And being a Christian doesn't give you immunity!

One big reason believers are often just as worn out as everyone else is that we too push ourselves over the limit. We work too much…and we allow ourselves to become physically depleted. Both of these things can cause us to be ineffective for Christ!

When they were rebuilding the walls of Jerusalem, Nehemiah and his fellow workers certainly experienced fatigue and weariness. Their strength was gone, and it seemed they just couldn't go on because of all the rubble they had to clear out. As a result, they lost the focus of their ultimate goal!

Do you ever feel that you have nothing left to give to Jesus? Have you experienced times when all you could think about was the pile of junk in front of you that had to be cleared off?

When those times of fatigue and weariness come around, look to Jesus for renewed strength. Keep your eyes on the ultimate goal He has for you, not on the obstacles in the way.

WHEN YOU'RE TIRED AND WEARY, KEEP YOUR EYES ON JESUS…NOT ON THE RUBBLE IN YOUR LIFE!

Day 122

"Yes, what they are building—if a fox goes up on it he will break down their stone wall!"

—Nehemiah 4:3

Don't you just love those who will find fault in almost anything? All of us know someone like that...someone who's a fault-finder...someone who seems to take delight in finding a problem with everything around them.

Nehemiah faced the same kinds of people when he was rebuilding the wall of Jerusalem. In fact, some of the fault-finders were his own people! As the verse says above, they criticized the job he was doing and predicted that even a fox could knock the wall down.

Sarcasm, criticism, and cynicism can be very defeating. In fact, someone may be criticizing you this moment. Maybe they've said some things that have hurt you and it's eating you alive.

Today I want to encourage you not to listen to the fault-finders and negative voices around you. Because I promise you, they will bring discouragement and defeat into your life!

Instead, I want to challenge you to meditate on God's Word when negative comments are thrown your way. Take some time today to read Psalm 37. This chapter has been a source of comfort for me many times, and I'm confident God's promises will help drown out the fault-finders in your life today.

MAKE A COMMITMENT TODAY TO FOCUS ON GOD'S PROMISES AND NOT ON THE FAULT-FINDERS IN YOUR LIFE.

Day 123

Forgetting what lies behind and straining forward to what lies ahead, I press on.

—Philippians 3:13-14

One of Satan's strongest weapons against Christians is to bring up our past failures and embarrassments to discourage us and tell us that we can't go on for Christ. The devil wants to pile up the rubbish and ruins from our past to block our progress.

Nehemiah and his fellow Jews who went back to Jerusalem to rebuild the city's walls encountered mounds of rubble and other debris from the city's destruction. The fourth chapter of Nehemiah describes the physical rubbish the workers faced, but the principle remains the same in the spiritual world.

The debris they were working around was a reminder of past failures and defeats for Jerusalem. But Nehemiah was there to claim victory, not moan over the past. And many times we must do as Nehemiah did—stand in the area of previous defeat and claim victory for Christ!

If you get caught up in all of the junk of the past, you'll he weighed down and not move forward. Don't let the evil one remind you of your failures...and fail to focus on the blessings of God in your life.

Have you lost confidence today because of failures that still haunt you? If so, I encourage you to follow Paul's advice and forget about them...and strain forward to what lies ahead!

DON'T LET THE PILES OF RUBBLE FROM YOUR PAST KEEP YOU FROM PRESSING ON FOR CHRIST.

Day 124

"Do not be afraid of them. Remember the Lord, who is great and awesome."
—Nehemiah 4:14

Few emotions are as powerful as fear. It can cause us to do things we wouldn't do under normal circumstances, and it can keep us from doing things we ought to do.

Nehemiah and his fellow wall builders in Jerusalem were being threatened with death. Talk about something to fill you with fear! A death threat would certainly get my attention.

But God doesn't want us to live in fear of others, because He knows it can hinder us from His work. Second Timothy 1:7 tells us that "God gave us a spirit not of fear but of power." What this means for you is that feelings of fear aren't from God, they're from Satan. Which means as a believer, you can defeat fear!

And Nehemiah gives us the key to combating fear in the verse above: "Remember the Lord."

When you're feeling afraid, remember the Lord. Remember His faithfulness. Remember His goodness. Remember that He's your shield and protector. Remember today that the God we serve is great and awesome, and He will not let you down!

DON'T FEAR, BUT "REMEMBER THE LORD"!

Day 125

I stationed the people by their clans.

—Nehemiah 4:13

Isn't it great to have family and close friends who encourage and uplift you? We all need people in our lives who are encouragers, enablers, and energizers.

But it's also very important for followers of Christ to have close friends who are also believers. We need fellowship with God's people! I'm talking about people who pray for us, love us unconditionally, and urge us on in our walk with Christ. We need the Lord, but we also need others who stir us up to love and good works (Hebrews 10:24).

Nehemiah understood the importance of this principle. He placed friends next to friends and families next to families as they worked on the walls of Jerusalem in order to get the most out of them. Everyone gets more done when they have the support of someone who loves and cares about them.

Are you walking in fellowship with other believers today? Are there people in your life right now who are aware of your spiritual victories and struggles?

If not, I want to encourage you to pray that the Lord would give you the determination and courage to invite people like this into your life. Because we all need the support of good, godly friends!

WE ALL NEED OTHERS WHO WILL STAND WITH US THROUGH EVERY VICTORY AND STRUGGLE.

Day 126

When our enemies heard...that God had frustrated their plan, we all returned to the wall, each to his work.

—Nehemiah 4:15

God can do amazing things with people who refuse to quit, who take their eyes off their present circumstances and look ahead because they believe God has something great in store.

That's what Nehemiah did when he was faced with a crisis in his wall-building work in Jerusalem. He never quit...even when the enemies of God's people plotted to stop their work. And God brought their plot to nothing. So Nehemiah looked ahead to the goal and sent everyone back to their work!

In other words, Nehemiah focused on the future. He refused to be discouraged by the present circumstances because he knew God was going to do something great.

Paul gives us the same encouragement in Philippians 3:13-14, when he says, "Brothers, I do not consider that I have made it my own. But one thing I do: forgetting what lies behind and straining forward to what lies ahead, I press on toward the goal for the prize of the upward call of God in Christ Jesus."

If you're discouraged today, think about this: God may just be letting you go through a down time to prepare you for a great victory tomorrow. So don't let your head hang low! Lift your eyes and take a forward look. Because God's blessing may be just around the corner!

BELIEVE THAT GOD HAS SOMETHING GREAT IN STORE FOR YOU!

Day 127

Half of my servants worked on construction, and half held the spears, shields, bows, and coats of mail.

—Nehemiah 4:16

As a Christian, God expects you and me to be productive. What a great example we have of this in the fourth chapter of Nehemiah. Once the plot to stop the work of rebuilding the wall of Jerusalem was foiled, everybody went back to work with renewed energy.

Even those who weren't actively rebuilding the walls kept armor and weapons ready in case the enemy attacked. Nobody sat around idly!

First Corinthians 15:58 tell us to "be steadfast, immovable, always abounding in the work of the Lord...."

And what exactly does "abounding in the work of the Lord" mean? For one, it means we're actively looking for ways to serve God and serve others. It means we're so busy thinking about what we can do next for the Kingdom that we have little time to think about ourselves, worry, and become discouraged!

Today I want to challenge you to go out of your way to serve someone. And don't just do it to do it. Let that person know you're helping them out because your service pleases the Lord you love! It will be a great testimony of a life that's sold out for Christ.

LOOK FOR WAYS TO SERVE AND LOVE OTHERS TODAY...AND EVERY DAY.

Day 128

But Jesus looked at them and said, "With man this is impossible, but with God all things are possible."

—Matthew 19:26

The Christian faith is a can-do faith! "I can do all things through him who strengthens me" was the apostle Paul's declaration in Philippians 4:13, and it should be ours as believers as well.

Jesus not only transforms our spirit when He saves us, but He transforms our way of thinking and looking at life.

Of course, there will be times when we're blue and discouraged, and even times when we are so down that we don't know which way is up! That's a normal part of being alive. But through it all, God's Word promises us that we can defeat discouragement through the power and victory that is ours in Jesus Christ!

When you know Christ, all things are possible. No matter what your past has been, what your current state of mind is, or what your current circumstances are, if you will come to Jesus Christ, you can rebuild your life. Don't let the devil or anybody else tell you that can't happen to you!

If you've never put your faith in Christ alone for salvation, or if you're not sure about your relationship with Him, I invite you to believe in the One who died on the cross for you. Put your faith in Christ, and receive Him as your Savior. And if you know Him, thank Him for new life and the can-do faith that He has given you!

THANK GOD TODAY FOR HIS POWER TO TRANSFORM AND REBUILD YOUR LIFE.

Day 129

But now, O God, strengthen my hands.

—Nehemiah 6:9

You have to give Nehemiah's enemies an "E" for effort. When their threats of violence didn't stop Nehemiah from rebuilding Jerusalem's walls, they resorted to lies in an attempt to slander Nehemiah.

They were simply doing the bidding of a greater enemy of God's people, the devil himself, who according to Jesus Christ is "the father of lies" (John 8:44).

The lie they used to slander Nehemiah was a big one: "Nehemiah, everyone knows you want to be king of Judah. The reason you're rebuilding this wall is because you're an egomaniac. You're in this for yourself, and we're going to tell the king of Persia on you!"

Nehemiah's enemies couldn't break his will by threats. So they sought to break his spirit by spreading rumors about him. And they used the devil's oldest attack of all—full-blown, blatant, bold-faced lies!

The rumor mill was working full time, but Nehemiah simply denied the charge. "No such things as you say have been done, for you are inventing them out of your own mind" (Nehemiah 6:8). And then Nehemiah prayed for the strength to finish his work.

At some point or another, someone has probably lied about you or spread rumors to hurt you. Have you forgiven them? Do you harbor bitterness towards them?

If you have been slandered, ask God for the grace to forgive. Then pray that God would strengthen your hands to finish the work He has given you to do without any bitterness in your heart.

ASK GOD TO GIVE YOU THE STRENGTH TO STAND AGAINST FALSE ACCUSATIONS...AND GO ABOUT THE WORK HE HAS FOR YOU.

Day 130

"I tell you, on the day of judgment people will give account for every careless word they speak, for by your words you will be justified, and by your words you will be condemned."

—Matthew 12:36-37

A famous pop song from the 60s said, "I heard it through the grapevine." May I suggest that in the Church of Jesus Christ, that vine needs to be pruned! Phrases like "I heard" and "they said" are potent ways to spread slander, innuendo, and rumors.

Nehemiah's enemies tried to slander him into quitting his work. The charge of treason they leveled against him in chapter 6 was designed to destroy him, because treason was punishable by death!

As believers, we need to be very careful with our words, because words can kill. Jesus was talking about the Day of Judgment when He said we will give an account of every careless word we speak.

Paul also warns us in Ephesians 4:29, "Let no corrupting talk come out of your mouths, but only such as is good for building up, as fits the occasion, that it may give grace to those who hear." Or in other words, ask yourself this question when you're tempted to gossip: "Does passing this information along honestly help solve the problem or help the parties involved?" If you can't answer with an affirmative "yes," then keep it to yourself!

You and I shouldn't pass on any information we can't sign our name to and stand behind. Determine in your heart today that the next rumor you hear will stop with you!

BE A RUMOR-STOPPER RATHER THAN A RUMOR-MONGER!

Day 131

"Blessed are you when others revile you…and utter all kinds of evil against you falsely on my account."

—Matthew 5:11

We all know that words can hurt us…and that unfair accusations or lies can sap us of spiritual and physical vitality. This is what Nehemiah's accusers hoped to do to him in chapter 6 by making very serious charges against him.

Nehemiah didn't have the words of Jesus to reassure him, but he did understand a very important principle: If you're living for God and someone accuses you falsely because of it, it's a sign of blessing. In fact, Jesus said, "Your reward is great in heaven" (Matthew 5:12).

Perhaps you're being accused of having wrong motives in your service for Christ. Or maybe someone is accusing you of saying or doing something that isn't true. If so, remember you can still have joy in the Lord! Like Nehemiah, you can rise above the rumors and stay the course in your service for the Lord.

Make the words of Hebrews 12:2 your prayer today: "Look to Jesus, the founder and perfecter of our faith, who for the joy that was set before him endured the cross, despising the shame, and is seated at the right hand of the throne of God." Look to Jesus, who also endured persecution and false accusations, and keep running the race!

FALSE ACCUSATIONS MEAN TRUE REWARDS WHEN YOU BEAR THEM FOR CHRIST!

Day 132

The wicked flee when no one pursues, but the righteous are bold as a lion.

—Proverbs 28:1

If the devil can't discourage and defeat you by slander or false accusations, he'll try to bring you down by tempting you to commit outright sin. And it takes incredible, God-given discernment to avoid Satan's traps.

That's the situation Nehemiah faced in verses 10-14 of chapter 6 in the book bearing his name. The plot against him was very clever. A false prophet said to Nehemiah, "God told me that your enemies are coming to kill you. Quick! Run and hide in the temple."

But Nehemiah was a discerning man. He knew God had not sent this so-called prophet. Nehemiah also knew if he listened to this man and hid in the inner recesses of the temple, that act would break the commandment of God and expose Nehemiah to all the people as a sinner.

So Nehemiah replied, "Should such a man as I run away?" (Nehemiah 6:11). It was a statement of holy boldness, not one of human braggadocio. Sometimes God's people are gullible and respond to any so-called message from Him. But Nehemiah knew the Word of God, so he could spot a sin when he saw one. Consequently, he wasn't fooled.

The same applies in your life today. Knowing God's Word gives you incredible discernment and will keep you from falling for Satan's traps. So don't go to bed tonight without spending time in your Bible today!

KNOWING GOD'S WORD WILL HELP YOU AVOID THE TRAPS OF SATAN.

Day 133

> "Fear not, for I am with you; be not dismayed, for I am your God; I will strengthen you, I will help you, I will uphold you with my righteous right hand."
>
> —Isaiah 41:10

One of the strongest drivers for us as humans is the drive for self-preservation. Even Job 2:4 says, "All that a man has he will give for his life."

Since this is the case, it only makes sense that one of the strongest human fears is the fear of death. The "devil in a prophet's suit" who came to Nehemiah in 6:10-14 tried to scare Nehemiah into disobeying God with this lie: "They are coming to kill you by night."

But Nehemiah knew this wasn't a message from God because it was a message of fear. This so-called prophet was a hired gun to get Nehemiah to give up and quit his God-given task to rebuild the wall of Jerusalem.

Perhaps you're being tempted to run away and hide today. Maybe you're ready to quit your job, ditch your church, or even bail out on your marriage and family. Don't run! That message of fear is not from God! His Word to you today is, "Fear not."

You can stand strong and not give in to fear because you aren't alone. God has promised never to leave you. If you're going to run, run to Him today. Confess your fear, and ask Him to replace it with the assurance of His presence and power.

GOD'S WORD TO YOU TODAY IS, "FEAR NOT."

Day 134

So the wall was finished…in fifty-two days.

—Nehemiah 6:15

In less than two months, what some people said was impossible was in fact completed! Under Nehemiah's leadership, the wall around Jerusalem was transformed from a pile of rubble into a formidable structure.

What may be the best part was that when it was done, even Nehemiah's enemies had to admit that "this work had been accomplished with the help of our God" (Nehemiah 6:16). When it was all said and done, this accomplishment was simply an expression of what God had done.

You know, I want to be a part of a work like that. Not something that's superficial, but something that is supernatural. Something that can't be explained any other way except by saying, "God did this."

When the work of Jesus Christ is done through the power of the Holy Spirit, those who observe it will be awestruck and amazed by the power of our God. And when it happens that way, the Lord Jesus Christ is lifted up and glorified.

Do you want to be part of a great work for God today? Then pray, "Lord, fill me with Your Holy Spirit and use me in whatever way You choose." Then be ready, because He will use you in a mighty way!

GOD WANTS TO DO GREAT THINGS THROUGH YOU.

Day 135

Will you not revive us again, that your people may rejoice in you?

—Psalm 85:6

If I could define revival, I would define it like this: Revival is all of Jesus Christ having all of His way all of the time in all of me. And what we need in America, in the church of Jesus Christ, and in our personal lives, is revival!

If you can't say today that Christ is having all of His way all of the time in all of you, then you're a candidate for personal revival. That's not an admission of weakness, but of reality. We all need times of revival and refreshing from the Lord.

Perhaps your greatest need and deepest desire today is for God to do a fresh work in your life. Then I have good news for you. God is ready and waiting to send you the showers of refreshment for which you long!

Revival is not just an event on your church's calendar. It's an event that happens inside you. And it can happen anywhere and at any time.

Substitute your name for "us" and "your people" in the verse above, and make this your personal prayer to the Lord today!

GOD IS READY AND WAITING TO SEND SHOWERS OF REFRESHMENT ON YOU!

Day 136

All the people gathered as one man into the square before the Water Gate.

—Nehemiah 8:1

After Nehemiah and his people had finished repairing and rebuilding the walls of Jerusalem, they gathered together for a time of spiritual renewal. And when they did, it impacted the entire city.

One of the wonderful things about revival is that when we are renewed in our relationship with God and His joy begins to flood our hearts, the overflow spills onto other people! That's why it's so important that we come together as the people of God to celebrate His goodness and seek Him for refreshment and revival!

The people of Jerusalem gathered "as one man." That is, they came with the same purpose to praise God, to hear His Word, and to observe the Feast of Tabernacles or Booths as God had commanded. And sure enough, great rejoicing and revival broke out!

There's something miraculous that happens when God's people come together. That's why it's so important that believers make corporate worship a consistent part of their lives.

Are you a part of a church where Christ is honored and the full counsel of His Word is believed and taught? If so, are you regularly taking part in corporate worship?

The Bible tells us not to forsake assembling ourselves as the body of Christ (Hebrews 10:25). It's my prayer that you will renew your commitment to Christ and His Church today.

SOMETHING MIRACULOUS HAPPENS WHEN GOD'S PEOPLE COME TOGETHER.

Day 137

I rejoice at your word like one who finds great spoil.

—Psalm 119:162

I love the picture the Scripture gives us of the revival that broke out when Nehemiah and Ezra gathered God's people to celebrate the completion of Jerusalem's walls. Ezra began to read from the Law, and the Bible says, "The ears of all the people were attentive to the Book of the Law" (Nehemiah 8:3).

Isn't that great?! In verse 1 of this story, we're told that the people asked Ezra to bring the Law and read from it! There was a famine in the land for the Word of God, and a deep hunger in their hearts to hear from Him.

Can the same thing be said of you today? Do have you have a passion and a hunger that cannot be satisfied by anything but Him? If we ever want to see true revival break out in our country, it must begin with personal revival in each of our lives.

Perhaps today you'd admit that you hunger for other things besides the Lord. Perhaps you've let other things get in the way of your relationship with Him.

If so, pray today that God will give you a passion for Him and His Word...and that you won't be satisfied with anything less than Him!

ASK GOD TO GIVE YOU A DEEP AND ABIDING HUNGER FOR HIM AND HIS WORD.

Day 138

And all the people went their way to eat and drink and to send portions and to make great rejoicing, because they had understood the words that were declared to them.

—Nehemiah 8:12

How would you describe true joy? Do you think you have it? The joy of the Lord is an inner sense of delight in Him that comes from knowing Him through Christ. But in the truest sense, joy can't be completely described. It can only be experienced!

As we see in the verse above, the Israelites experienced this kind of joy when they heard Ezra read from the Scriptures. They understood what was read to them and its significance for their lives.

When we experience true joy like that, the celebration is in our hearts! It's an inward joy that can't be shaken.

Now, I want to make sure you understand the difference between joy and happiness because these two terms are not synonymous. This difference should be what separates you and me as Christians from the rest of the world.

Happiness is just a feeling, an emotion that's based on circumstances and the environment around us. But joy is the heartfelt and internal confidence, peace, and contentment of a believer. It's something that can be found in Christ alone!

So let me ask you, are you living each day with joy…or mere happiness? If you don't know the joy I'm talking about, I invite you to come and share in the true joy of the Lord Jesus Christ.

The only way you can live each day with true joy and celebration in your heart is by knowing Him!

TRUE JOY CAN ONLY BE FOUND IN KNOWING CHRIST!

Day 139

"The joy of the LORD is your strength."

—Nehemiah 8:10

Remember the old saying, "Time flies by when you're having fun"? I think there's a lot of truth to this statement.

When things aren't going the way we want, or if we're bored, time seems to slow down to a crawl. But when we fill our lives with things we enjoy, time just zooms by. I believe the same is true of us in our Christian lives.

Nehemiah 8:10 says that the joy of the Lord is our strength. This means that as believers we should be strengthened and encouraged by our relationship with the Lord. He should be the reason we serve and His glory should be the goal of everything we do.

Unfortunately, when we are out of fellowship or out of touch with Christ, we usually lose the joy of serving. At that point, serving God and worshiping Him become tasks we dread and events that just seem to go by in slow motion.

However, when we're in vibrant fellowship with Christ, we enjoy serving and worshiping Him…and the time goes by so quickly that we are hardly aware of the passing of the hours!

I pray that you will feel great joy in serving the Lord today and every day. He promised us that He will be our strength each and every hour if we will remain in Him.

ASK GOD TO RENEW YOUR JOY AND STRENGTH THROUGH HIM TODAY.

Day 140

"You are the LORD, you alone. You have made heaven, the heaven of heavens, with all their host, the earth and all that is on it, the seas and all that is in them."

—Nehemiah 9:6

The Lord wants us to approach Him with an attitude of awe and humility. Nothing less is appropriate when we realize that we don't measure up to the standards of an all-powerful, holy, and sinless God. We need to come with a sense of awe and wonder before the God of the universe.

This is really where true prayer begins. There's a great example of this in chapter nine of Nehemiah. After Ezra read the Law, the Israelites realized just how awesome God was, and how far short of His glory they fell.

They came to confess their sins, but first they did something that I believe we forget to do quite often, which is to spend time telling the Lord just how mighty and wonderful He is.

People today try to ignore God, and deny their need of Him by filling their lives with pleasures, possessions, and other things that can't fill the void. We can try to escape the inevitable, but sooner or later we all have to come before a holy God and confess that we have no hope for today or tomorrow apart from Him.

When we reach that point of selflessness, and come to grips with who God really is, we cannot help but truly humble ourselves in His presence. When you come to the end of yourself, you realize that it is either Jesus or nothing!

The Israelites fell on their faces in worship, and covered themselves with rags to show God their unworthiness and need of Him. When was the last time you fell on your face, or even your knees, to adore the Lord for His greatness and confess your sins?

MAKE TODAY AN AWESOME DAY BY SPENDING TIME IN ADORATION OF GOD!

Day 141

"God opposes the proud, but gives grace to the humble." Submit yourselves therefore to God.

—James 4:6-7

In Nehemiah chapter 9, we see God's people fasting, praying, and approaching God with sincerity and humility.

They weren't concerned with their self-esteem, but came confessing their sins and seeking forgiveness. God accepts our worship when we come to Him with true humility that recognizes our total dependence on Him.

How do you feel when you're dealing with a proud, arrogant person? Most of us are frustrated when we meet people who are so full of themselves that they don't even think of anyone else.

It's unfortunate that true brokenness is considered a weakness in today's society. To God, however, our brokenness shows true strength in Him. When we come before God and rid ourselves of selfishness and pride, He gives us immeasurable strength to continue in His name.

We actually become much stronger and more capable when we approach the Lord with humility!

What about you? Are you living with pride today? You don't have to be arrogant or parade your accomplishments to be proud. Pride is simply saying "no" to God because we think we have a better plan.

Ask God to help you approach Him with a broken, humble spirit today…and allow Him to give you a new measure of strength in your life today!

HUMILITY BEFORE GOD IS ESSENTIAL IF YOU ARE TO GAIN HIS STRENGTH IN YOUR LIFE.

Day 142

You in your great mercies did not forsake them in the wilderness.

—Nehemiah 9:19

Isn't it great to know that no matter how unfaithful we are, God is always faithful and merciful to us? His love is astounding and amazing to me, even as it was to the Israelites, as we read in chapter 9 of Nehemiah.

But that doesn't mean we can take sin lightly. God's love and mercy can only become real to us when we see them against the backdrop of our own sinfulness and lack of faith.

As the people of Israel looked back over their history and realized that they had rebelled against God, they were struck by the reality of sinfulness and the true magnitude of God's great mercy towards them.

As Christians, we need to be reminded of the seriousness of sin. Sin is not simply breaking a rule, but breaking trust with God. We rupture our relationship with God when we sin. That's why it is so heartbreaking to the Lord when we rebel against Him.

Of course, this breaking of trust doesn't mean we aren't believers anymore. But it does create a breach in our intimacy with Christ. In a sense, we start walking backward or a little farther away from God when we sin, making our relationship weaker.

But the good news is that when we are repentant, turning back to Christ and renewing our commitment to Him, that intimacy is restored. I encourage you, walk toward the Lord today...and rejoice in His faithfulness!

EVEN THOUGH SIN BREAKS OUR INTIMACY WITH CHRIST, REPENTANCE RESTORES IT!

Day 143

If we confess our sins, he is faithful and just to forgive us our sins and to cleanse us from all unrighteousness.

—1 John 1:9

D o you want to experience God's forgiveness?

The best place to start is to assume personal and total responsibility for your sins. Don't blame others—not your parents, society, or even God—for your problems. Just say "Lord, I'm guilty and I need Your forgiveness."

This is exactly the formula the Israelites used to seek God's forgiveness in the story of Nehemiah. They looked back over their actions, owned their sins, and admitted they deserved God's judgment, not forgiveness.

But when they came to God in humility and confession, He forgave them!

Even though we all deserve God's judgment, we all can receive His forgiveness. God is both just and merciful, which is why we receive grace and forgiveness, not what we deserve. That's why John says that if we confess our sins and take responsibility for them, God will forgive us and clean us from our unrighteousness!

Are you ready to take responsibility for your actions, confessing your sins to God and asking for His forgiveness? He has promised to forgive you because forgiveness is the gift He gave us when He hung on the cross!

YOU CAN EXPERIENCE TRUE FORGIVENESS WHEN YOU TAKE RESPONSIBILITY FOR YOUR SINS.

Day 144

As far as the east is from the west, so far does he remove our transgressions from us.

—Psalm 103:12

One of the most effective tricks Satan plays on Christians is to convince us that our sins aren't really forgiven…despite the promise of God's Word.

But if you've trusted Jesus as your Savior, that uneasy feeling of wondering whether or not you are forgiven comes straight from the devil.

Many believers can quote verses that tell of the forgiveness of Christ…they can feel bad about their sins…and even confess and turn from them. But deep in their hearts, they don't really believe they are fully forgiven.

You see, Satan wants to remind us of our past transgressions, and he uses those to prove that God couldn't possibly forgive or restore us. The devil's attacks make it a challenge for us to simply rest in the promises of God and trust His love.

But Psalm 103 tells us that God not only forgives our sins, but removes them completely from His presence. This is a very difficult concept for human beings to grasp, which is why I think it's so easy for us to worry and wonder about forgiveness instead of just accepting it.

Do you still worry about the sins in your past? Do you ask for forgiveness, but still have an uneasy or guilty feeling? Give those doubts to the Lord today, and rest in His promise of forgiveness.

REST ON THE PROMISE OF GOD THAT YOUR SINS ARE FORGIVEN!

Day 145

"We will not neglect the house of our God."

—Nehemiah 10:39

The Christian life is really a series of new beginnings. That's what makes being a Christian so interesting and exhilarating. We should be excited about our next opportunity to serve, lead, grow, and follow God through another open door.

But be careful! There's a danger here.

It's easy to rest on our success and become stagnant after reaching a new level of growth. We need to be aware of what I call the perils of the plateau. That's the danger of settling for where we are and becoming stagnant, rather than moving onward and upward for the cause of Christ.

We must not, as Nehemiah put it, "neglect the house of our God." Instead, let's continue to look for the next opportunity and not get comfortable, lazy, or satisfied with our current level of spiritual growth. Nothing is worse for a Christian than being dormant and still in our spiritual life.

Have you hit a spiritual plateau, or are you still excited and eager for your next opportunity to grow spiritually? Tell the Lord you want Him to show you the next spiritual mountain to climb. Enjoy the Christian life, and live it to the fullest, without settling or stopping!

THE CHRISTIAN LIFE IS A SERIES OF NEW BEGINNINGS.

Day 146

Bear fruit in keeping with repentance.

—Matthew 3:8

I'm sure that you've heard the old saying, "Actions speak louder than words."

I believe this is exactly what God is saying to us sometimes. God wants us to worship Him with our mouths and voices, but He also wants us to act upon those words.

This is especially true of repentance. The Bible tells us to confess our sins with our mouths…but it also says that God wants to see the change in our lives. The challenge is to move from repentance to commitment!

How can you tell if someone is genuine in what they say? Check and see if their actions match their words. As Matthew 3:8 says, we must bear fruit that is consistent with our repentance. That simply means living in a way that matches our verbal commitments to God.

The only reliable, outward sign of true repentance is a changed life. Tears, emotions, and words are many times outward signals of inward change, but those can be deceiving. Genuine repentance is displayed when our actions match our words.

You probably already know to confess your sins to God to experience His forgiveness. But think about this today. In what ways has that repentance resulted in a change in your life?

It's wonderful to be able to confess our sins to God and experience His forgiveness. Let's just make sure that what we do after we say "Amen" matches up with the words we just spoke to the Lord.

THE SIGN OF AUTHENTIC REPENTANCE IS A CHANGED LIFE.

Day 147

The rest of the people...join with their brothers, their nobles, and enter into a curse and an oath to walk in God's Law that was given by Moses the servant of God, and to observe and do all the commandments of the LORD our Lord and his rules and his statutes.

—Nehemiah 10:28-29

Many times in the Bible, when the Israelites made a commitment to the Lord, they did so publicly. This is something the church still practices today in a variety of ways...baptisms, weddings, communion, and altar calls. Why? Because of the level of commitment it represents.

In chapter 10 of Nehemiah, God's people made public commitments to Him for their families, finances, and many other issues. They made a promise, or covenant to the Lord to be faithful to their vows.

The Lord has already made a covenant with us in His Word, the Bible. The vows and commitments we make in His presence and the presence of others are ways we express our pledge back to the Lord.

But often I find that too many Christians are secret believers. They don't make a public confession of their commitment and faith in God.

When we do, everyone knows the promises we have made, and those around us can encourage us to keep our commitments faithfully. That's why people are baptized in front of the whole church, and why we invite hundreds of close friends and family to weddings—for public commitment and accountability!

Don't be a secret believer today. Make a public commitment to the Lord to show your dedication to Him!

DON'T BE A SECRET BELIEVER IN CHRIST...STAND BOLDLY AND PUBLICLY FOR HIM.

Day 148

Join with their brothers, their nobles, and enter into a curse and an oath to walk in God's Law that was given by Moses the servant of God, and to observe and do all the commandments of the LORD our Lord and his rules and his statutes.

—Nehemiah 10:29

I wanted to revisit this verse today, because it has a powerful truth we must not fail to see. As the people of God, there needs to be something clearly different about us as we live our daily lives.

After the Israelites vowed to always follow the Lord, they made vows to live life differently than the people around them.

In the same way, Christ calls His followers to live sanctified lives, set apart from the unsaved world.

But there's more to being set apart for Christ than just refraining from certain activities. Too many Christians are known for what they don't do instead of for their love, compassion, and service to others.

Sometimes we become so focused on avoiding things that displease God that we forget to do the things that please Him.

Being separate from the world is a call to live such holy, blameless, and God-honoring lives that people are drawn to Christ as they see Him in us.

And if your desire is to live a set-apart life for Christ, I commend you. But let me ask you, are you making an impact for Him in your world? Commit yourself today to be a positive, attractive influence for Christ!

CHRISTIANS SHOULD BE KNOWN FOR WHAT THEY DO, NOT JUST WHAT THEY AVOID!

Day 149

But as he who called you is holy, you also be holy in all your conduct.

—1 Peter 1:15

The goal of a lot of Christians these days is to be healthy and happy. And there's nothing wrong with that. But it makes me wonder why so few Christians endeavor to be holy.

Now, holiness is much easier said than done. But it should be the goal we're striving for as followers of Jesus Christ. Christ has called us to be holy and to live under His authority and lordship. We should have a burning desire to live by the Word of God and apply it to our lives.

And this requires more than just reading the Bible or listening to God's Word preached. Have you ever known anyone who hears everything, but doesn't really listen to much of anything? That is exactly how we are sometimes with the Scripture. We know it and can probably quote it, but we don't always listen to it and apply it to our lives.

The old hymn says, "Trust and obey, for there's no other way to be happy in Jesus!" We've sung it a thousand times, but have we taken those words home and applied them?

God says He will bless those who obey and trust Him. It means that you and I must trust God and obey Him in every area of our lives.

Is He Lord over the way you speak, the way you react, the way you lead your family, the way you do your business...even the way you drive??

Obeying Christ is not always easy, but it makes you more like Him. I encourage you to make your prayer today be, "Lord, make me holy as You are holy."

HOLINESS REQUIRES NOT JUST HEARING THE WORD, BUT LIVING IT.

Day 150

For where your treasure is, there will your heart be also.

—Luke 12:34

Did you know that your dedication to Jesus Christ should affect your checkbook?

The issue of what we do with our money is so important that Jesus talked more about it than He did any other single topic in the Scripture.

We know it costs money to operate a church, which is why believers are required to support their local church body. To put it simply, being a Christian requires a financial commitment!

Now, that may sound blunt and even somewhat scary to you, but Jesus teaches that He will provide for us when we put Him and His work first financially. And when we get to the point that we can give regularly to the Lord without worrying about how we're going to meet our own needs, this is a sign we are growing in our faith. Because Jesus said our hearts will follow our treasures.

Many people treasure money the most…which is why Jesus addressed the subject so often. He knows the love of money is an easy trap for us to fall into…that it can capture our hearts and make us treasure it more than we do Him.

So here's something to think about…does the way you spend your money show that you treasure God over everything else in your life? Does the way you contribute to your church and God's work show Jesus, your family, and your friends that God is Lord over your finances?

THE WAY YOU SPEND YOUR MONEY SHOWS HOW MUCH YOU TREASURE GOD.

Day 151

We obligate ourselves to bring the firstfruits of our ground and the firstfruits of all fruit of every tree, year by year, to the house of the LORD.

—Nehemiah 10:35

A small child requires constant care and feeding. But when that child grows up healthy and matures, all the time and effort spent is worth it!

It's the same way with the Church of Jesus Christ. The Church is a living, growing body that requires many commitments. But when its members grow strong in Christ and are able to reach others, all the effort is worth it.

Near the end of the tenth chapter of Nehemiah, the Israelites made a commitment to faithfully nurture the work of God and help it grow. They understood what so many believers here in America need to take to heart. In order for the Church to be an influence in society today, it must be supported and grown by everyone in the body of Christ.

Supporting your church doesn't mean just darkening the door a few times a year. Truly supporting your church as a Christian means praying for your church and its leaders, serving it, and committing your families and finances to it as well.

This may sound like a lot to give for Christ, but remember everything He gave for you!

The Church is God's earthly instrument to reach the lost and share His love with them. And it needs to be supported so it can grow and become a strong influence for Christ in this dark and hopeless world!

THE CHURCH IS A LIVING, GROWING BODY THAT NEEDS YOUR CONSISTENT SUPPORT.

Day 152

By faith Moses, when he was grown up, refused to be called the son of Pharaoh's daughter, choosing rather to be mistreated with the people of God than to enjoy the fleeting pleasures of sin.

—Hebrews 11:24-25

Your character can be defined as the summation of all the choices you make in life. Choices can be powerful and they can shape your life. Someone once said, "First you make your choice, and then your choice makes you."

Moses' decision to forsake the pleasures of Egypt as Pharaoh's son is a wonderful example of how our choices can lead us in a different direction and shape our ultimate destiny for Christ. In a society of many celebrities, but few real heroes, Moses stands out to us as a real hero of faith who made the right decision.

Even though Moses lived like a prince in Egypt, he knew he was a Jew, and he decided to follow God by identifying with His people.

At about age 40, Moses knew God was calling him to do something important. So, instead of taking the easy way out and staying with his life of luxury, Moses said, "Yes, Lord." And he followed God in faith.

Like Moses, God often calls you and me to stand up in the midst of difficult situations and say, "Yes, Lord!" It may not always be easy, but I challenge you to follow God regardless. Who knows? A wise choice you make today could change the rest of your life!

BE WILLING TO SAY "YES, LORD," AND FOLLOW HIS LEADING IN FAITH.

Day 153

"No servant can serve two masters, for either he will hate the one and love the other, or he will be devoted to the one and despise the other. You cannot serve God and money."

—Luke 16:13

Many people spend the first 20 or 30 years of their life having fun, enjoying their success and worldly possessions. But as they approach mid-life, they start to seriously ponder life's deeper issues, realizing what promised to fulfill their lives has let them down.

God doesn't mind if we have fun and enjoy things in life, but He wants us to spend our lives making eternal investments in things that will matter when we leave this earth. We need to understand that having worldly success is no guarantee of eternal reward.

That's why all the fun in the world leaves a void and does not satisfy our souls!

Sooner or later, the earthly and heavenly worlds will collide, and you'll have to decide where you are going to invest your life. That's why Jesus said we can't give all of our energy to worldly pleasures and expect to gain heavenly rewards.

Our heart only has room for one master. It will either be Christ or the temporary things of this world.

I pray today that you are not trying to keep one foot in the world while the other is in heaven. Because that's a balancing act no one can pull off! Stop straddling the fence…and come over to the side that Christ is calling you to even now!

MAKE AN ETERNAL…NOT TEMPORARY…INVESTMENT WITH YOUR LIFE.

Day 154

He considered the reproach of Christ greater wealth than the treasures of Egypt, for he was looking to the reward.

—Hebrews 11:26

How often do you think about the future?

It's important to see where you're headed, especially if you want to leave a legacy of blessing for future generations.

That's what Moses did when he took a hard look at the struggles of his enslaved people, the Israelites, and knew he could not just sit back and enjoy his luxurious life in Pharaoh's palace and let them suffer as slaves.

Moses realized this was not the future God had in mind for him...or his people.

My prayer for us is that we will look ahead and see not only our future, but the future of the people God has called us to reach. We need to have a burden that compels us to do something about the spiritually lost people around us, knowing that they face a hopeless future and eternity without Christ.

As believers, we have a wonderful future awaiting us in heaven. But we can't just sit back and enjoy the good things of God while unbelievers all around us are heading to a horrible future!

Remember, non-believers have an eternal future too—a very bleak and painful one. I truly believe that when we as Christians comprehend the significance of that fact, we become absolutely desperate to share Christ with others.

Moses saw into the future and decided to do something about it. Why not follow Moses' lead today and reach out to that unsaved friend or neighbor?

SHARE CHRIST TODAY WITH SOMEONE WHO COULD SPEND AN ETERNITY SEPARATED FROM GOD!

Day 155

Then Moses was afraid, and thought, "Surely the thing is known."

—Exodus 2:14

Moses was a high-ranking member of Egyptian society since he was raised in the palace of the Pharaoh. But even though he was well-cultured in the local way of life, he was Jewish…and he had a heart for the suffering of his people.

One day, Moses saw an Egyptian beating a Jewish slave. Overcome with anger, Moses ran over and killed the Egyptian.

Moses realized later that his deed was known, and that Pharaoh would be out for his head. So he fled to the wilderness in fear. You see, Moses was genuinely concerned for the Jewish people, but he reacted in his own strength…and failed.

Instead of waiting for the Lord's timing to free the Hebrew slaves, Moses took matters into his own hands. The result was that Moses went from living a charmed life in a palace to being an outlaw roaming a desolate and foreign land before he could be used for God's service.

Like Moses, you and I can often be tempted to do things in our own time and in our own way. It can be very difficult to wait for God's timing and leading. So I challenge you today to learn from Moses' mistake.

Make sure you hear from God before attempting to do something for God!

WAIT FOR GOD'S TIMING INSTEAD OF TRYING TO DO THINGS IN YOUR OWN STRENGTH.

Day 156

But Moses said to God, "Who am I that I should go to Pharaoh and bring the children of Israel out of Egypt?"

—Exodus 3:11

In the third chapter of Exodus, we find Moses tending flocks in the desert when God speaks to him in a burning bush.

God calls Moses to lead the Israelites out of Egypt, but Moses protests multiple times. He asks God what makes him so special that he was picked for this formidable task.

God answers that He will be with Moses all the way. Which, by the way, is the same answer God would give you and me if we asked the same question! God didn't tell Moses how special Moses was, but how special He, God, was!

If God can speak through a small, burning bush and use an outlaw shepherd to lead a nation of people from slavery to freedom, why can't He use you to do amazing things? The answer is, He can!

But like Moses, you and I often make excuses why we're not qualified or capable of accomplishing God's task for us. We need to realize that as children of God, He's qualified us to do great things for Him!

Today, I challenge you to follow God's leading…even if what He asks you to do seems impossible or improbable.

GOD CAN USE YOU TO DO AMAZING THINGS FOR HIM BECAUSE YOU ARE HIS CHILD.

Day 157

And he said, "Throw it on the ground." So he threw it on the ground, and it became a serpent, and Moses ran from it. But the LORD said to Moses, "Put out your hand and catch it by the tail"—so he put out his hand and caught it, and it became a staff in his hand.

—Exodus 4:3-4

Moses put his life squarely in God's hands when God told him to pick up a live, slithering snake. God instructed Moses to throw down his rod, which turned into a snake, and then pick up the snake by the tail.

When Moses did that, it became a rod in his hand. If anyone else had tried to pick up a snake by the tail, they probably would have had a very nasty surprise!

Why did God ask Moses to risk his life? Because God wanted Moses to demonstrate his complete dependence upon Him. Moses had a stick in his hand, but God wanted him to obey Him and throw it down to teach Moses not to depend on anything but God alone.

We all carry things in our hands, so to speak, that can hold us back from totally depending upon God. It may be our possessions… or other people…but whatever it is, we need to let go of them. We need to "throw them on the ground" and let God use them as He sees fit.

What are you holding on to today for security? If it's keeping you from depending on God, I challenge you to throw it down and put your complete trust in Him.

HAVE YOU COME TO THE POINT OF COMPLETE DEPENDENCE UPON GOD?

Day 158

If possible, so far as it depends on you, live peaceably with all.

—Romans 12:18

Tolerance is the key word of our culture today. The world teaches us that we should be tolerant and accepting of others' beliefs and behavior...or whatever it is that one defines as truth.

But the tolerance Paul speaks of in the 12th chapter of Romans is a different kind of tolerance. He's encouraging us to make allowances for the differences between people. But he's not condoning a blind tolerance for those who disregard the truth as revealed in God's Word.

Jesus was forgiving of others and tolerant of those who thought differently than He did. He never attacked them or resorted to personal insults. And you and I are to follow His example in this area.

But we also need to realize, as Jesus did, that tolerance only stretches so far.

In our world today, Satan has done a masterful job of twisting the concept of tolerance to mean we should be accepting...and even embrace...anything the world tries to pass off as truth.

But the fact is, we should have absolutely no tolerance when truth is at stake!

Today I encourage you to stand firm in the truth of what Jesus taught...regardless of how unpopular you might be in the world's eyes. And don't let popular opinion change your mind!

AS A FOLLOWER OF CHRIST, YOU ARE CALLED TO DEFEND TRUTH...REGARDLESS OF HOW UNPOPULAR IT MIGHT MAKE YOU.

Day 159

> Therefore, preparing your minds for action, and being sober-minded, set your hope fully on the grace that will be brought to you at the revelation of Jesus Christ.
>
> —1 Peter 1:13

In the verse above, we have a mighty motivator for living the life we discussed in yesterday's devotional…a life that's different, that's separated from sin. That motivation is the expectation of Jesus Christ's soon coming.

"The revelation of Jesus Christ" refers to the second coming of Christ. And in view of His soon return, we ought to be motivated to live godly lives!

As a matter of fact, the Scripture says in 1 John 3:3, "And everyone who thus hopes in him purifies himself as he is pure." If you really believe that Jesus is coming, you will live a holy life!

What if you knew beyond a shadow of a doubt that Jesus was coming today? That before this day was done, He would come and take us to be with Him?

Would there be some things in your life you need to change? Would you have to scurry around to make sure some things were settled between friends or family members?

Would you have to rush out and tell someone about Jesus?

When we get married, every decision, every plan, every thought is focused on the day when we'll stand at the altar. In the same way, as the bride of Christ, the Church, you and I should live every day with the expectancy of His return.

CHRIST'S IMMINENT RETURN SHOULD IMPACT THE WAY YOU LIVE YOUR LIFE TODAY.

Day 160

"You shall be holy, for I am holy."

—1 Peter 1:16

If I could sum up the character of God in one word, that word would be *holy*. I realize that we have had a number of devotionals on this issue, but it is that important!

Our God is a holy God! And as His children who love Him, you and I should be motivated to obey Him and live holy lives.

As followers of Christ, you and I are partakers of His divine nature. So it makes sense that if the divine nature of God is living in you, then His holiness will be displayed in your life…that His character will be reproduced in your life.

My earthly father gave me his nature. And regardless of where I go, at least in the physical realm, I am a Graham. That's my name and that's my nature! I am the child of my father. And it always did me a lot of good every now and then when someone would say, "He's just like his dad."

In the same way, people ought to say of you and me, "He's just like his heavenly Father." "She's just like her Lord." Our love and obedience to our Father should manifest itself in a Christ-likeness that people notice.

I simply ask you today, does your life reflect the nature and Spirit of our God who is holy? Would others ever say that you're just like your heavenly Father?

GOD'S HOLINESS SHOULD BE DISPLAYED IN YOUR LIFE.

Day 161

Be blameless and innocent, children of God without blemish in the midst of a crooked and twisted generation, among whom you shine as lights in the world.

—Philippians 2:15

In the verse above, Paul encourages us as Christians to live pure lives in a polluted world. To live a life that is blameless—not sinless—because no one can do that this side of heaven.

Being blameless means being real, authentic, genuine...not saying one thing and then doing another.

Paul says to be real, to be blameless, to be pure. Being pure means having "inexperience with evil." A believer should have a certain naiveté of the world.

In today's society, do you ever wonder how you can do this? Is it an unrealistic expectation?

Well, it's not unrealistic when you remember that it is God who is working inside you to maintain a pure heart, mind, and lifestyle. You can't do it, but He can!

By walking a straight path in a crooked world, others will see that your faith is real. And it's that kind of faith...that muscular Christianity...that is both courageous and contagious.

So I encourage you to be genuine, to be real, so that your life will draw others to Him!

BY WALKING A STRAIGHT PATH IN A CROOKED WORLD, OTHERS WILL SEE THAT YOUR FAITH IS REAL.

Day 162

Holding fast to the word of life, so that in the day of Christ I may be proud that I did not run in vain or labor in vain.

—Philippians 2:16

What does it mean to hold fast to the word of life? It means to get the message out! And what is that message? LIFE! We're to share the message of LIFE together as a Church, but we're also called to do it independently and individually.

And to help you do this, I want to give you a simple tool...an acronym...that will help you share the message of LIFE with anyone:

- **L** – God *loves* you and has a wonderful plan for your life (John 3:16).
- **I** – You are *isolated* from God by your sin (Romans 3:23).
- **F** – You can be saved through *faith* in the Lord Jesus Christ. You do this by turning from your sins, believing that He died on the cross to save you from your sins and that He was raised on the third day (Ephesians 2:8-9).
- **E** – *Eternal life* begins the moment you receive Jesus Christ (Romans 6:23).

I want to challenge you to use this LIFE tool with someone you know over the next week!

Perhaps this means taking a napkin and jotting this down for a friend over coffee. Or sharing it in a conversation with your lost loved ones. Whatever you do, take time to show someone you know how they can have LIFE in Jesus Christ!

YOU ARE CALLED TO SHARE THE MESSAGE OF LIFE INDEPENDENTLY AND INDIVIDUALLY!

Day 163

Even if I am to be poured out as a drink offering upon the sacrificial offering of your faith, I am glad and rejoice with you all. Likewise you also should be glad and rejoice with me.

—Philippians 2:17-18

In the family of God, we should live as a band of brothers…to be there for one another. This is especially important to restore the fallen, lift the bruised and broken, and encourage one another in the faith.

Friends are available and friends are accountable. And each of us needs those friends who are both available and hold us accountable.

Do you have people in your life you can look to when you are in need? If not, I encourage you to make finding those friends a priority. And are there people who depend on you? Not only do we need friends, we need to be a friend. We need accountability and to hold others accountable.

Now, let me leave you today with this one final thought. In the Bible, we are told that God has called us His friends! As a believer, you are a friend of God. It's a phenomenal thought, but that is exactly the relationship He gives us!

Life is meant to be lived in relationship…a relationship with God, with His people, and with the family and friends we share in Christ. These relationships are among the greatest treasures of life itself!

AS CHRISTIANS, WE SHOULD BE A BAND OF BROTHERS WHO ARE ALWAYS THERE FOR ONE ANOTHER.

Day 164

Indeed, I count everything as loss because of the surpassing worth of knowing Christ Jesus my Lord.

—Philippians 3:8

In Philippians 3, we discover that true happiness comes from a relationship with Christ.

While Paul wrote the book of Philippians when he was in jail, imprisonment could not imprison his spirit! Paul didn't let his circumstances dictate his attitude because he was free in Christ.

Unfortunately, far too few Christians today know the kind of joy that Paul had. Too many of us are walking around tripping over our bottom lips!

Rather than worshiping God, we're whining. Rather than praising, we're pouting. Satan often attacks us at the point of our joy because he knows that the joy of the Lord is our strength.

I want you to know that you can know the same joy that Paul did if you know the Lord. You see, Paul understood that joy isn't in our circumstances. It isn't found in ourselves.

True joy is something so much deeper! It's a different way of looking at life and thinking about life. It's positive, hopeful, and optimistic.

Because real joy is only found in our relationship with Christ!

DON'T LET CIRCUMSTANCES DICTATE THE LEVEL OF JOY IN YOUR LIFE.

Day 165

Not that I have already obtained this or am already perfect, but I press on to make it my own, because Christ Jesus has made me his own. Brothers, I do not consider that I have made it my own. But one thing I do: forgetting what lies behind and straining forward to what lies ahead, I press on toward the goal for the prize of the upward call of God in Christ Jesus.

—Philippians 3:12-14

The apostle Paul said the meaning of life was the pursuit of Christ. And Paul focused on that goal with incredible intensity.

So often we don't win in life because we don't know the difference between what is good and what is best. There are many good things we can do, but God has called us to higher things, to the better things, to the best things in our lives. And we need to do those best things, rather than being constantly distracted by our own over-commitments.

In Hebrews 12:1, the writer encourages us to "lay aside every weight"…to take off the things that drag and pull us down.

So what is slowing you down? Working too much? A hobby? Channel surfing? A sin? Maybe it's just a distraction that's keeping you from focusing on God because you don't have the time to spend with Him. Is there something in your life today that's causing you to take your eyes off the prize?

Every successful person has a focus in life…and they opt for the best things over the good things. I hope today you'll lay aside your weights, you'll focus on the best things…the things of God…and that you'll press toward the prize of your calling in Christ!

MAKE THE FOCUS OF YOUR LIFE THE BEST THINGS…THE THINGS OF GOD!

Day 166

Rejoice in the Lord always; again I will say, Rejoice.

—Philippians 4:4

Pay attention to the key phrase that the apostle Paul uses over and over again in the book of Philippians: *in the Lord.* Now, why should that bring you joy? Because if you're a believer, you are in Christ. And in Christ, there is security, there is strength, and there is peace.

As a follower of Christ, you should find your joy in Him...not in your circumstances.

Now, I'm not talking about putting on a plastic smile and pretending to be happy or being superficial and phony. I'm talking about a joy deep within us that can't help but come out. It's what Chuck Swindoll calls "outrageous joy." Wouldn't you love for the joy of the Lord to be so strong in you that it could be called outrageous?

Keep in mind that Satan knows there is joy in the Lord, and he diligently tries to steal it from you. He wants to rob you of that joy through disappointments, defeat, and discouragement. He wants to make you weak and vulnerable, because it's your joy in the Lord that keeps you strong and draws others to Christ!

Jesus is the source of all joy. So when your circumstances don't make you feel all that joyful, rejoice in the Lord. Praise Him, because when you exalt Christ in your life, you'll find joy.

The joy of the Lord is your strength.

AS FOLLOWERS OF CHRIST, WE SHOULD FIND JOY IN CHRIST—NOT IN OUR CIRCUMSTANCES.

Day 167

Do not be anxious about anything, but in everything by prayer and supplication with thanksgiving let your requests be made known to God.

—**Philippians 4:6**

What do you worry about? Money? Your job? Your family? You know, if you think about it, worry really is useless. It has never solved a problem, never dried a tear, and never changed anything. And most of us spend most of our time worrying about things that will never happen or circumstances we can't change anyway!

Worry saps your strength, destroys your spirit, and robs you of the joy in life. It takes its toll physically, emotionally, and spiritually.

Someone once said, "Worry is assuming responsibility that God never intended for you to have."

Yet it seems so much easier to worry about things instead of sharing those concerns with God. But that's exactly what He wants you to do! He wants you to offer your concerns up to Him in prayer.

Today, I want to encourage you to stop worrying about your future, because God's in control of your future! Don't worry about your life, because He holds your life in His hands. Don't worry about anything, but rather, pray about everything!

There's nothing too great for God. There's no problem too hard for God to solve and there's no problem too small for God.

Pray confidently, and ask, seek, and knock continually. Because only in trusting God will you find true contentment in this life.

"WORRY IS ASSUMING RESPONSIBILITY THAT GOD NEVER INTENDED FOR YOU TO HAVE."

Day 168

And my God will supply every need of yours according to his riches in glory in Christ Jesus.

—Philippians 4:19

Too many of us today are missing out on God's blessings because our life is absorbed in trying to meet our own needs.

Rather than trusting God to meet our needs, too often we go out and buy what we think we need…only to go into debt doing it! Then, saddled with that debt, we can't be a blessing to others.

Can you relate? Are you missing out on being a blessing?

Well, you can change that! Begin trusting God, wait on Him, and just see how He will supply what you need!

You'll never experience the power of God to meet your needs if you don't trust Him for what He can do. God's strength, grace, and power are available to you. Like Paul said in Philippians 4:13, "I can do all things through him who strengthens me."

Remember, God knows what you need even before you ask for it. When you pray, asking for God's provision, you put yourself in the position to receive from God all He wants to give you. When you pray expectantly, you can pray confidently that you will receive from God what He desires to give you!

Today, I want to challenge you to elevate your expectations of God. Begin each day in worship and ask for God's provision. Believe Him for great things in your life. When you do, you will begin to see how your life can indeed become a blessing to others.

TRUST GOD TO MEET YOUR NEEDS…AND SEE WHAT HE WILL DO.

Day 169

"Do not lay up for yourselves treasures on earth, where moth and rust destroy and where thieves break in and steal, but lay up for yourselves treasures in heaven, where neither moth nor rust destroys and where thieves do not break in and steal."

—Matthew 6:19-20

In America today, there's the constant pressure to spend, spend, spend! We have to have the big house...the newest car...and the most expensive clothes. Our culture promotes and glorifies excessive spending.

And as a result, many Americans...and far too many Christians...are swimming in a sea of debt.

Yet the Bible teaches that we are to save money and prepare for the future. We are to be wise in the management of our money and not live beyond what God has given us. That's why I would advise you to deal aggressively with excessive debt in your life.

And what does excessive debt look like? Excessive debt is any debt that grinds you down, any debt that creates pressure in your family, or any debt that keeps you from giving as God would have you give.

There are many Christians who can't begin to give what God would have them give because they're so bound up in debt!

Each of us needs God as a partner in our finances. And today, I would challenge you to open your finances up to God if you haven't already...and ask Him to speak to you about how you're handling your money.

Do you have excessive debt? Then put a plan together today to begin to deal with it. Are you investing in the future of the kingdom? If not, begin to do so!

GOD EXPECTS US TO MANAGE OUR MONEY WISELY AND NOT "DEVOUR" IT.

Day 170

When I was a son with my father, tender, the only one in the sight of my mother, he taught me and said to me, "Let your heart hold fast my words; keep my commandments, and live."

—Proverbs 4:3-4

The book of Proverbs teaches us what wise families look like. But sometimes…in the crush of day-to-day life…it's easy to just operate on autopilot and not engage with our families. Yet if we as parents aren't engaged with our kids, who will engage with them?

Your children will be influenced by someone. And wouldn't you rather it be you?

Today's world is not an easy place to grow up. Our children are constantly exposed to outside influences that encourage them to grow up too fast. They're bombarded by images you would prefer they never see and pressures that are unbelievable.

And if you aren't there to show them the alternative, they will embrace the world's values as their reality.

What's the best way to model Christ for your children? Know Him yourself. Spend time with your heavenly Father. Make it a priority. There's nothing more important.

Then you will be able to pass on the legacy of God's love and grace, and you'll be able to show them that Christ is where they'll find real contentment and peace.

Be a mom or dad that your child will one day call blessed!

YOUR KIDS WILL BE INFLUENCED BY SOMEONE, SO MAKE THAT PERSON YOU!

Day 171

Wine is a mocker, strong drink a brawler, and whoever is led astray by it is not wise.

—Proverbs 20:1

My goal today is not to condemn anyone for drinking alcohol. But if you drink, my challenge for you today is to ask yourself, does my drinking glorify Jesus Christ?

With the kind of alcohol that is used and abused in our culture today, can you honestly say your drinking glorifies God?

Of course we have liberty as followers of Christ. But I want you to make a greater statement than your liberty as a Christian! I want you to make a statement of Christian love, because it trumps liberty every time.

The facts are clear: Alcohol causes much harm to many people; it's highly habit-forming; it's not healthy; it can ruin your witness for Christ; and it has the potential to cause a weaker brother to sin or stumble.

Given such clear evidence of alcohol's negative consequences, is it worth the risk you take to continue to drink?

God promises pleasure and an abundant life in Christ. But alcohol is a substitute for the real life, the real joy, and real pleasure you can have in Him! That's why I hope you will consider saying "no" to alcohol…and "yes" to a truly abundant life in Christ!

MAKE A STATEMENT OF CHRISTIAN LOVE, BECAUSE LOVE TRUMPS LIBERTY EVERY TIME!

Day 172

Train up a child in the way he should go; even when he is old he will not depart from it.

—Proverbs 22:6

As Christian moms and dads, we are to train our children…to teach them how to live life. We are to teach them to be upright, to be honest, moral, and most importantly, to love God.

There are two worldviews today: Either God is in control or man is. Don't be fooled into thinking your child won't be influenced by our humanistic society. You can't isolate them that much!

What you can do is teach them…train them…show them how much God loves them…and pray for them. That's the best protection you can give your kids.

Deuteronomy 6:7 says to impress the commandments of God on the hearts of your children. Talk to them about the things of God when you're hanging out at home or when you're taking them to school. Make God a part of your everyday conversation!

Your children are a wonderful gift…and responsibility…from God. Why would you not want to be heavily involved in the people they become? Work to raise wise children who love God. There's no better gift you could give your child!

MAKE IT A PRIORITY TO TEACH YOUR KIDS TO LOVE GOD.

Day 173

Death and life are in the power of the tongue, and those who love it will eat its fruits.

—Proverbs 18:21

More than 90 times in the book of Proverbs, Solomon uses words to describe communication.

We can use our words like medicine to strengthen and soothe those who need it the most…or we can use our words like missiles to destroy and to devour.

That's why we need to ask ourselves, do our words strengthen and soothe or do they destroy and devour? The words we are to use should impact and influence those around us. These words should encourage and edify…build up, rather than tear down.

Imagine the new sense of joy and excitement in your home and family if you would cut out all the negative and strife-filled words and begin speaking the nourishing words of God!

Remember, the words you speak show what's really in your heart. And in order to speak those nourishing words of God, you must be connected with Him as your source—the center of your life.

When the Word of God gets in us, we breathe it out, and help those around us. As it says in Proverbs 16:24, "Gracious words are like a honeycomb, sweetness to the soul and health to the body."

It is my prayer today that your words will reflect the One who dwells in your heart!

MAKE YOUR WORDS STRENGTHEN AND SOOTHE…RATHER THAN DESTROY AND DEVOUR.

Day 174

By wisdom a house is built, and by understanding it is established; by knowledge the rooms are filled with all precious and pleasant riches. A wise man is full of strength, and a man of knowledge enhances his might, for by wise guidance you can wage your war, and in abundance of counselors there is victory.

—Proverbs 24:3-6

In Matthew chapter 7, Jesus tells us a story about two men. One built his house on the rock and the other man built his house on the sand. And when the storms came, the house that was built on the rock stood strong. But the one that was built on the sand fell! In fact, Jesus said, "Great was the fall of it."

What I've come to learn over the years is that in life, you're either in a storm, coming out of a storm, or about to go into a storm. So it's vital that you build your life and the life of your family on a solid foundation…the Rock of Jesus Christ!

What foundation are you building your family on today?

Perhaps you'd admit that your family is built on the sand of worldly wisdom. Perhaps you've allowed the sewage of our contemporary culture to seep into your home. Or perhaps you'd acknowledge that you've been too lax about making sure your family is plugged into a local church body.

Today, I want to challenge you as a Christian mom or dad to build your house on the solid Rock of Jesus Christ. Because I can guarantee you that the storms of life are going to rage…and their harsh winds are going to blow!

And you will need the foundation of Jesus Christ to keep your family strong.

BUILD YOUR FAMILY ON THE FOUNDATION OF JESUS CHRIST AND HIS WISDOM.

Day 175

Therefore let us be grateful for receiving a kingdom that cannot be shaken, and thus let us offer to God acceptable worship, with reverence and awe.

—Hebrews 12:28

How are you and I as Christians to respond to the gift of God's unshakable Kingdom? How are we to show Him how thankful we are? By living for eternity here and today.

So how do you do that?

Well, first, you must live with an expectant attitude! You should be living on tiptoes with excitement and anticipation, looking forward to Christ's return. Because Jesus says in Revelation 22:20, "Surely I am coming soon."

That means suddenly...rapidly...at any time, at any moment. It was my friend Adrian Rogers who said, "We ought to live as though Jesus died yesterday, rose this morning, and is coming back this afternoon."

We ought to get up every day and think, "Lord, perhaps today is the day I see you!" I promise, it will transform your thinking...and it will transform your living when you live with an excited, joyous, expectant attitude.

The reason this kind of thinking transforms our living is because it gives us a new vantage point...a new vision for life and for the future.

This means no matter what happens to you...no matter what you may go through as a believer...you have this reference point. And you have the amazing hope of an eternity with Christ!

LIVE YOUR LIFE IN LIGHT OF ETERNITY AND DON'T BE WEIGHED DOWN BY THE HERE AND NOW.

Day 176

Give thanks in all circumstances; for this is the will of God in Christ Jesus for you.

—1 Thessalonians 5:18

As followers of Christ, you and I have an amazing hope in a future spent forever with Him...in a Kingdom that cannot be shaken.

And one way we are to respond to this is to live with a grateful heart today...and every day!

You know, a lot of people talk about having an attitude of gratitude. But I believe there's a longitude and latitude of gratitude as well. Here's what I mean by that.

If, as the psalmist says, you bless God and praise God and worship God and give thanks for all things, then eternity does not even limit the length and the depth of your blessings!

In the Psalms, the psalmist is up in the heavenlies worshiping God. He's down in the depths of Sheol worshiping God. He's on the seas; he's riding in a cloud; he's celebrating in the mountains; he's worshiping in the desert; he's crying out to God in anguish, even in times of anger, frustration, and disappointment. And he's crying out to God in times of joy.

His life is made large because every experience in life is an opportunity to give thanks to God.

And when you're a grateful person, the whole world becomes your sanctuary! Every experience in life is enlarged and elevated when you lift Him up. And as you do, you get lifted up...especially when you're thankful "in all circumstances"!

BE THANKFUL IN EVERY CIRCUMSTANCE IN WHICH YOU FIND YOURSELF.

Day 177

For our God is a consuming fire.

—Hebrews 12:29

Living life in thanksgiving and expectation are two ways we as Christians are to respond knowing that we have the hope of heaven.

A third way we're to respond is to live with a sober, serious mind.

The verse above speaks of the judgment of the holy God. And in view of the fact that God is going to judge this world, we should be "serious minded."

I'm not saying we don't have joy. But there's is a sobriety when we think about the future...and the future of our family and friends who may not know Christ.

Jesus...who is incarnate love...spoke more about hell than any other person in the Scripture. In fact, 13% of the words of Jesus had to do with judgment and separation from God.

Fiery judgment is sure, and we dare not spiritualize the truth concerning judgment. It's a serious matter to deny, to dilute, and to distort the truth about heaven and hell.

There's a great deal of confusion out there today. Many voices are vying for our attention about what happens when we die.

That's why I want to challenge you to read and study your Bible so you can know what you believe and why you believe it.

And it's my prayer that you'll love your unsaved friends and family enough to tell them what Jesus says about rejecting Him!

MAKE SHARING CHRIST A PRIORITY IN YOUR LIFE.

Day 178

"And when he had removed him, he raised up David to be their king, of whom he testified and said, 'I have found in David the son of Jesse a man after my heart, who will do all my will.'"

—Acts 13:22

Have you ever wondered why David was called "a man after God's heart"? It was because he sought after God with everything he had.

When David was a young teenager tending to the sheep in the fields, he spent a lot of time seeking God through prayer. And I think that's a lesson that stayed with him. That precious habit of spending time with God made such a difference in the leader he would eventually become.

David was a true man of prayer. Before he made a move, David went to God to find His will. And as a result, God used David—and He used him powerfully.

Let me ask you a question: In today's crazy world, do you take the time to get alone with God every day? It's so easy to get caught up in the whirlwind. And unfortunately, we can often make decisions based on what feels right instead of seeking answers from the Creator of the universe.

Today, make it a priority to find time to slow down and spend time with God. Even if you have to, schedule it in your planner! Whatever you have to do, just keep that daily appointment with God.

There's nothing in this world that is worth missing what God has for you. So spend time in prayer. Seek Him in every move you make. And like David, become a man or woman after God's own heart!

MAKE A PRIORITY OF SPENDING TIME ALONE WITH GOD.

Day 179

It happened, late one afternoon, when David arose from his couch and was walking on the roof of the king's house, that he saw from the roof a woman bathing; and the woman was very beautiful. And David sent and inquired about the woman. And one said, "Is not this Bathsheba, the daughter of Eliam, the wife of Uriah the Hittite?" So David sent messengers and took her, and she came to him, and he lay with her.

—2 Samuel 11:2-4

Imagine a sleepy-eyed David strolling out on his balcony for a breath of fresh air. Perhaps he accidentally caught a glimpse of Bathsheba. But he didn't have to keep watching! His greatest sin started innocently enough, but it didn't stay innocent.

David opened the door, and Satan waltzed right through it!

Are there doors in your life that you've cracked…only to have the enemy kick them wide open? Are there attitudes you shouldn't have, or sin that needs to be addressed?

David repented, and God forgave him completely. So what is stopping you from doing the same thing?

Your sin, whatever it is, doesn't have to continue taking you downhill. The same God who loved and forgave David loves and will forgive you. All you have to do is ask and turn from your sin.

How much does God want to forgive you and bring you back to Himself? So much that He gave His only Son just for you!

Today I encourage you to soften your heart. Allow God to cleanse and forgive you. Remember, it's God who loves you, made you, and wants you in fellowship with Him. This is the life for which He designed you! Don't settle for anything less.

THE SAME GOD WHO FORGAVE DAVID'S SIN WILL FORGIVE YOU.

Day 180

Saul answered, "Am I not a Benjaminite, from the least of the tribes of Israel? And is not my clan the humblest of all the clans of the tribe of Benjamin? Why then have you spoken to me in this way?"

—1 Samuel 9:21

When you look at the life of Saul, you see a man who had everything life had to offer. He was good-looking. Humble. A leader. And God's Spirit rested upon him. But he squandered it all because of the choices he made and the life he lived.

Saul's fatal flaw was his own selfishness. He was determined to do his own thing and not wait on God. This selfishness transformed into stubborn disobedience, and it cost Saul everything. His stubborn will wasn't worth the price he paid.

How often are we determined to do things our own way? To have what we want just because we want it. When we do, we take our eyes off God and plow ahead blindly.

Hopefully though, we'll learn from the actions and hearts of both Saul and David!

David, like Saul, also wandered far from God. But David was also very different from Saul. David's heart sought after God. He had the will to obey Him, and that made all the difference in David's life.

You may be walking in disobedience and defeat, but you don't have to stay there! Seek God. Seek His forgiveness. Become a man or woman after God's own heart. Because that is the life of true victory!

IS YOUR HEART MORE LIKE DAVID'S…OR LIKE SAUL'S?

Day 181

For the sake of Christ, then, I am content with weaknesses, hardships, persecutions, and calamities. For when I am weak, then I am strong.

—2 Corinthians 12:10

You know, we often take comfort in this verse. But what do you do when the enemy attacks you at your strongest point?

David was a man who was known for his integrity…a man who the Bible says was after God's own heart. Yet the characteristics that God used to raise David to the position of king over of Israel were the exact same characteristics where the devil attacked him!

Today I want to ask you, what do you think your strongest characteristics are? Are there any areas of you life where you think, "Oh, I've got that thing covered…it's under control. I'm safe here"?

Don't let your guard down like David did. Protect yourself with the armor of God (Ephesians 6:13-17)…armor that's really all about Jesus.

Remember, as believers, He's standing in our shoes and we're standing in His. We're standing in His peace…His truth…His righteousness…His faith…and in His Word. Praise God that He's not only strong when we are weak, but that's He's stronger where we think we are strong!

DON'T LET YOUR GUARD DOWN, BUT PROTECT YOURSELF WITH THE FULL ARMOR OF GOD.

Day 182

And when Jesus was baptized, immediately he went up from the water, and behold, the heavens were opened to him, and he saw the Spirit of God descending like a dove and coming to rest on him; and behold, a voice from heaven said, "This is my beloved Son, with whom I am well pleased." Then Jesus was led up by the Spirit into the wilderness to be tempted by the devil.

—Matthew 3:16-17, 4:1

That must have been an amazing sight when John baptized Jesus in the Jordan River. God blessed Him in an audible voice from heaven, and Jesus' earthly ministry began.

Now, you wouldn't expect the next part of His story to include His greatest temptation, but that's exactly what happened!

Satan often attacks us with temptation just after we've won a spiritual victory…just like he did Jesus. The devil knows our triumph leaves us more vulnerable, and he wants us to miss out on God's blessings in our lives.

The only way you can defeat Satan is to protect yourself by putting on the battle fatigues God has provided for you. Those fatigues are found in Ephesians 6:13-17.

When Jesus went out to the desert after His baptism, He was protected. He had on His armor. When Satan came after Him, Jesus used His shield. He used His sword. Satan took three shots, but Jesus knocked him down each time!

And just like Jesus, you can overcome the attacks of Satan in your life today. It's my prayer you'll take advantage of the armor God's given you as His child…so that you can win every battle for Him!

PUT ON THE BATTLE FATIGUES GOD HAS PROVIDED SO YOU CAN OVERCOME THE ATTACKS OF SATAN IN YOUR LIFE TODAY!

Day 183

"Come, I will send you to Pharaoh that you may bring my people, the children of Israel, out of Egypt."

—Exodus 3:10

When God made this declaration to Moses, it was a frightening moment for him. It's the last thing he thought God would ask him to do!

Moses had a challenge he had to face if he was going to be what God wanted him to be. He had to break free from his fears if he was going to return to Egypt to set the Israelites free from their slavery to Pharaoh.

Moses didn't want to leave his "comfort zone" in the wilderness, but God called Moses to be His witness and representative to the world.

You see, like Moses, most Christians have to face their fears if they are going to be a strong witness for God in today's world. Satan wants us to keep our feet planted in the things of the world. He wants us to do absolutely nothing that will stick out or make an impact, but to quietly blend into the fabric of society.

The devil tries to convince us that it's too risky to take a courageous stand for the Lord or that if we try to tell others about Jesus, they will reject us or cause us trouble. So we often find it difficult to break free from our fears to be the witness God wants us to be.

Don't be afraid to step out and follow God's leading to tell others that you believe in Jesus, both by your lips and your life. If we truly believe He is the only way to heaven, we have a message the world needs to hear!

DON'T BE AFRAID TO STEP OUT AND FOLLOW GOD'S LEADING TO SHARE CHRIST.

Day 184

He leads me in paths of righteousness for his name's sake.

—Psalm 23:3

Have you ever set out to go somewhere, only to realize that you were heading in the wrong direction? There's nothing quite like the experience of a trip that ends up going in a direction different then you thought it would.

That's how it is at times in our Christian lives. We are called to follow Christ, which sounds easy enough. But there are times when it feels like He is taking us in a different direction than we thought He would. That's when we need to cling to the Bible's promise that Christ will indeed be with us and lead us every step of the way.

When Moses led Israel out of Egypt, God instructed him not to take the quickest and most direct route to Canaan, but to follow the path He would lead him on. I'm sure Moses wondered many times what was going on and why God was having the nation of Israel trek so many extra miles to reach the Promised Land.

But God was working out His plan in His way. In fact, in Deuteronomy 8:2, Moses says this about God's leading in the wilderness: "And you shall remember the whole way that the LORD your God has led you these forty years in the wilderness, that he might humble you, testing you to know what was in your heart, whether you would keep his commandments or not."

Be assured God is at work in your life no matter how strange His leading might seem at the moment.

So if you're not sure where you're heading today, just get close to Christ and don't give in to the temptation of giving up or going the way you think best. We don't have the promise of an easy and clear journey, but we do have the promise of His guidance!

GOD HAS PROMISED TO GUIDE YOU EVERY STEP OF THE WAY!

Day 185

"Fear not, stand firm, and see the salvation of the LORD."

—Exodus 14:13

Panic can be a response to fear...especially when we are confronted with seemingly impossible situations. But as Christians, our first reaction to impossible situations should be prayer, not panic. Because the antidote to fear is faith. I don't mean blind hope or belief, but true faith built solidly upon Christ and His Word.

As the Israelites came to the Red Sea with the Egyptian army behind them, I'm confident that panic gripped the hearts of the people. They knew that if they were caught, it would be death for most of them and slavery for the rest. But at that moment of panic, Moses spoke the words in the verse above, calling the people to resist panic and stand firm, waiting for the salvation of the Lord.

Faith is a learned response, developed through the hard experiences and trials in our lives. But as we grow in faith, our tendency to panic will subside. Even when a trial comes suddenly, we can choose to respond in faith instead of panic. Remember, faith and fear can't coexist in our hearts at the same time. We will either be consumed by one or the other.

Faith is a gift from God, but it's a gift that is supposed to grow. Is your faith growing? When pressed against the wall of life, do you panic or rest in the promises of God? Make a commitment today to spend time with God in prayer and studying His Word, so your faith will continue to grow and you will be able to resist the urge to panic.

WHEN YOU FEEL THE URGE TO PANIC, PRAY FOR THE FAITH TO STAND FIRM.

Day 186

Be watchful, stand firm in the faith, act like men, be strong.

—1 Corinthians 16:13

We all face those moments in life when we find ourselves in an unexpected situation. And it can seem like things are out of control. Yet, our difficult situations are on God's calendar, and He knows the very day, hour, and minute they will happen. He has a reason for allowing them to happen at that precise moment.

Isn't it great to know that God is sovereign over all? Although we have our calendars, day timers, and schedules, we have to come to grips with the fact that there are some things we just can't control. As much as we would like to, we can't manage every minute of our days.

But as schedule-driven beings, we often want to simply work our way out of difficulties. But sometimes God wants us to stand still in the middle of a problem and seek His leading because we are just where He wants us to be.

When you stand still and allow God to work in you...standing firm in your faith...you'll begin to see His timetable unfold and you'll come out the other end even stronger in your faith.

I know the temptation is strong to try and take control when hard times hit. Today, pray that God will give you the ability to stand firm and allow Him to work in His time.

WHEN FACED WITH A DIFFICULT SITUATION, GIVE IT TO GOD AND TRUST HIM TO WORK!

Day 187

"The LORD will fight for you, and you have only to be silent."

—Exodus 14:14

The great missionary David Livingston once said, "I'll go anywhere, as long as it's forward." That's the attitude that Christ wants us to have in our relationship with Him. For a believer, if we are growing spiritually, there really is no other way to go but forward!

People who step out in faith and make a difference for Christ don't fade away or move backward, but press forward in the name and power of Christ. Many times it is our own fear and lack of faith that keep us moving sideways or even back into sin.

But our God is the God of the impossible! He can give you the strength to advance even against the toughest foes. Just as the Lord fought for Israel against the Egyptian army, He'll fight for you. God cleared the way for Moses and the Israelites to cross the Red Sea, and He took care of Pharaoh's forces. All the Israelites had to do was move out in faith.

Whenever you're having a Red Sea experience of your own, when your back is against the wall, God is ready to part the waters and fight the battle for you if you will just step out in obedient faith. Set your mind and heart to follow Him—and watch Him part waters in your life that threaten to trap you or swallow you up!

The formula is really pretty simple. First believe God in your heart, and then obey Him with your feet. Have you ever gone forward into turbulent waters, only to see God open them up and make a dry path for you to follow? Recall the thrill of that faith-building moment today, and ask God to help you do it again.

BELIEVE GOD WITH YOUR HEART, AND THEN OBEY HIM WITH YOUR FEET!

Day 188

And God spoke all these words, saying, "I am the LORD your God."

—Exodus 20:1-2

I think it's safe to say that too many Christians today don't value the largest portion of God's Word—the 39 books of the Old Testament—as they should. Somehow we have the idea that the Old Testament Scriptures are not quite as important as the New Testament. But this isn't at all true.

Not only is it important for us as Christians to know the Old Testament, it is virtually impossible to truly understand the New Testament without it! The history of God's chosen people, the Jews, is our history too, because we are the direct heirs of the faith of Abraham.

Perhaps the most important part of the Old Testament is found in Exodus 20, where we read the Ten Commandments as God gave them to Moses. I'm not sure how many Christians could name these ten foundational laws of God—but we should be able to. In fact, we should be studying and learning all of God's Word as if our lives depended on it, because they do!

The Old Testament may seem out of date and irrelevant in the 21st century. But nothing could be further from the truth. The truths of the Old Testament still apply to us today.

Make it a point to spend time studying the entire Bible, including the incredible story of previous generations of God's people as told in the Old Testament! Learn to value all of God's revelation!

VALUE ALL OF GOD'S WORD BY MAKING A PRIORITY OF STUDYING BOTH THE NEW AND OLD TESTAMENTS.

Day 189

Woe to those who call evil good and good evil, who put darkness for light and light for darkness, who put bitter for sweet and sweet for bitter!

—Isaiah 5:20

Even though the Ten Commandments were handed to Moses thousands of years ago, they are more up-to-date and relevant than today's newspaper. The Ten Commandments are not obsolete, they're absolute! They are the very heart and mind of God...not of Moses or any other human being.

The problem is that people today don't really like to be commanded. They want to come up with their own list of acceptable behavior and live by that. After all, we're told, everything is just a matter of choice anyway.

It's sad that most people see the Ten Commandments as a list of "don'ts" designed to squash everyone's fun. God is perceived as being a cosmic killjoy trying to make everyone toe the line. But the Ten Commandments are far from being a list of prohibitions. They are, in fact, an infallible guide to help us find true contentment and happiness

As believers, we need to commit ourselves to live our lives by God's clear directives, and through that obedience, help those around us see what happens when we live according to God's plan.

When others see God at work in our lives in such a positive and life-changing way, they will want the same peace, joy, and satisfaction they see in us.

PUT THE TRUTH OF GOD'S WORD FIRST IN YOUR LIFE SO OTHERS WILL SEE THE JOY, PEACE, AND SATISFACTION IT CAN BRING!

Day 190

> "Do not think that I have come to abolish the Law or the Prophets; I have not come to abolish them but to fulfill them."
>
> —Matthew 5:17

"If it feels good, do it" is an all too common belief floating around today. It reflects what people believe, like, "What may be right for you isn't right for me," and, "There's no such thing as truth, just opinion."

These ideas aren't just wrong, they're dangerous!

My friend, the foundations of Christianity in America are shaking. While this country was founded on the principles of God's Word…even our laws reflect the values and commandments of the Bible…we are quickly moving from that foundation.

But even though this world has passed on the concept of absolute truth and decided to adopt a philosophy of moral relativism, it doesn't mean that such a belief is right. Yes, over two-thirds of Americans say they don't believe in absolute truth…and have rejected the possibility that there is an unwavering standard of truth and righteousness. But that doesn't make it the truth.

This moral decay is undermining our society. And now, more than ever, we must stand firmly on the truth God has revealed to us in His Word.

If God's people will stand up and show the way, we can point this great nation back to the Lord. Join me today in praying for America. Ask God to help us…His children…express clearly the Lordship of Jesus Christ and that in Him is the truth…the way… and the life!

STAND FIRMLY ON THE TRUTH GOD HAS REVEALED TO US IN HIS WORD.

Day 191

I can do all things through him who strengthens me.

—Philippians 4:13

A re Christians perfect? Of course not...but we can be powerful! We are tempted and tested just like everyone else, but we can overcome temptation and triumph over trials because we have Christ living within us.

Every once in a while, you have one of those days that just seems to be a struggle from the moment you wake up. Maybe today is one of those days for you! If so, I've got some encouraging news for you. Even though we all have struggles and fall short from time to time, we have the power of Christ at work within us every moment to help us get past the problems and...in spite of those problems...still accomplish great things!

The key to tapping into this power is to keep our eyes on Christ and try not to compare ourselves to someone else.

Here's what I want you to remember today. The verse above says that we can do anything for the Lord because He gives us strength. We may struggle and stumble, but with Christ, we can rest assured that we are heading toward greater things because He is always with us.

Do you really believe you can accomplish anything Christ wants you to accomplish? Tell Him so today, and thank Him for His promise of strength for every situation.

YOU CAN DO ANYTHING TODAY THROUGH THE STRENGTH GOD GIVES YOU!

Day 192

"You shall love the Lord your God with all your heart and with all your soul and with all your mind. And a second is like it: You shall love your neighbor as yourself."

—Matthew 22:37, 39

The Bible teaches that love is the most important thing on earth. God's Word also teaches us to express love in the proper way.

First, it means loving the Lord with all the passion of our being…and then it means loving others the way we love ourselves. In fact, this is how Christ Himself summarized the entire Law of Moses!

Christ was saying love is so important that, in fact, love is what the Ten Commandments are all about. Did you know that the first four commandments deal with our love for God, and the next six deal with our love for and relationships with others?

When it comes right down to it, the only thing that matters is love—the love of Christ for us, the love we are to have for Him, and the love we need to show to others. These ways of loving should define our lives.

We are on this earth to love and form relationships with Christ and others. Make sure to put love first today in everything you do. It's the best way to point someone to Christ, the greatest love of all.

LOVE THE LORD WITH ALL YOUR HEART, SOUL, AND MIND…AND LOVE OTHERS AS YOU LOVE YOURSELF.

Day 193

If I give away all I have, and if I deliver up my body to be burned, but have not love, I gain nothing.

—1 Corinthians 13:3

You and I won't progress or succeed in life unless we learn how to love…to be loved…and to give love. Today's verse is even stronger: Our lives add up to nothing without love for Christ and a love for people that flows from our love for Christ.

Too often we see other people through the lens of our own opinions instead of seeing them through Christ's eyes of love, forgiveness, and compassion. But when we truly experience the love of Christ in our own lives, we are set free to see others as Jesus sees them.

When you reach that point in your walk with Christ, you won't feel a need for self-promotion; you'll be too busy with Christ-promotion! You'll lose your worries about whether or not you're getting the attention you feel you deserve, and you'll be free to love others the way Christ wants you to love them.

And when you reach this point, you'll find more personal success and spiritual satisfaction than you can imagine as you truly love others, no strings attached. This is true in business and personal relationships…and it is even truer of our relationships with the ones we love the most, our closest friends and family members.

So my question to you today is this: Do you look at people through the lens of your personal experiences and opinions, or do you see them as Jesus sees them? Let me challenge you to think of someone you really have a hard time loving, and then ask God to help you see that person through the eyes of Jesus Christ. When you do, you will love as Christ loves…and your life will be richer for it!

ASK GOD TO HELP YOU SEE…AND LOVE…SOMEONE THROUGH THE EYES OF CHRIST TODAY.

Day 194

It is right for me to feel this way about you all, because I hold you in my heart, for you are all partakers with me of grace, both in my imprisonment and in the defense and confirmation of the gospel.

—Philippians 1:7

L ife is not meant to be a solo journey. Christ didn't intend for us to walk this road without any fellow travelers. Sooner or later, we will all discover that we can't make it alone. And when we figure that out, we'll be a lot better off!

One place where we need each other is in the Church. The work of Jesus Christ advances through a network of relationships and friends. Paul considered his fellow believers as partners with him in sharing the Good News of Christ with others.

Paul knew how important the believers at Philippi were as his spiritual brothers and sisters in Christ who encouraged him in his Christian life…even as he encouraged them.

As Christians, we are a spiritual family. Paul felt this way toward the members of the church at Philippi. This is why he thanked the Lord for the privilege of knowing and serving with them.

We need friends and supporters in life—it's just that simple. Christ puts people in our lives to encourage and strengthen us in our walk of faith…and for them to receive those blessings from us.

Is there someone in your life who has been a special friend and encourager to you? Thank the Lord for that person today. Do you know someone who needs you to be a friend and encourager today? Reach out with that helping hand.

THANK THE LORD FOR YOUR SPECIAL ENCOURAGER—AND TAKE THE TIME TO ENCOURAGE SOMEONE ELSE TODAY!

Day 195

I am sure of this, that he who began a good work in you will bring it to completion at the day of Jesus Christ.

—Philippians 1:6

What really matters to you? Is it your relationship with Christ and with others, or is it your accomplishments and accolades?

One of the ways God is preparing you and me for heaven is by teaching us that the relationships we have formed here on earth are the only things we can take with us when we go to be with the Lord.

Discovering what truly matters in light of eternity is a lesson we have to keep learning and relearning as we go along. And learning that is part of what Christ does as He works in our lives each and every day. It's so encouraging to know that He will never give up on us!

With this assurance to stand on, let's learn today that Christ is working in us to get us ready for heaven. And part of being ready means not wasting our time on things that we won't care about when we are knocking on heaven's door.

As a Christian, you are on your way to heaven—no doubt about that! But what are you doing in the meantime that will matter for eternity? Take a look at your schedule and ask yourself how much of your time is devoted to building your relationship with Christ, loving and serving others, and helping the lost know Christ. If the answer to this question bothers you, be ready to make some adjustments.

ASK GOD TO HELP YOU FOCUS TODAY ON WHAT WILL MATTER FOR ETERNITY.

Day 196

It is my prayer that your love may abound more and more.

—Philippians 1:9

The Christian life is not a self-improvement plan or a do-it-yourself project. It's letting Christ take control of your life as you cooperate with Him and allow Him to do His perfecting work in you.

Perfection in the Christian life doesn't mean we never sin, but it does mean that we are becoming more and more like Christ. And since love is at the heart of what it means to be like Christ, Paul's prayer for the loving church at Philippi is that they would grow even more in their love for Christ and for one another.

My friend, we need to pray for and encourage one another in this process of growing in love. This prayer of Paul's is for the whole Church; the words in today's verse are plural. We can't do it alone. We need our brothers and sisters in Christ who God has put around us in the Church.

And when the Church is functioning as it should, the results are spectacular. The word picture in Philippians 1:9 of the word *abound* suggests we are standing under a gigantic waterfall with the love of Christ just pouring on us, and splashing over us onto other people. Whether it's your love for God or for people, you can't love too much!

May your love abound more and more!

PRAY THAT THE LOVE OF CHRIST MAY GROW MORE AND MORE IN YOUR LIFE EACH DAY.

Day 197

For to us a child is born, to us a son is given...and his name shall be called Wonderful Counselor.

—Isaiah 9:6

Today, I want to help you understand the importance of this verse...and its significance for your life.

Wonderful is a word that in the original Hebrew means beyond our comprehension. Part of what this means is that Christ is far beyond our thinking and understanding. It's simply mind-boggling who Christ is—and what He has done. He is uncommon, unique, and distinctly different from everyone else.

Jesus is called "Wonderful Counselor" by the prophet Isaiah. A counselor is someone who can help us put the broken pieces back together and make sense out of our lives. And because Jesus is Counselor above all others, life makes sense when we know Him! This also means that without Him, nothing makes sense.

This is why so many people can be miserable even in the most joyous of times. They are filled with anger, self-absorption, and other spiritual poisons. They're also battling emotional and psychological problems that result from their spiritual needs. People think they need medications and counselors, but they're only partly correct. What they really need is the Wonderful Counselor!

Take time today to thank God that He sent His Son...the Wonderful Counselor...to help you put the pieces of your life together!

PRAISE GOD HE HAS GIVEN US A COUNSELOR FAR BEYOND OUR UNDERSTANDING TO PUT THE PIECES OF OUR LIVES TOGETHER!

Day 198

In the beginning was the Word, and the Word was with God, and the Word was God.

—John 1:1

Today I want to invite you to take a moment to reflect on what makes the birth of Jesus unique from every other.

First, we need to remember that even though Jesus is the eternal God, He was born as a baby here on earth. But more than that, He was born of a virgin, a truth that no one before or after Him can claim.

Now, you might wonder if it really matters that Jesus was virgin-born. Absolutely! If Christ had been born the same way as everyone else, He would have no claim to be of God. John said Christ existed as God before time began—a statement of His eternal pre-existence as co-equal with God the Father...hence the power of the virgin birth!

If there was human blood running through the veins of Jesus, He would have just been another child born to a poor Jewish family in first-century Israel. But there was heavenly blood running through His body! Praise God, because the virgin birth of Christ opens heaven for us.

What a glorious story: the infant, eternal God in the arms of young Mary. Yes, the birth of Jesus was supernatural! God became man that He might purchase our salvation!

TAKE TIME TODAY TO THANK GOD FOR JESUS CHRIST, HEAVEN'S GREATEST GIFT TO US.

Day 199

For it was indeed fitting that we should have such a high priest, holy, innocent, unstained, separated from sinners, and exalted above the heavens.

—Hebrews 7:26

Jesus lived a sinless life. Stop and think about that for a minute! This mind-bending truth separates Jesus from all others who have walked on this earth. He was the perfect God-man who NEVER sinned!

The apostle John wrote that no book could contain all of the wonders of the life of Jesus. There is no human explanation for His miraculous birth and perfect life apart from the fact that He is who He claimed to be—the eternal Son of God and Savior of the world.

Yet, this wonderful fact of the sinlessness of Jesus doesn't mean that He can't relate to you and me as sinners. Remember, He took on human flesh as a baby in Bethlehem. Even though He lived a separate and sinless life, Jesus touched the lives of helpless sinners everywhere He went. And He was tempted as we are…yet without sin.

Jesus was born to save an imperfect, unsaved world. And unless He had lived that perfect life, we would be doomed! So praise God today for His precious gift of His perfect Son. He bought our salvation through His sinless blood that flowed on the cross to pay the price for our sin.

EVEN THOUGH HE IS SINLESS, CHRIST LOVES SINNERS LIKE YOU AND ME AND REDEEMED US THROUGH HIS DEATH ON THE CROSS!

Day 200

All we like sheep have gone astray; we have turned every one to his own way; and the LORD has laid on him the iniquity of us all.

—Isaiah 53:6

Why would the eternal Son of God leave the splendors of heaven to be born as a helpless baby into the world that He created? As the old gospel song says, "He did it all for me."

All of us have experienced spiritual death because of our sins. And it was because of the death sentence on us that Christ died! He is unique and worthy because He gave up His own life so that we would not have to pay the penalty of death for our sins.

Christ was born with one purpose in mind: to die upon a cross and redeem those who believe in Him.

Christ was our replacement, our substitute upon the cross. That should have been you and me up there, but Christ did what no one else could do. He took our place and our punishment. That's why even the Roman soldier who witnessed the crucifixion of Christ stood in amazement and said, "Truly this man was the Son of God!" (Mark 15:39).

So today, rejoice that Jesus was not only born into this world, but that He was born to take your place on the cross. He is worthy of your worship each and every day of the year.

JESUS BORE THE PUNISHMENT FOR OUR INIQUITY. PRAISE HIM TODAY FOR TAKING OUR PLACE ON THE CROSS.

Day 201

At the name of Jesus every knee should bow, in heaven and on earth and under the earth, and every tongue confess that Jesus Christ is Lord.

—Philippians 2:10-11

Other people have died noble deaths, so what makes the death of Christ so special? He didn't stay dead very long! He rose from the grave after only three days, and that is something that only He can claim! That is why His influence is still strong in the lives of millions of people around the world today.

You see, when most spiritual and political leaders die, their ideas and direct impact die soon after, but not so with Jesus Christ. That's why, two thousand years later, we still celebrate and observe Christmas and Easter. We celebrate during these special times because Jesus was born into this world to die for us...but He also rose from the dead, and is coming back for us. And He still guides us and instructs us from on high!

What a message we have to share with our world today!

Let's make sure that each and every day we tell everyone possible the Good News that the Son of God came to live and die for them. And that the One who died will be coming back just for them.

I challenge you to make a commitment today to be a bold witness for the Lord. There's no better way to demonstrate your gratitude for the One who came to live and die for you. His resurrection was not only spectacular, but it proved that everything He said in His 33 years of ministry was true.

It is a story worth sharing!

ONLY CHRIST CAN LOVE YOU ENOUGH TO NOT ONLY DIE FOR YOU, BUT COME BACK FOR YOU.

Day 202

If I go and prepare a place for you, I will come again and take you to myself, that where I am you may be also.

—John 14:3

The story of Jesus Christ did not end 2000 years ago. The Savior who came into this world in the manger of Bethlehem, died for you and me on the cross of Calvary, and rose from the dead, is coming again for us!

But this time, Jesus will not come to a cradle in a lowly manger, but to a throne. He will be wrapped in glory, not in swaddling clothes, on His final return.

We look forward with great joy and anticipation to that day. But in the meantime, Jesus is our wonderful Savior and Lord who keeps us every day. Did you know that right now, Christ is at the right hand of the Father, interceding and praying for you? He is on your side; He wants to give you sound counsel and wise advice. And He is your legal representative before the courts of heaven.

When you place your life in Christ's hands, you can rest assured that you will receive grace and not judgment because of what Christ did for you. Christ has saved you, and one day soon He will return for you and bring you into His holy presence in heaven!

That is why Christ is unique as the One who reigns on high, and will reign forever and ever!

PRAISE THE LORD TODAY FOR THE GLORIOUS TRUTH THAT HE WILL RETURN ONE DAY TO TAKE YOU TO HEAVEN TO BE WITH HIM.

Day 203

For to me to live is Christ, and to die is gain.

—Philippians 1:21

What does it mean to be totally alive? How would you describe "living large"? Paul said in Philippians that the purpose and passion of life should be to live every moment as Christ would live it…to magnify Jesus Christ.

This passion is a strong, unyielding commitment to live life in such a way that we glorify God in everything we do. The love of Christ should be our motivation, and we should get excited about the same things that Christ gets excited about.

What I find is that too many believers aren't happy because they are waiting to live; they are waiting for something great to happen or for that next big step. The only problem with waiting is that it doesn't fit with Christ's call to serve Him every day right where we are.

Many of us hope for that day when we "arrive," but Christ wants us to experience fulfillment on the journey today…right now…in whatever place or circumstance that He has placed us. His desire is that we live every moment walking with Him and for Him.

What makes you excited? What motivates you to get up in the morning? I hope it's the things of Christ…living for and walking with Him. Don't just endure life hoping you'll arrive at some great place some day. Live large starting today by living every moment as Christ would live it…seeking to bring glory to Him in every way!

LIVE EVERY MOMENT AS CHRIST WOULD LIVE IT.

Day 204

I want you to know, brothers, that what has happened to me has really served to advance the gospel.

—Philippians 1:12

One of the ways to gain that unique perspective on life that will bring you the joy God desires for you is found in Scripture.

I encourage you to spend some time reading the book of Philippians, which is all about living a life of joy. The apostle Paul may have been in prison when he wrote this book, but he shows us what it means to have genuine joy despite circumstances.

How could Paul be excited about what God was doing in his life when he was going through such suffering? Why should we be joyful when we are undergoing physical, emotional, or financial struggles? Again, it's the unique perspective God has given us. For example, God's Word tells us that when we are weak, Christ is strong.

Paul knew that in his weakness Christ's power was being displayed. And that gave Paul joy because He could trust God to work through him and to bring about His purpose. And that purpose is ultimately to bring glory to the name of Jesus Christ!

I pray you will gain the perspective today that God has a good purpose behind every struggle in your life, and that you will rejoice that Christ is in control.

YOU CAN HAVE UNSPEAKABLE JOY AS YOU GAIN GOD'S PERSPECTIVE ON LIFE.

Day 205

Most of the brothers, having become confident in the Lord by my imprisonment, are much more bold to speak the word without fear.

—Philippians 1:14

Salvation is truly an extreme makeover…a makeover that changes us from the inside out.

Paul is a perfect example. Before Paul knew God, Paul was known as Saul. He hated Christians and made it his life's work to rid Israel of every believer in Christ. But what a changed person we meet in the book of Philippians! Saul, the persecutor of Christians, was now Paul, the apostle who willingly went to prison and endured beatings for the name of Jesus!

And what an impact Paul's life…and his bold walk with Christ…had on other Christians. His joy, faithfulness, and strong sense of purpose gave many of the Christians in Philippi greater courage to witness for the Lord despite persecution.

Paul was a wonderful example of the truth that when we know Christ and realize He has a purpose for our troubles, we can praise Him and be faithful to Him. And God will use our boldness to strengthen other believers.

Like Paul, you and I should constantly be lifting our eyes up to Jesus…and our hands out to others…so that they may know the Jesus we know. When Paul was changed, he didn't just stop what he was doing and close up, but opened the door of his life to others and ministered to any who were in need.

If you have experienced the "extreme makeover" of salvation in Christ, then let me encourage you today to share the Gospel with someone who needs it! And remember, other Christians will be inspired by your example to do the same.

LIVE IN SUCH A WAY THAT OTHER CHRISTIANS ARE STRENGTHENED BY YOUR EXAMPLE.

Day 206

What you have learned and received and heard and seen in me—practice these things, and the God of peace will be with you.

—Philippians 4:9

People live for all kinds of things. Some believe life is about pleasure, parties, and fun—just being happy. Others go hard after careers, possessions, and climbing the ladder of success.

You probably know some people who believe that fame, power, and wealth are all that matter. There is nothing particularly wrong with any one of these, but they should not be the sum of life, especially for a believer in Christ.

One day, when this life is over, each of us will give an account to the Lord for our lives. Make no mistake, He won't be looking at our financial portfolio. All the money, power, and fame accumulated over the years will disappear and be forgotten the day we stand before Christ. The things that excite us today will be left behind tomorrow.

Like the apostle Paul, we need to pursue those things that will bring glory to God. And we should model those things in how we live so that we can say, like Paul, that other Christians ought to live like we do if they want to honor God.

What a different focus and a different drive than the world around us! Rather than our goal in life being to exalt our own name or fame, as Christians, our goal is to bring the name of the Lord fame.

So let me ask you. What are you pursuing today? What motivates you? Can you say, like Paul, "What you have learned and received and heard and seen in me, practice these things"?

MODEL FOR OTHERS HOW THE CHRISTIAN LIFE OUGHT TO BE LIVED.

Day 207

For the sake of Christ, then, I am content with weaknesses. . . . For when I am weak, then I am strong.

—2 Corinthians 12:10

What's powerful enough to bring even strong and prideful men to their knees? The answer is Jesus Christ and His powerful love.

Now, it's great to talk about Jesus and His great love, but I want to tell you today that it's only when we come to the end of ourselves that we really begin to experience His love and power!

No matter how strong we may think we are, we'll all come to the end of ourselves someday. We'll all come to the point of saying to the Lord, "I can't do it on my own. I need you, Jesus." Whether it's earthly struggles or spiritual warfare that brings us to our knees, we need to learn that Christ is all we need.

Have you ever been in a position where the only way out was a miracle? There is nothing like seeing God make a way where there is no way. That's why it's sad to see believers who struggle to fix problems on their own without the help of God.

We need to understand that Christ brings us to the point of weakness not to break us or discourage us, but so that we might learn how to tap into His supernatural power! Christ wants us to turn to Him as our first reaction, not as our last resort.

I don't know if you're riding high or flying low today. But whatever your situation, make things easier on yourself. Don't try to do it all or fix every problem by yourself. Let Christ do His work in you today.

GOD BRINGS US TO THE END OF OURSELVES SO THAT WE CAN EXPERIENCE HIS SUPERNATURAL POWER IN OUR LIVES.

Day 208

I am hard pressed between the two. My desire is to depart and be with Christ, for that is far better.

—Philippians 1:23

I love a win-win situation! There's nothing better than being in a situation where you come out on top no matter what you do. This is exactly what Paul describes in today's verse.

Paul knew that the churches he had established needed him, and that staying on earth would mean more fruitful ministry. But he also had an overwhelming desire to be with Christ.

This is the ultimate win-win situation for Christians. If we live, we have another day to serve and please Christ. And even if we die, we will be with Him in paradise for eternity!

So how should we respond to this? The way Paul did. He wanted to go to heaven, but he also wanted to take as many people as possible with him. So Paul decided he would make every day he had count for Christ, serving Him and bringing Him glory…and let God decide when it was time for him to go home to be with Him for eternity.

My friend, if you're a Christian, you have the best of both worlds! You have a sure future and eternity in the presence of God, and you have another day to serve Him until then.

I challenge you today to make the most of each day God gives you to bring Him glory…and bring others to Christ.

PRAISE GOD FOR GIVING YOU THE ULTIMATE WIN-WIN SITUATION—A LIFE THAT COUNTS FOR HIM TODAY AND A FUTURE TO BE WITH HIM FOREVER.

Day 209

It is appointed for man to die once, and after that comes judgment.

—Hebrews 9:27

The end of life is not usually a fun subject. I don't know too many people who like to talk about or look forward to death. But unless my math is incorrect, I believe the death rate is right at 100%.

That's why I think it's terribly foolish to live life unprepared for death. Which is why, I believe, the author of Hebrews gives us the perspective in the verse above. In essence, I believe he is saying that you're not ready to live until you're ready to die!

Scripture also tells us that life is like a vapor, which means it's far too short and precious to waste time trudging through pointless and worthless activities. We need to set our sights and hopes on things above, not just on what's here in front of us.

That's why as a pastor I urge Christians to spend their lives seeking heaven. Jesus Himself said in Matthew 6:19-21 to store up treasures in heaven, not on earth, because we aren't here for very long. We don't have anything to fear from eternity, even though most of the world around us fears death and doesn't like to think about it. But we have been delivered from the power and the sting of death through Christ.

I hope the thought of death doesn't scare you. We don't know all there is to know about eternity, but I do know that because of Christ we can live in hope and anticipation of being with Him…forever!

LIVE YOUR LIFE PREPARED FOR ETERNITY.

Day 210

Set your minds on things that are above, not on things that are on earth.

—Colossians 3:2

When we were young, we thought the best day of our lives was the day we could leave home and be our own person. But for the Christian, the best day is not leaving home, it's coming home...because the very best day you and I will ever have as Christians is the day we see Jesus face to face.

I believe God gives Christians a strong desire for heaven, where we will be in His glorious presence forever. The apostle Paul had it. He said he preferred to go and be with Christ even though he knew he was still needed in Christ's work on earth.

The great thing about a desire for heaven is that it can, and should, impact the way we live on earth. When we desire God, we find ourselves also desiring those things that we know please Him. I think it's interesting that if we have a strong desire for those things that are good, pure, and holy, we don't have room for the wrong kind of desires. It's what I call being "heaven-hearted."

The best way I know to be ready for heaven is to have a pure heart and desires that are fixed on God and His Kingdom. So let me ask you, what is your mind set on today? If your strongest desire is to live for Christ and see His work done on earth, then you are well prepared for the best day you will ever have as a Christian.

MAKE TODAY THE BEST DAY IT CAN POSSIBLY BE BY SETTING YOUR MIND ON THINGS ABOVE.

Day 211

And if I go and prepare a place for you, I will come again and will take you to myself, that where I am you may be also.

—John 14:3

When a Christian dies, we shouldn't say they're gone, because the fact is they aren't gone. They're just out of our sight for a while. Although we, of course, grieve, there should be little sadness when a believer goes to be with the Lord because that person is more alive than ever!

Think about it. When we get to heaven, we will lose all of our limitations. Here on earth, we are limited by many things, including our bodies, but in heaven we will praise God with no limitations or constraints.

Can you imagine doing the thing you love the most all the time, without end or limitation? That's exactly what heaven is all about. We're not just going to sit on a cloud and be served by angels in heaven; we are going to be actively praising and serving God.

Heaven is a move from limitations to freedom, from questions to answers, and from tents (our aging bodies) to mansions!

Everything on earth will all make sense in heaven. We will get to spend eternity in God's presence. So what is there to be sad about?

The great evangelist Dwight L. Moody said on the day he drew his last breath, "This is my coronation day!" My friend, we can live today with excitement because our coronation day is coming, too.

AS A BELIEVER, JESUS HAS PREPARED A PLACE FOR YOU IN HEAVEN!

Day 212

Beloved, we are God's children now, and what we will be has not yet appeared; but we know that when he appears we shall be like him, because we shall see him as he is.

—1 John 3:2

As a pastor, one of the realities of life I try to help people deal with is the fact that there are questions we simply don't have the answers to. No matter how hard we ponder the imponderables of life, we will never be able to figure everything out.

That's one reason I'm looking forward to heaven. In heaven, our eyes will be opened to see and comprehend things that are mysteries to us down here. Heaven will be a wonderful time of discovering all that God was doing in our lives...to use us on earth and fit us for heaven.

Just because we don't have all of the explanations here on earth doesn't mean that the explanations aren't there. In fact, I think we will be saying, "Aha," a whole lot in heaven!

To me, one of the best parts of the transformation we will undergo in heaven is our transformation from faith to sight. Right now we live by faith, but sometimes our faith falters. When we see the face of Jesus, though, we will have no more questions or doubts, only praise for His infinite goodness and wisdom.

So what should the anticipation of heaven do for you and me on earth today? For one thing, it should motivate us to continue living by faith, knowing that God not only has a perfect purpose for our lives, but also that one day we will see and understand that purpose and have all of our questions answered...once and for all!

SOMEDAY YOU'LL HAVE THE ANSWERS TO ALL YOUR QUESTIONS!

Day 213

It is my eager expectation and hope that I will not be at all ashamed, but that with full courage now as always Christ will be honored in my body, whether by life or by death.

—Philippians 1:20

Have you noticed lately how many people seem to be sick and tired? I'm serious! The number of people who either seem to be sick all the time or live in a constant state of fatigue represents a growing trend that is having a huge, negative impact on workplaces, families, and ministries.

That's why I believe it is imperative for us to be both spiritually and physically fit. Paul himself said that Christ should be honored in our bodies. It is both biblical and practical to take care of ourselves physically. Our bodies are the temple of Jesus Christ, so they must be kept pure, strong, and vibrant.

Christians are supposed to do everything in the name of and for the glory of Christ, so why shouldn't we take good care of our bodies for His sake and His glory? We should be vital in our faith and our fitness! Look at Jesus Himself. He was no pale weakling. He was a strong, vibrant Man who had the strength to stand up to sinners and endure the pain of the cross.

Fitness is a biblical concept. We don't necessarily need to obsess and stress over it, but we should make an effort to honor God by honoring His temple in the way we care for our bodies through exercise, proper diet, and adequate rest.

HONOR CHRIST BY BEING PHYSICALLY FIT.

Day 214

Do you not know that your body is a temple of the Holy Spirit within you, whom you have from God?

—1 Corinthians 6:19

If you're a Christian, then the Holy Spirit is living inside of you right now! I don't know about you, but I am amazed by that truth! The God of the universe is dwelling in you and me, making our bodies His earthly home!!

One of the implications of this is that we should consider our bodies as holy. I doubt if any Christian would even think of committing some sin right in the middle of a church service while people are worshiping God. I'm sure we would consider that despicable—but that's really the same kind of thing we're doing when we commit a sin against our own body.

We should treat our body with respect, much like you would a church. Doing something physically harmful to your body dishonors the Lord and the place that He chose to live in. Besides this, when you misuse your body or fail to care for it, you minimize your effectiveness for Christ.

A Christian is made up of body, mind, and spirit. These three must be "in sync" for us to be maximally effective for the Lord.

If physical fitness is not a part of your regular routine, choose today as the day you start taking better care of God's temple. You don't have to do it all at once. Start with a walk around the block, or set a goal to be more watchful in what you eat.

Make sure you are doing everything you can to live a healthy and productive life for Christ!

HONOR YOUR BODY AS A TEMPLE OF THE LIVING GOD!

Day 215

Whatever you do, do all to the glory of God.

—1 Corinthians 10:31

Yesterday we focused on how our bodies are the temple of the Holy Spirit…the place God chooses to dwell here on earth. And while it's important to be careful what we put in our bodies, we also need to be careful what we put on them!

God's Word gives us a general dress code when it says we should use "greater modesty" (1 Corinthians 12:23) to cover the parts of our bodies that are not meant to be exposed. The biblical principle is modesty in the way we dress, which honors the Lord.

This means dressing in a way that shows self-respect and dignity. Others should not be so distracted by what we wear that they don't focus their attention on what we say or how we act.

Like so many other decisions we make, the desire to show proper modesty in what we wear starts in the heart. We choose each day what we want to wear, and we know the effect we want our dress to have. Christians who dress immodestly to attract the attention of the opposite gender are forgetting that as believers, our audience is God, not other people.

What we put on is a very important concept in the Scriptures. We are told to put on the armor of Christ, to put on the goodness of God, and to clothe ourselves in righteousness. The local body of Christ, the Church, is supposed to be dressed in these things, and I believe the Church must also affirm and support modest, wholesome standards of dress.

We hear a lot about dressing for success. But since everything we do, including the way we dress, reflects on our Lord, then the ultimate in dressing for success is to make sure that even our wardrobe reflects His glory!

MODESTY IN THE WAY WE DRESS IS A GOOD REFLECTION ON OUR LORD!

Day 216

It is good not to eat meat or drink wine or do anything that causes your brother to stumble.

—Romans 14:21

Not everyone in the body of Christ is at the same point of spiritual maturity. Some Christians are either very young or still relatively immature in the faith, and thus may be more easily influenced by the actions of others. Instead of disregarding them, the Bible teaches us to be careful to make decisions that will not negatively impact them. This should be a very serious consideration for believers, who are called to be examples.

Little eyes are always watching you, waiting to see what you choose to do. Even if you can control your habits, can you guarantee that those around you will be able to control the habit that you helped start in their lives?

These are tough questions, but I believe we need to ask them so we can hold ourselves to the highest standards of Christian conduct. We are to be above reproach and to set an example to believers and nonbelievers alike. Are you sending the right messages through your actions?

Let me urge you to live with an acute awareness of those around you who may be at a different point of maturity in their walk with Christ.

REMEMBER, YOUR ACTIONS WILL INFLUENCE HOW OTHERS MAY CHOOSE TO ACT!

Day 217

This is the day that the LORD has made; let us rejoice and be glad in it.
—Psalm 118:24

If you're around negative people very much, you know what a downer they can be. Some people just seem to always see the negative side of things, and refuse to embrace hope or happiness.

But as Christians, we need to get rid of those negative attitudes. That's exactly what Paul did in his writings. He was even in prison when he wrote several of his letters, but he chose to rejoice in the Lord! Paul would agree that your attitude will determine your outcome.

Every day, we should make a decision to rejoice and thank God, no matter our situation. Christians should be the most insanely joyful people on the earth! We don't need to struggle all day with fear or worry because we know that Christ has everything in His hands, and He won't let us go.

Learning to rejoice in the day is a process of training and disciplining ourselves to serve Christ and live in the joy of His love and grace. We may get irritable and stressed at times, but if the determination of our hearts is to rejoice in the Lord, we can find the good in everything—even in the little delays and frustrations of the day that so often upset us.

There is a wonderful little children's chorus that begins, "This is the day, this is the day that the Lord has made. We will rejoice, we will rejoice and be glad in it." That would be a good daily anthem to sing.

Choose to live your life today in the shadow of God's grace, and rejoice that He has given you another day of life to serve Him.

CHRISTIANS SHOULD BE THE MOST JOYFUL AND POSITIVE PEOPLE ON THE EARTH. ARE YOU?

Day 218

While bodily training is of some value, godliness is of value in every way, as it holds promise for the present life and also for the life to come.

—1 Timothy 4:8

I see people all the time outside jogging, running, and biking down the street. That's great, because it's important for us to take care of our bodies. I just wonder sometimes if these people care as much about staying in good spiritual shape as they do about staying in good physical shape.

For the Christian, it's not an either/or situation. As we have discussed over the last few days, the Bible urges us to stay in top shape both physically and spiritually.

It's a matter of having balance in life. We make an effort to work out and stay in shape so that we can live longer, healthier, and more productive lives. The same should be true spiritually.

Having strong, healthy bodies prepares us to deal with the physical world we live in. In much the same way, strengthening our spirits through regular times of prayer, Bible study, worship, and service to the Lord will prepare us for the spiritual atmosphere of heaven, where we will worship and serve the Lord forever!

Just as athletes do, we must practice to be ready for the big game, which in our case is heaven! We're practicing for the big event, so let's give the Lord our best today—whether it's in our prayer life, the study of His Word, or our service. Practice hard every day, and you'll be prepared and in shape when the time comes to enter heaven.

Don't neglect your daily spiritual workout!

MAKE TIME FOR YOUR SPIRITUAL WORKOUT EVERY DAY!

Day 219

I pray that all may go well with you and that you may be in good health.

—3 John 1:2

When was the last time you thanked God for your health? It's probably been a while, because most of us take our health for granted.

One interesting thing to me about physical health is the powerful impact that our minds can have on the way we feel. By that I mean if we are always entertaining thoughts about how sick we are, or if we're afraid of how sick we might become, the chances are we're going to be sick.

Now please don't misunderstand. I'm not making light of real illnesses. I'm just saying that the way we think and the attitude we take toward life has a tremendous influence on how we feel.

When I was in seminary, I ran an impromptu field test where four or five of us went up to another student who was perfectly healthy and told him, "Boy, you look sick," just to see how it would affect him. Sure enough, before the day was over he went home sick!

My point is simply this: Live with a healthy attitude. Don't worry about whether you might catch the latest "in" disease. Just thank God for the strength He gives you each day.

THANK GOD TODAY FOR THE STRENGTH HE GIVES YOU TO FOLLOW AND SERVE HIM.

Day 220

Contend for the faith that was once for all delivered to the saints.

—Jude 1:3

Many people want to add works or rules to the Gospel; that is, they distort it to fit their own ideas of what it takes to be saved. Others try to water down the Gospel by removing or downplaying the need for confession and repentance.

The problem is that when unbelievers hear multiple versions of the Gospel, they usually don't know which one to believe. Or even worse, they just simply choose the one that sounds the best!

There will always be those who try to make the Gospel less… or more…than it is. The challenge for us as believers is to make absolutely sure that we are clear when we present the truth of Christ.

That means being truthful with people about their sin and need of a Savior. Beware of the teaching, even in some so-called Christian circles, which says that everything will be fine if you just try to do your best, because God loves you no matter what and will accept your best efforts.

That's not the Gospel! Nor is it the Gospel that somehow we can work our way to heaven.

It's only when people come to realize their desperate need for Christ that they are truly coming to grips with the message of Jesus Christ. And it's only when people realize God's grace covers their sin that they can fully appreciate the Gospel message.

The Bible calls us to stand firm for the truth. Don't stand for a distorted or diluted Gospel.

BE CLEAR IN PRESENTING THE TRUTH OF GOD'S SAVING GRACE FOR THE SIN OF MANKIND.

Day 221

Let your manner of life be worthy of the gospel of Christ.

—Philippians 1:27

Character is something you can't fake or manufacture on the spot. We can try to cover up and act like someone we really aren't, but it doesn't work. In fact, Jesus called the fake and pious masks that people wear hypocrisy.

I've been a pastor for over 35 years, and I've met many people who claimed to be righteous men and women of character. But the truth always comes out sooner or later, because life has a way of revealing what we really are on the inside.

That's why if you're a person of solid Christian character, your life will ring true.

Have you ever wondered what happens to people who seem to have this very sudden fall from grace as they get caught up in sinful and immoral behavior? The truth is that the fall was probably not all that sudden. Instead, it was probably the culmination of a long line of small compromises that were made in secret before the problem ever became public knowledge.

That's why personal character is such a big issue. One small compromise can lead to another, which in turn leads to another, and so on. Eventually, these small lapses in character turn into a full-fledged scandal.

Our lives are to make the Gospel of Jesus Christ attractive to others, and one of the best ways to do that is to exhibit true Christ-like character. This means we need to pay attention to how we live each day, since character is not something you can pick up quickly when you need it; it's a way of life you develop and keep.

COMMIT TO BE A PERSON OF SOLID CHRIST-LIKE CHARACTER!

Day 222

In every way, whether in pretense or in truth, Christ is proclaimed, and in that I rejoice.

—Philippians 1:17

Having Christ-like character is vital in the life of the believer because what's inside us will come out when we are under pressure or facing opposition. It's at times like these when others see who we really are.

If we are going to lead someone else to Christ, or be a positive example, we have to be people of integrity and credibility. Nobody wants to follow someone they don't trust or who is not completely believable. Your message must be livable if it is to be believable.

It's important to remember that we are either bringing credit or discredit to the holy name of Christ by the things we do and say each day. If the people around you know that you are a Christian, then what you do and say is a representation to them of Jesus.

That's challenging to think about, but if Christ is in you, you have everything you need to be a positive example. After all, the best argument for Christ is a faithful follower of Him!

There's really nothing mysterious about being a good example of the Christian faith. Just let your walk match your talk. Make your personal witness for Christ believable and trustworthy, so others will be willing to follow the example you set.

THE BEST ARGUMENT FOR CHRISTIANITY IS A FAITHFUL FOLLOWER OF CHRIST.

Day 223

And my God will supply every need of yours according to his riches in glory in Christ Jesus.

—Philippians 4:19

When Paul wrote to the people of Philippi, he knew they weren't rich. As a matter of fact, the apostle Paul says these compassionate Christians gave out of their poverty so that his needs would be met. But they were doing so much more than just meeting his needs. They were making a spiritual investment!

In the same way today, when you give to the work of the Lord, you too make a spiritual investment. Not simply a contribution, but an investment in something that will truly last.

Here's something to think about: If God doesn't really need your money, why should you give? Because He wants you to be a part of His redemptive work in the world today! When you give, your focus is on others and on His Kingdom work. And He knows that when your focus is on you, life gets very, very small.

Even if you think you don't have very much to give, look around! Do you have time? Then plant the seeds of time. Even the smallest investment in others can make such a difference. Even the smallest of gifts can transmit hope, encouragement, blessing, and strength to others.

The Philippian believers were not a rich people...but they were rich towards God and they sowed into the life and ministry of the apostle Paul. They gave...and God blessed them as a result!

If you become rich towards God...if you become a giver...He'll do the same for you!

MAKE A SPIRITUAL INVESTMENT BY CONSISTENTLY GIVING YOUR TIME AND RESOURCES TO THE WORK OF THE LORD.

Day 224

Again Jesus spoke to them, saying, "I am the light of the world. Whoever follows me will not walk in darkness, but will have the light of life."

—John 8:12

When I was a boy growing up in Ft. Worth, Texas, I remember seeing a beggar on the street around Christmas one year.

It was apparent that the man was blind, and he held a sign that read, "The sun is shining, but I cannot see." And you know, there really are a lot of people like that beggar in the world today. There's a Light to be seen…but so many people are blind to it.

All of us know what it's like to be in a pitch-dark room where you can't see your hand in front of your face. Where you have vision…but you can't see. Where there is sight…but no light.

Maybe you feel like your life is filled with darkness today…and the light of reason, the light of logic, the light of conscience have all failed you.

If so, remember you have light through Jesus Christ…the One who is "the light of the world." So focus on Him!

As the old hymn says,

> O soul, are you weary and troubled?
> No light in the darkness you see?
> There's a light for a look at the Savior,
> And life more abundant and free!
>
> Turn your eyes upon Jesus,
> Look full in His wonderful face,
> And the things of earth will grow strangely dim,
> In the light of His glory and grace.

IF YOU ARE WEARY AND TROUBLED, LOOK UP TO JESUS TODAY!

Day 225

Keep your conduct among the Gentiles honorable, so that when they speak against you as evildoers, they may see your good deeds and glorify God on the day of visitation.

—1 Peter 2:12

Is there anything in your life…anything about your faith in Jesus Christ…anything about what has happened to you since you encountered Jesus Christ the Son of God…that makes people stop and say, "What on earth happened to you? Who did this to you? Why are you such a changed person?"

You know, I'm afraid we live so blandly…and blindly…that people often don't know that anything has happened to us! Our Christianity is so concealed and our faith is so shut up that no one is ever prompted to even ask about our faith!

Today, I want you to think about one person you know who needs the love of Jesus. Just one person! It could be a friend…a neighbor…a coworker…anyone!

Now, what's one way you could intentionally reach out to that person with the goal of showing and sharing Christ with them this week?

Does your friend need a word of affirmation? Does your neighbor have any work that needs to be done around his or her house? Does your coworker need some work offloaded? Whatever the need, offer to help out…and then, when they ask why you're doing what you're doing, say what's motivating you to do it!

DOES ANYTHING IN YOUR LIFE CAUSE OTHERS TO WANT TO GLORIFY GOD?

Day 226

"The thief comes only to steal and kill and destroy. I came that they may have life and have it abundantly."

—John 10:10

The reason Jesus came to earth is so you and I could have the life He wants us to have. A life that's overflowing, that's bubbling over with joy and peace. God deeply loves us and has a wonderful, abundant plan for our lives.

But we also have an adversary who wants us to live the un-abundant life…a life that's unproductive, deficient, and inadequate. And far too often, we choose that life instead!

Today I want to ask you, are you truly living the abundant life Jesus talked about? Are you finding meaning and purpose in your relationship with Him? Or have you given in to the lies of the enemy that tell you that meaning and purpose is to be found in other things?

If you know Christ, but feel like you aren't living the abundant life, I encourage you to do two things today. First, begin to pray He'll clearly show you His direction for your life. Second, spend time every day in His Word, not just reading but listening. If you will do these two things, just watch…your life will become much more than you ever thought it could be!

DON'T MISS OUT ON THE ABUNDANT, EXTRAVAGANT LIFE YOU CAN HAVE IN CHRIST!

Day 227

He said to him the third time, "Simon, son of John, do you love me?" Peter was grieved because he said to him the third time, "Do you love me?" and he said to him, "Lord, you know everything; you know that I love you." Jesus said to him, "Feed my sheep."

—John 21:17

Not long after Christ's resurrection, we find Peter back on the shores of the Sea of Galilee—the very place he'd first met Jesus. And there on that shoreline, the risen Christ came to Peter...forgave him...and completely restored him.

Have you ever felt like Peter? Have you ever felt like you let God down...that you've done something so wretched you feel like your relationship with Christ could never be the same?

If so, I want you to remember, Jesus loves you...and He loves you perfectly. The great Shepherd is your caretaker and He will lovingly, carefully restore and renew His sheep that fall away. And this includes you!

If you know Christ, but you've wandered or lost your way, your Shepherd is seeking you and deeply desiring to restore you.

No one knows you better than your perfect Shepherd. He knows your name. He knows your thoughts. He knows your needs. He knows the worst thing about you and loves you anyway! And He'll never leave you or forsake you! Like I said, He loves you perfectly.

IF YOU FEEL LIKE YOU'VE WANDERED FAR FROM GOD, REMEMBER YOUR GREAT SHEPHERD IS SEEKING TO RESTORE AND RENEW YOU.

Day 228

For I am sure that neither death nor life, nor angels nor rulers, nor things present nor things to come, nor powers, nor height nor depth, nor anything else in all creation, will be able to separate us from the love of God in Christ Jesus our Lord.

—Romans 8:38-39

Do you ever worry that you could lose your salvation? That you could do something so awful that you would no longer be saved?

The fact is, when you make a decision to accept Christ as your Savior, your eternal future is made secure. His work is finished! Thanks to what Jesus did on the cross, God has wiped away any sin that separated you from Him. In fact, Psalm 103:12 tells us, "As far as the east is from the west, so far does he remove our transgressions from us."

But maybe you still feel guilty for what you've done in the past…or for what you're currently doing. Maybe your deep sense of regret is stopping you from turning back to God now.

If so, I want to point you to what Paul says in Romans 8:38-39…that nothing can separate you from God's love. Death can't do it. Life can't do it. Neither can angels, governments, or powers. Nothing in your past, your present, or your future can separate you from God's love. Not one single thing!

So I encourage you to claim this promise from God today…and commit Romans 8:38-39 to memory. Then the next time Satan tempts you to doubt your standing in Christ, say these verses out loud…and stand on God's promises!

NOTHING CAN SEPARATE YOU FROM THE LOVE OF CHRIST.

Day 229

Do not be conformed to this world, but be transformed by the renewal of your mind, that by testing you may discern what is the will of God, what is good and acceptable and perfect.

—Romans 12:2

One of the best ways to renew your mind is to memorize the Word of God and then make it your own. For example, if you find yourself worrying, remember Matthew 6:33, which says, "But seek first the kingdom of God and his righteousness, and all these things will be added to you."

Or if you have an important decision to make, you might recall Proverbs 3:5-6, which says, "Trust in the LORD with all your heart, and do not lean on your own understanding. In all your ways acknowledge him, and he will make straight your paths."

Once you have memorized a verse, let me encourage you to use it when you have a crisis or a need. Recall it for strength and direction.

Remember too that being conformed to the Word of God is so much more than just reading the Bible here and there. It means really taking the time to study God's Word...to comprehend it and to meditate on it.

Make a commitment to spend time every day in His Word...to make that a consistent habit. And then take a verse each week to memorize from what you read. Finally, strive to conform to what God is teaching you from His Word so that you can know Him intimately and abide in Him each day.

MAKE A COMMITMENT TODAY TO MEMORIZE SCRIPTURE FOR STRENGTH AND DIRECTION.

Day 230

For a wide door for effective work has opened to me, and there are many adversaries.

—1 Corinthians 16:9

There are dozens of preachers today who claim that making a decision to follow Christ will mean that your life will be easier...or that you'll be materially or monetarily blessed because you're a Christian.

Well, I'm going to shoot straight with you. While the Christian life is full of God's blessings, it's also full of opposition. And many people become disillusioned when they encounter trials and difficulties as they walk with Christ.

If you attempt to do something in particular for the glory of God, you will discover opposition and confrontation.

In fact, as believers, we're called to a life that will be filled with conflict. Because when the people of God attempt to lead and do great things in His name, the forces of evil will attempt to stop it by discouraging us. The devil is a liar, a murderer, an accuser of the brethren, and a destroyer! He will oppose you!

Perhaps today you'd admit that you're a little discouraged by how difficult the Christian life can be. If so, I want to offer you a word of encouragement: The opposition you face is actually a sure sign that you're doing something right! Because if the devil leaves you alone, that means you must not be worth trying to discourage!

When you set out to do something great and glorious for God, expect opposition. And take heart with these words from Romans 8:31: "If God is for us, who can be against us?"

IF THE DEVIL IS ON YOUR CASE, IT'S A SIGN YOU'RE DOING SOMETHING RIGHT!

Day 231

Little children, you are from God and have overcome them, for he who is in you is greater than he who is in the world.

—1 John 4:4

Satan doesn't want you to know this, but as a follower of Christ, you are victorious!

Yes, you have a very real and very deadly enemy. Yes, you're engaged in a spiritual battle with him every single day. But you are victorious in Jesus Christ! The battle is already won.

As believers, we fight from a position of strength, not from a position of weakness. We fight from victory...not for victory. When Jesus cried out "it is finished" (John 19:30) on the cross, Satan was finished. And because of the cross, we have victory in Jesus.

That's our victory in Jesus and that's why we can say we fight, not for victory, but from victory, from the strongest possible position of strength! According to God's Word, through Jesus Christ we are invincible against the attacks of the enemy...invincible.

For the Scripture says in 1 John 2:17, "Whoever does the will of God abides forever."

I want to leave you with one last thought today: Satan may frighten you...but he cannot hurt you. Because as God's child, you are in His omnipotent grip! As it says in 2 Corinthians 4:8-9, "We are afflicted in every way, but not crushed; perplexed, but not driven to despair; persecuted, but not forsaken; struck down, but not destroyed"!!

It's my prayer that the Lord Jesus would encourage you with these words...no matter what you may be going through today.

AS BELIEVERS IN THE LORD JESUS CHRIST, OUR BATTLE IS ALREADY WON!

Day 232

"And there is salvation in no one else, for there is no other name under heaven given among men by which we must be saved."

—Acts 4:12

Jesus came to earth to be our Savior…the Savior of our hearts. Because of our sin we were all lost!

Now, I know this isn't a popular statement to make in our culture today. No one really wants to hear that they're a sinner, much less that they're lost on their own. We all want to believe that we're self-sufficient.

But that's not what the Bible tells us. In fact, if I could reduce the message of the entire Bible down to two words it would simply be, "Jesus saves." The Father sent the Son to be the Savior of the world. This was promised and provided in Christ only.

The salvation spoken of in today's verse includes everyone. No one is excluded! Jesus didn't die just for a select few. He died for you and He died for me. Jesus came to be the Savior of the world, and God's desire is that every man, woman, boy, and girl be saved.

God is not willing that any should perish, but that all should come to repentance! So take time today to thank God for sending us His Son…and for the eternal life you have in Him. And take the time to share that good news with someone who needs to hear it today!

TAKE TIME TO PRAISE AND THANK GOD FOR THE SALVATION YOU HAVE IN JESUS CHRIST.

Day 233

And this is the confidence that we have toward him, that if we ask anything according to his will he hears us. And if we know that he hears us in whatever we ask, we know that we have the requests that we have asked of him.

—1 John 5:14-15

There's no doubt that prayer changes things. It's a clear promise from the Scripture. But prayer also changes you and me. It changes our priorities…and it gets our lives in sync with God's plan.

There's a great formula for prayer I learned from my fellow pastor and friend, Dr. Ed Young from Houston. It's the acronym SELF:

S stands for *surrender.* Each day, you and I must surrender our lives to the Lord.

E stands for *empty.* Once you surrender your life to Christ each day, you must empty yourself of self and sin and anything else that would keep you from fulfilling God's plan and purpose for your life.

L stands for *lift.* Once you surrender your life to the Lord Jesus and empty yourself of everything that would hinder your relationship with Him, you must lift your heart in praise, petition, and thanksgiving.

F stands for *fill.* This is when you ask God to fill you with His Holy Spirit so that you will live in the fullness of His power and His blessing.

So SELF is surrendering, it is emptying, it is lifting, and it is filling. And if you do these things in prayer every day, not only is your relationship with Christ going to be that much sweeter, you'll make an eternal impact on the world for Jesus Christ!

PRAYER IS A VITAL PART OF GETTING OUR LIVES IN SYNC WITH GOD'S PLAN.

Day 234

As soon as I heard these words I sat down and wept and mourned for days, and I continued fasting and praying before the God of heaven.

—Nehemiah 1:4

It's been said that when life sweeps you off your feet, get on your knees. And that's exactly what Nehemiah did. When he was swept off his feet by the solemn news of what was happening in the city of Jerusalem, he got on his face before God.

Before he could do anything, Nehemiah knew that he had to first pray. And that should be our reaction as well. In fact, I believe the reason most major goals are never achieved is because we spend our time doing second things first…instead of doing the first thing first, and that's to pray!

Nehemiah…the leader…understood that he was required to do the first thing first, and the first thing was to pray to the God of heaven.

Why is prayer so important to be an effective leader? Because it's in prayer that we surrender and align our will with the will of God. It's in prayer that we get our marching orders and we get our strategies. And it's in prayer that God leads us and helps us to know what we're to do.

Nehemiah prayed to the God of heaven…to our great and awesome, covenant-keeping, promise-keeping God. And in 52 short days, the walls of Jerusalem were rebuilt!

Perhaps today you're trying to rebuild your marriage…or your business…or even your reputation. Whatever you're trying to rebuild, remember to follow the leadership example of Nehemiah: Seek the God of heaven in prayer!

THROUGH PRAYER YOU SURRENDER AND ALIGN YOUR WILL WITH THE WILL OF GOD…AND CAN REBUILD WHATEVER IS BROKEN IN YOUR LIFE.

Day 235

"I have loved you with an everlasting love; therefore I have continued my faithfulness to you."

—Jeremiah 31:3

There are four things about the love of God that I'd like you to meditate on today.

First, God loves you. He loves you more than anyone else could ever love you!

Second, God's love for you is eternal. Time cannot erase it. God loves you and He will always love you.

Third, God's love for you is unconditional. This concept is hard to completely understand at times because of how conditional human love can be. Sometimes human love is dependent on how we feel about someone…or it's dependent upon someone loving us in return. But God's love is unconditional. Nothing you do or don't do can alter it.

Lastly, God's love is incomprehensible! It's immeasurable. What's most remarkable about the love of God is that in spite of your sin and my sin…despite our failure and brokenness and worthlessness…He reached down and showed us His love by sending His Son to die in our place on the cross!

It's my prayer that you'll remember just how much God loves you today…and that as a result, you'll be motivated to share God's love with others.

GOD'S LOVE FOR YOU IS ETERNAL, UNCONDITIONAL, AND IMMEASURABLE!

Day 236

But all things should be done decently and in order.

—1 Corinthians 14:40

Inspiration without organization leads to frustration.

It doesn't matter what kind of organization you're leading—whether it's a leading Fortune 500 company or leading your kids to clean up their room—inspiration without organization equals frustration. This is one of the most important principles of leadership.

Now, there are some who think that organization is of the devil, that organization is somehow not of God.

Yet even when God created our bodies, He put everything in order—the skeletal system, the muscular system, the delivery systems of the body. You and I are fearfully and wonderfully made (Psalm 139:14). The hand of God in the creation of the universe is one of complexity and beauty, and it's highly organized.

God is a God of organization...and even His Church should reflect that quality. But that can only happen if you and I make the commitment to get plugged in to the local Church! The hand of God moves through the hands of His people. And many hands organized together can accomplish what no hand can do by itself!

I challenge you today to look at your life and honestly assess where you are not properly organized. Commit that area to God in prayer and begin to take steps to become more effective for Him.

INSPIRATION WITHOUT ORGANIZATION LEADS TO FRUSTRATION.

Day 237

Therefore, since we are surrounded by so great a cloud of witnesses, let us also lay aside every weight, and sin which clings so closely, and let us run with endurance the race that is set before us, looking to Jesus, the founder and perfecter of our faith, who for the joy that was set before him endured the cross, despising the shame, and is seated at the right hand of the throne of God. Consider him who endured from sinners such hostility against himself, so that you may not grow weary or fainthearted.

—Hebrews 12:1-3

As Christians, one of the best ways to defeat Satan…the enemy of our souls…is to know how he operates.

Far too many believers today are unaware of or don't fully appreciate how deadly this enemy is…and to what lengths he will go to thwart and destroy God's people and God's plan! So it's important each of us know our enemy so we can better prepare ourselves for his attack.

Of all the schemes and tactics Satan uses against the people of God, his greatest tool is probably the tool of discouragement. Satan knows that if he can pry open your heart with discouragement, he can make you quit.

Galatians 6:9 reminds us, "And let us not grow weary of doing good, for in due season we will reap, if we do not give up."

If you're a believer and you're discouraged today, it's because Satan is on your trail. Are you thinking about throwing in the towel on your marriage…or giving up on your kids…or giving in to that recurring temptation? Don't do it! Don't give in!

You may want to quit at times, but that's when you need to push on through the pain and push on to finish the work God has called you to do. Don't grow weary in doing good!

DON'T LET DISCOURAGEMENT KEEP YOU FROM DOING GREAT THINGS FOR GOD.

Day 238

Your words were found, and I ate them, and your words became to me a joy and the delight of my heart, for I am called by your name, O LORD, God of hosts.

—**Jeremiah 15:16**

Someone has said that true revival is all of Jesus getting all of me. And I think that's a great definition!

But I wonder today how many people who call themselves followers of Christ can really say that Jesus has absolute lordship over every area of their lives.

In the book of Nehemiah, we see that there are certain things that must happen in the life of a believer and in the Body of Christ for true revival to take place. And one of the most important elements is applying the Word of God to your life…letting it affect the way you think and live and breathe!

You know, I often wonder how much of what we know in our heads as believers really ever gets into our hearts and affects the way we live our lives.

Which leads me to a question today: When was the last time you read the Word of God and it made you think twice about your attitude or actions? When was the last time God's Word convicted you of sin in your life?

Today, it's my prayer that you will give God time to let Him help you respond to His Word. It's my hope that you will be able to say along with Jeremiah, "Your words were found, and I ate them, and your words became to me a joy and the delight of my heart."

CAN YOU TRULY SAY THAT THE LORD IS LORD OVER EVERY AREA OF YOUR LIFE?

Day 239

Jesus said to them, "I am the bread of life; whoever comes to me shall not hunger, and whoever believes in me shall never thirst."

—John 6:35

Back when the children of Israel were wandering in the desert and needed food, God miraculously supplied their needs. He provided bread for them that appeared on the ground every morning, which they called "manna." And that manna fed them and sustained them in the wilderness.

I believe that the manna was a picture of Jesus Christ. Just as the manna came from God...so did Jesus. God Himself descended and came to earth that we might know Him...that we might have spiritual life...not just physical life.

Now, in the Old Testament you had a choice. You could either walk over the manna...or you could pick it up and eat it. And the same choice is yours today! The Bread of Heaven has come down. The Bread of Heaven is available. But it's up to you to take that Bread...Jesus Christ...and make Him the source of nourishment and power.

Jesus tells us in John 6:27, "Do not labor for the food that perishes, but for the food that endures to eternal life, which the Son of Man will give to you."

Are you laboring for "food that perishes"? Or are you feasting on the Bread of Life each and every day? The choice is yours!

DON'T SETTLE FOR "FOOD THAT PERISHES." FEAST ON THE BREAD OF LIFE TODAY!

Day 240

Jesus said to him, "I am the way, and the truth, and the life. No one comes to the Father except through me."

—John 14:6

There are three essential truths that all believers must remember in order to walk closely with the Lord Jesus. They're truths that we as Christians must fearlessly defend and declare when we tell others about Christ.

First, as Jesus says in today's verse, He is the only way to God. Standing up and declaring that Jesus Christ alone is God…that there's only one name given among men where by we must be saved…is an explosive truth that divides people. But it's a truth you and I must be willing to tell others.

Second, Jesus' death on the cross atoned for the sins of the whole world. In our day and time, you can get away with talking about Jesus being a great moral teacher, an influential leader, or even a revolutionary. But start talking about Jesus dying for our sins, and people bristle.

Third, God is sovereign over the destinies of human beings. He has chosen each of us who is saved (Ephesians 1:3-4).

Now, when you share Christ, someone may say, "How do I know I am chosen?" The answer is simple—ask Jesus into your life right now and you will know you are chosen!

So I hope you will take time today to share the Good News of Jesus Christ with someone you know. It is the only truth by which any man or woman can be saved!

TAKE TIME TODAY TO SHARE THE GOOD NEWS OF JESUS CHRIST WITH SOMEONE YOU KNOW.

Day 241

"If anyone's will is to do God's will, he will know whether the teaching is from God or whether I am speaking on my own authority."

—John 7:17

Here's what Jesus is saying in today's verse: "If you really want to know Me...if you really want to know if I'm speaking the truth of God...if you want to know if I'm just making this up or if this is reality, you can know because God will reveal Himself to you!"

Ultimately, knowing Jesus isn't a problem of the intellect. It's an issue of the heart.

If a person waits until he or she gets it all figured out, they may never come to Christ. At some point each person has to decide on the evidence. Is Jesus a liar? Is He a lunatic? Or is He Lord? If you say, "Well, I'm not sure yet," then simply say, "Jesus, if You are real, show Yourself to me." Then examine the evidence, and ask God to show you if it's true or not. I believe if you ask Him, He will absolutely make it clear to you!

Thousands, even millions, through the ages will testify to the reality of Jesus Christ in their lives. And I know that I can personally testify to the reality of Christ in my life. In fact, I'm banking my life and my future on the fact that it's true!

The Good News of Jesus Christ is the best news ever given to mankind. That He came...lived a perfect, sinless life...died on the cross...and rose again that you and I can be saved and forgiven.

Jesus is not a liar...nor a lunatic...but Lord. And that's good news!

IF SOMEONE YOU KNOW IS UNSURE ABOUT JESUS, ENCOURAGE THEM TO ASK GOD TO REVEAL HIMSELF...AND HE WILL!

Day 242

On the last day of the feast, the great day, Jesus stood up and cried out, "If anyone thirsts, let him come to me and drink. Whoever believes in me, as the Scripture has said, 'Out of his heart will flow rivers of living water.'"

—John 7:37-38

When the Spirit of God fills you and overflows in and out of your life, you're going to live in obedience to Him. You will have the power to please Him and live for Him from the inside out.

My constant daily prayer is that I will be filled with the Holy Spirit of God...and as a result, that I will please God, that I will grow stronger in my faith, that I will grow more powerful in resisting temptation, that I will be more dedicated in my prayer, and more faithful in my witness.

There's always more power to live the Christian life when the Holy Spirit captures our hearts. And when the Spirit of God is in control of our hearts, He is in control of our attitudes and ultimately our actions.

I've discovered when I'm full of the Spirit, I don't worry about demanding my rights and doing what pleases me. My primary concern is to please God when I'm walking in the fullness and the freshness of the Holy Spirit. And that, my friend, is a life of victory!

So let me ask you today: As a believer, are you walking in the Spirit? Are you living a life full of His power...that wants to please Christ in your thoughts and actions? Are you living a victorious life?

It's my prayer that God will enable you to live a spirit-filled, victory-filled life today and every day.

WHEN YOU LIVE A LIFE THAT IS FILLED WITH THE POWER OF THE HOLY SPIRIT, YOU WILL LIVE IN OBEDIENCE TO GOD.

Day 243

Jesus said to them again, "Peace be with you. As the Father has sent me, even so I am sending you."

—John 20:21

There's no sin that can keep you out of heaven. And there's no religion in the world that can get you in.

The only way you can go to heaven is through the pardon brought about through the death and resurrection of Jesus Christ. And when you accept that pardon, Jesus takes you and changes you...and then He empowers you by His presence for a truly abundant life!

In the New Testament, this is called conversion. It's called the new birth. It's called salvation, getting saved. And this new birth is for everyone. That's why you and I as believers are on a mission of mercy...the same mission that brought Jesus to this earth.

We are to go into the world where people are living in their brokenness and sin. We are to go into this world on a mission of mercy and say, "Jesus loves you, and He will forgive you because of what He's done on the cross and by the power of His resurrection."

Most of the people in the world today believe God is angry at them...that because of their sin they can never be saved. But we have a message of hope and grace...that God loves them and desires that they be saved. Which is why Jesus voluntarily gave His life!

Are you willing to voluntarily give your life as a mission of mercy so that others may know Him?

LIKE JESUS, WE ARE TO GO INTO THE WORLD ON A MISSION OF MERCY WITH A MESSAGE OF HOPE AND GRACE.

Day 244

"Blessed are those whose lawless deeds are forgiven, and whose sins are covered; blessed is the man to whom the LORD shall not impute sin" (NKJV).

—Romans 4:7-8

One of the great truths of salvation is that you and I are able to forget the guilt of the past and the stained pages of yesterday…and begin life anew!

How awesome it is to know the forgiveness, the glorious love of Jesus Christ. And in today's verse, King David…one of the greatest figures in all of human history…talks about knowing that joy of forgiveness.

David was someone who experienced that joy for himself. He was someone who delved deeply into sin, and yet in his great sin found great forgiveness.

Now, the Scripture uses many illustrations to describe salvation and eternal life. And one of these terms is a word we find in today's verse: impute. The word *impute* means "to reckon" or "to credit one's account."

When you go to the bank and make a deposit, an imputation takes place. And that's what God does for us and to us when we come to Jesus Christ! A great imputation takes place wherein we are credited with the righteousness of Christ. In fact, that's how we are forgiven.

Today, thank God that all your sins…past, present, and future…are forgiven because of God's imputation in your account!

PRAISE GOD THAT THROUGH CHRIST'S FORGIVENESS, YOU WERE ABLE TO BEGIN LIFE ANEW!

Day 245

For all have sinned and fall short of the glory of God.

—Romans 3:23

The easiest way to understand what Christ did for you and me on the cross is to think about two bank books. At the top of one bank book is the name of Jesus Christ. It belongs to Him. At the top of the other bank book is your name.

When you look at Jesus' bank book, you see that the record is perfect. There are no marks or imperfections. Jesus Christ, the God Man, never sinned against God! And on the record of Christ there are no debts to be paid because He is pure, perfect, and righteous.

But when you look on your page, the record isn't perfect. In fact, today's verse tells us there are many marks of imperfection there. When you look at your bank account and read the bottom line, you find that you are spiritually bankrupt. Every man and woman ever born is drowning in spiritual debt!

But do you know what happens to your bank book of sin when you come to Jesus Christ? It's cleared! When Jesus died on the cross for your sins and when you come to Him for forgiveness, He absolutely takes away your sin and debt and they're gone forever!

Where do they go? I don't know! But they're gone forever. Your record is clear! This is why Romans 8:1 says, "There is therefore now no condemnation for those who are in Christ Jesus."

As a Christian, praise God today that your "bank book" is clean...that He has fully paid your debt!

WHEN YOU COME TO CHRIST, HE TAKES AWAY THE DEBT OF YOUR SINS...AND IT'S GONE FOREVER!

Day 246

For when I kept silent, my bones wasted away through my groaning all day long. For day and night your hand was heavy upon me; my strength was dried up as by the heat of summer.

—Psalm 32:3-4

There are several different ways people try to deal with their sin on their own. Some people ignore it. Others try to change themselves and become "a better person." And others think, "I'll just destroy the record."

But the thing is, we can't destroy the record of our sin on our own. We wish that we could just blot them out, forget about them, move on, and think positively. But that's impossible because our record book is in God's hands...and we can't change it.

No one knew this better than King David. After he fell into sin with Bathsheba, and he made her pregnant, David arranged the murder of Bathsheba's husband to cover up what he had done. It was all a big cover-up!

And David thought he could hide the record from God. But in the middle of his hiding and running from God, he was miserable.

Thankfully, though, God began to deal with David and work to bring him to a place of repentance. And God will do that for every believer!

Let me ask you a question today: Are you hiding a sin in your life from God? Are you running from Him?

Whatever we cover, God uncovers. But whatever we uncover, God covers. When we get honest with God...when we're willing to confess our sins and become clean before a holy God...then His love will cover our sin.

WHATEVER SIN WE COVER, GOD UNCOVERS. BUT WHATEVER SIN WE UNCOVER, HE COVERS.

Day 247

As far as the east is from the west, so far does he remove our transgressions from us.

—Psalm 103:12

Today's verse is a wonderful promise of God. When we come to Christ, He forgives us and cleanses us from all sin.

Yet many Christians are still keeping books on themselves! If you have come to Jesus Christ…if you have experienced His salvation… you need to recognize that the books are closed on your account.

Some Christians are always remembering what God has forgotten. And on the other hand, some Christians are always forgetting what God wants us to remember.

But do you know what God has forgotten? He has forgotten your sin. When God forgives, He forgets. Now, it's good for us to ask God to search our hearts and to see if there is any wicked way in us, according to Psalm 139. And we need to always be transparent with God and open to God.

But we shouldn't keep recording our sins that are forgiven and cleansed by the power of Jesus Christ! God doesn't keep a record of them, so why should we?

You know what would be a good confession for you to make every morning of your life? When you have your time with God, make these three confessions. Say, "I am forgiven!", "I am filled with the Spirit of God!", and "I am forever secure in the righteousness of Jesus Christ!"

Stop keeping books on your past sin…sin that has already been forgiven by God.

DON'T LET YOURSELF FEEL GUILTY FOR SINS THAT CHRIST HAS ALREADY FORGIVEN.

Day 248

So God created man in his own image, in the image of God he created him; male and female he created them.

—Genesis 1:27

Our attitude toward the origin of the earth is essential to our attitude toward life. To a great degree, how we live our life is determined by what we believe about who we are and where we came from. In fact, our very understanding of God Himself is also at stake in this issue.

For instance, why would there need to be a God if we just evolved, are really just animals, and everything happens purely by chance? If the entire universe is just a random set of events and a collection of beings with no purpose, then having a Creator is unnecessary.

But as Christians, we believe that life is not random. We believe there is a personal God that is involved with His creation.

But here's the real issue: Even though it's important to know where we came from, it's even more important to know where we are going! Our past is only a precursor to our future. We must know that we came from the hand of God, and that someday we will stand before Him!

Genesis 1 is a great week-long story of how God loves us and created us. Just make sure you not only know where you came from, but where you're going. And share with others this week the good news that God loves them, and invite them to come to know Jesus as their Savior so someday they can stand before Him as His child.

IT'S IMPORTANT TO KNOW WHERE YOU CAME FROM, BUT IT'S EVEN MORE IMPORTANT TO KNOW WHERE YOU ARE GOING!

Day 249

God called the light Day, and the darkness he called Night. And there was evening and there was morning, the first day.

—Genesis 1:5

The first chapter of the Bible is the amazing story of how God created everything in the world in just six days, capping off His work with the creation of man and woman. This was without a doubt the most productive week in history!

Throughout Genesis 1, there are references to six separate days of creation. There are disagreements as to whether the days of creation are literal 24-hour periods, or just the Bible's way of speaking of long periods of time. I happen to believe that the Scriptures talk of actual 24-hour days, because that's what the Word says.

This truth should make us stand in awe of God every day. When you wake up tomorrow morning, the air you will breathe, the sunrise you will see, and the plants you will pass by all came directly as a result of God's handiwork in just a six-day period!

Genesis 1:16 shows us just how awesome and majestic God is. This verse states that He made the sun, the moon, the stars, and all the galaxies of this universe. Think of it. The stars all came into being with just a word from God, a wave of His holy hand! The multiplied millions of galaxies that we still know so little about were created instantly in God's creative work.

This verse is quite an understatement! God's creative power is awesome! But here's the best part of the story: This God who created the world also made you and loves you. Let that thought fill your mind today, and everything you do will take on new meaning.

THE GOD WHO MADE THE ENTIRE UNIVERSE CREATED YOU AND LOVES YOU!

Day 250

Then God said, "Let us make man in our image, after our likeness. And let them have dominion over the fish of the sea and over the birds of the heavens and over the livestock and over all the earth and over every creeping thing that creeps on the earth."

—Genesis 1:26

There is one large question that looms over the creation story: Why? Why did God create the material world and create us in His own image? He had to make a decision to spend six days creating all of this, so what was His reasoning?

I think that first and foremost, God created us for His pleasure. It pleases Him to have a relationship with us. It's not that God was lonely. He has hosts of angels worshiping Him. And He is self-sufficient, so we don't give Him anything He lacks. But God delights in having a relationship with us.

I also believe that God made everything for His praise. The Bible states in many different passages that all of creation praises Him. Every man, woman, and creature praises God either here on earth or eventually in His presence at the gates of heaven.

Besides His pleasure and His praise, God also made us for a specific purpose. The Bible says in Romans 8:28-29 that we were created and redeemed so that we might be conformed to the image of Jesus Christ.

I want you to keep this in mind today as you go about the activities of the day. Remember that the God of the universe desired so much to have a relationship with you that He created you to be like His own Son! Thank God today that you are known and loved by Him.

YOU WERE CREATED FOR THE PLEASURE AND PRAISE OF GOD, AND TO FULFILL HIS PURPOSE FOR YOUR LIFE.

Day 251

Heaven and earth will pass away, but my words will not pass away.

—Matthew 24:35

Despite the Bible's clear teaching of God's creative work, there remains a strong denial of creation in the world today. Many people continue to deny that the heavens and the earth are the handiwork of a personal and powerful God. They believe the answers to our origins are found in science.

But the truth is that true Scripture and true science never clash. There's no contradiction between what God says and the realities of science.

However, I do believe that science must be subservient to Scripture, for a very important reason. Science is constantly changing. New theories and ideas are being proposed, revised, and discarded all the time. That's why scientific theories about how the world came into existence must bow to the constant and eternal truth of the Bible.

Evolution is, of course, the main opponent of creation. The problem is that evolution is simply a theory. And yet, despite this most obvious fact, many people teach it and believe it as if it were a proven reality. But the theory of evolution is not scientifically true because none of it has been proven, and it is increasingly rejected by many brilliant and capable scientists.

Science is always looking for the starting point of life. But we already know where it is, in the opening chapters of the book of Genesis. Don't be fooled or influenced by the pseudo-scientific fantasies and false theories of this world. You're on solid ground scientifically when you stand on the truth of God's Word.

TRUE SCIENCE AND TRUE SCRIPTURE NEVER CLASH.

Day 252

And God said, "Let the earth bring forth living creatures according to their kinds—livestock and creeping things and beasts of the earth according to their kinds."

—Genesis 1:24

Why should we reject evolutionary ideas? Besides the fact that they are unproven scientifically, the bigger problem is that evolution takes God out of the picture and turns this world into a pointless and random universe. It's important not only to reject evolution, but to know why we should reject evolution.

We should reject it first for logical reasons. It takes more faith and stretching of the mind to believe the absurdity that life spontaneously began than it does to believe that a powerful and purposeful God created it. The order and complexity we see in creation argues for a Creator.

We should also reject evolutionary theory for moral reasons. If we deny that we are created by a God who made us in His image, then human life has no ultimate value. We're just animals without a purpose.

Most important of all, we should reject evolution in all its forms for biblical reasons. The Bible clearly states that we are created by God, which makes evolution contrary to what God's Word teaches. That should be reason enough for believers.

As Christians, our faith is built upon God being who He says He is. You were created by God's loving hand, which means you are of infinite value to Him. Let that truth give new meaning and purpose to everything you do today.

YOU ARE NOT THE PRODUCT OF RANDOM EVOLUTIONARY FORCES! EVERYTHING YOU ARE AND EVERYTHING YOU DO MATTERS TO GOD.

Day 253

For God, who said, "Let light shine out of darkness," has shone in our hearts to give the light of the knowledge of the glory of God in the face of Jesus Christ.

—2 Corinthians 4:6

Genesis 1 tells us that at the beginning of the creation, the earth was without form and void of any light. I believe that this statement is also a perfect description of a person who is without Christ.

The great king Solomon, the wisest and wealthiest person who ever lived, would agree that life without God is empty, futile, and constantly enveloped in darkness. Solomon explains in the book of Ecclesiastes how he tried to fill his life with money, pleasure, sex, and even work. But nothing brought fulfillment. And Solomon came to the conclusion that any pursuit without God is worthless—or in the words of Genesis 1, dark and formless.

Why? Because God created us with souls that are designed with a need for their Creator. Every person feels this need, but many people try to fill it with earthly pleasures that ultimately fail. The inescapable truth is that our lives are empty and dark without the loving light of Jesus Christ to shine in and take control.

But when Christ takes over a soul, that person becomes a new creation! That isn't figurative language; we really become different people.

Here's what I hope you will do today in light of this truth: Help shine the light of Christ into someone's life. There are people all around you who are living dark, formless lives without Christ. Do a friend or coworker a huge favor by sharing the exciting news that Christ can fill the void in their soul.

EVERY PERSON HAS A GOD-SHAPED HOLE IN THEIR HEART. DO SOMEONE A FAVOR TODAY AND TELL THEM HOW CHRIST CAN FILL IT.

Day 254

Your eyes saw my unformed substance; in your book were written, every one of them, the days that were formed for me, when as yet there were none of them.

—Psalm 139:16

The birth of a baby is a special and wonderful moment when a new life enters the world. Every baby is truly a tiny miracle, because the Bible says God creates each baby and knits it together in its mother's womb.

The human body is so complex and intricate that it's mind-boggling to realize how every part works together. We could spend the rest of this day discussing how teeth develop, how bones grow, and how the human body just knows what to do and when to do it.

The wonder of Psalm 139 is that God's creative work in our lives begins at the very moment of conception. Even in our embryonic stage, God is at work shaping us to be the person He wants us to be. And it's just as incredible to realize that after we are born, God continues to form our bodies.

When we stop to think about what an astounding work of creation the human body is, it's no wonder that God said it was good when He created us. Our bodies are far more complex than any computer or other manmade invention.

And by the way, our bodies are constantly growing and maturing, which tells us that God is still at work in us every day. That should give you a reason to praise Him today. Take a moment right now to thank God for loving you before you ever entered this world, and for loving you every day thereafter!

GOD HAD HIS HAND ON YOU BEFORE YOU WERE BORN—AND HE STILL HAS HIS HAND ON YOU TODAY!

Day 255

And God said to them, "Be fruitful and multiply and fill the earth and subdue it and have dominion over the fish of the sea and over the birds of the heavens and over every living thing that moves on the earth."

—Genesis 1:28

I believe the human mind is one of the most incredible parts of God's handiwork in creation. The animals have a certain level of mental capacity, but none can compare to human beings. The difference is clearly stated in the first chapter of Genesis.

God gave humans dominion and power over all the animals of the earth. There are some animals we call smart, but they can only be trained, they don't necessarily learn. Being taught an idea or a concept is unique to human beings because God gave us a unique mind that gives us self-consciousness and God-consciousness.

God gave us the ability to think and be creative. We can play beautiful music, write a great story, paint a picture, and build a magnificent skyscraper. God does give animals many internal instincts, such as a beaver's ability to build a dam, and a bird's ability to build a nest. But animals don't have the desire for growth and learning.

What's even more amazing to me about the human mind is that we are told we only use about 10% of our brain capacity. Think of the potential God has given us to think and act and respond to Him. What a challenge to us to maximize the mind God has given us.

Your hopes, joys, and desires are all things God has given you the ability to develop and pursue. Do you have a dream or a goal that you believe is from the Lord and will glorify Him? Go for it with all that you have!

MAXIMIZE YOUR POTENTIAL TO THINK, RESPOND, AND LIVE FOR GOD.

Day 256

For what does it profit a man to gain the whole world and forfeit his life?
For what can a man give in return for his life?

—Mark 8:36-37

By far the greatest marvel of human life is the marvel of our eternal soul. Man was made as an eternal and spiritual being, which is what it means to be made in God's image.

The Bible also calls this resemblance we have to God being made in His likeness. This doesn't necessarily refer to our physical appearance, but to the fact that we have an immaterial part called the soul or spirit that allows us to understand and respond to God.

This incredible spiritual capacity to know God is one of the main distinctions between humans and animals. We may have a similar physical structure to some animals, and eat the same foods that some animals eat, but we are made distinctively different.

That means we are not descended from any animal. You and I were created by the hand of God! It's true that we will die physically someday just as animals do. But even in death the profound differences between humans and the rest of creation continue, because we were made for eternal existence…for life with God forever.

Our spirits never die, but will exist forever in either heaven or hell. God made us to be able to spend eternity with Him. Share that good news with someone you know today.

GOD HAS GIVEN US LIFE SO THAT WE MIGHT SPEND IT WITH HIM FOR ETERNITY.

Day 257

And God said, "Behold, I have given you every plant yielding seed that is on the face of all the earth, and every tree with seed in its fruit. You shall have them for food."

—Genesis 1:29

Even though some people try to deny and ignore it, deep within every person is a craving to seek and to know God. We were given a God-consciousness at our creation; God implanted some of Himself in each and every one of us. That's why humans are the only creation of God that seeks Him and has an inner need for Him.

For example, one way we are like God is that we are called to reflect His dominion over the earth. God has all power over creation. He can tell lightning when and where to strike and command the seas to do His will. We have a small part of this power that God gave us to subdue and rule the earth.

Another way we are like God is that we have the capacity to make choices. Unfortunately, because we're all sinful, we have made wrong choices, but sin has not canceled out our capacity to accept or reject God's commands.

Giving us the gift of choice was a risky and costly decision for God, because it cost Christ His life. But it was worthwhile for God because He wants us to choose Him, not be programmed by Him. He loved us, chose us, and saved us, and He wants us to love and choose Him.

The bottom line is you and I were made for God. He wants us to make the choice to accept His Son as our Savior so that we will be with Him forever. If you haven't done so already, I challenge you to do that today.

CHRIST PAID A HIGH PRICE FOR OUR FREE WILL. HAVE YOU MADE THE CHOICE TO ACCEPT HIS LOVE AND SACRIFICE BY PLACING YOUR FAITH IN HIM?

Day 258

Therefore, if anyone is in Christ, he is a new creation. The old has passed away; behold, the new has come.

—2 Corinthians 5:17

Everyone has a worldview, whether they are aware of it or not. Your worldview is your basic belief system, the way you look at the world through the lens of your own mind and life. Your worldview is important because it determines both your attitude toward life and your actions in life.

It is that driving force behind everything we do—that thing inside of us that motivates us to follow a certain path in life and make the decisions we make, good or bad.

We can boil every worldview down into one of two basic categories: either Christ-centered or man-centered. If you are a Christian, then your view of life should be Christ-centered. This simply means that Christ is your sufficient and sovereign Lord in every area of life. This view places Christ at the center of every idea and decision.

But unfortunately, many people place themselves at the center of life. The man-centered view says that humans are basically good, capable of making it fine on their own, and therefore have no need for God.

What's the driving force behind your life? How does your worldview impact the decisions you make and the actions you take every day? Those questions are worth thinking about. If you live with Christ at the center of your life, you will experience joy, peace, and fulfillment beyond your greatest imagination.

Make sure your worldview is centered on Christ.

OUR LIVES ARE EITHER CHRIST-CENTERED OR MAN-CENTERED. WHO IS THE CENTER OF YOUR WORLD?

Day 259

For he knows our frame; he remembers that we are dust.

—Psalm 103:14

The almighty God of this universe made us with His own hands. What an incredible thought! The Bible says that God stretched out the universe and flung the stars into the sky with just a word. But when it came to the creation of mankind, God seemingly knelt down and lovingly created us from the dust of the ground—just like a potter, creating something beautiful out of a lump of unformed clay.

This means that God purposely and creatively constructed us! He made us wonderfully and beautifully, even though the main ingredient He used was dirt!

I think it's interesting that Genesis 1-2 speaks of man's creation in such lofty terms as the image and likeness of God, yet also records that we are made of perhaps the most common element of earth, the dust of the ground. That's why we should be careful to remain humble. We are not only made from the dust of the earth, but Scripture says that our bodies will also return to dust one day.

Does that mean our bodies don't matter to God? Not at all! Our bodies are the temple of God here on earth. Everything we do with our bodies is a matter of great importance to Him. In fact, the Bible teaches that we are the workmanship of Christ and therefore our bodies are not our own, to do anything we want to with them.

My friend, you are the magnificent creation of God—spirit and body. So live your life and treat your body in a way that honors God and reminds you that you belong to Him!

YOUR BODY IS GOD'S PERSONAL CREATION. BE CAREFUL HOW YOU TREAT IT.

Day 260

The LORD God took the man and put him in the garden of Eden to work it and keep it.

—Genesis 2:15

The desire to work is built into everyone. Now I know what you're thinking: If that's true, then why are there so many lazy people out there? I certainly can't account for every case of laziness, but I believe our need, desire, and capacity for work are God-given.

The creation account in Genesis says that God placed Adam in a perfect place called the Garden of Eden. Eden was a real, physical place, not just an imaginary garden. Other than being in the Mesopotamia region, we don't really know where it was. But it was real, and Adam lived there and cared for it.

Work is not, as some would like to believe, a part of the curse that came about from mankind's sin. God means for us to find purpose and satisfaction in work, and He gives us the desire to succeed and be productive in that work.

That's why the Bible says in Colossians 3:23 that whatever our job may be, we are to work hard at it and do it for the glory of God, as if we were working for Him and not just for the boss.

When we fulfill our purpose in life, then we are in a sense giving it back as a gift to God. That's why whether you are the CEO of a large company or a part-time clerk, God wants you to give it your all and glorify Him with your effort.

How might your day be different if you were to work with the awareness that you are working for the Lord? Are you honoring Him by giving everything you have to your work? It's amazing to think that we can bring God glory every day right where He has placed us.

WORK TODAY LIKE YOUR JOB MATTERS TO GOD—BECAUSE IN TRUTH, IT DOES!

Day 261

Of the tree of the knowledge of good and evil you shall not eat.

—Genesis 2:17

Today's verse gives us the first prohibition of the Bible. This is the first time that God says "you shall not" with regard to any part of His creation. Lots of people wonder what was wrong with the tree of the knowledge of good and evil. But there was probably nothing wrong with it, other than God told Adam not to eat from it.

You see, the problem didn't lie with the fruit hanging from that tree. The problem was with the two humans down on the ground. Adam and Eve were given their first choice to make. They could either follow God or disobey Him.

It might seem as if it would have been easier if God had simply not given them the choice. But that's not what He wants. God gives us His rules for life, along with the freedom to make choices, with the goal that we will honor Him in what we choose.

To the outside world, rules may seem to make us enslaved. But having the ability to make choices for God and His will actually frees us to be holy people.

The concept of freedom is terribly skewed in the world today. Most people see freedom as a life of no rules or regulations. But that's chaos, not freedom. Human freedom is a gift from God, not permission to rid ourselves of God! True freedom is the freedom to do what is right, not whatever we want.

Thank God that He didn't make us into robots, programmed to tell Him what He wants to hear. He wants a loving relationship with us; He wants us to choose Him. When we do, we will experience true freedom and joy. I hope and pray that you are living in the freedom of Christ today.

REAL FREEDOM IS FOUND IN MAKING THE CHOICE TO FOLLOW AND OBEY CHRIST.

Day 262

For the LORD God is a sun and shield; the LORD bestows favor and honor. No good thing does he withhold from those who walk uprightly.

—Psalm 84:11

I remember how much it used to bug me as a child when my parents gave me rules to follow, and held me to them. I thought those rules were unfair, and were only meant to keep me from doing fun things. But as I grew older, I came to realize that my dad and mom laid down those rules for my own good.

That's exactly how it is with our heavenly Father. He sets up boundaries to keep us from hurting ourselves. But more than just that, He also gives us rules so that we can have the freedom to run within those safe boundaries.

Would you let your child run across a busy street? I know you wouldn't. And I'm also sure that your child doesn't always understand what's wrong with that. When a parent gives this rule to a child, are they trying to control and frustrate the child? Of course not; they are trying to do what's best to protect their child.

We need to remember that when we disobey God and "run into the street," we are not only rejecting His authority, we are putting ourselves in harm's way. God's commandments and instructions are not there to constrain us, but to free us from the worry of harm or danger.

Make up your mind today to follow God's instructions in His Word, knowing that they aren't there to trap you, but to set you free!

WHEN WE DISOBEY GOD, WE NOT ONLY REJECT HIS AUTHORITY—WE PUT OURSELVES IN HARM'S WAY.

Day 263

Then the LORD God said, "It is not good that the man should be alone; I will make him a helper fit for him."

—Genesis 2:18

I firmly believe that the Bible is absolutely the best source for a happy marriage. Married couples can learn so much from the strength and the wisdom of the Word. It's really our only hope to keep marriage as a vital and strong institution.

We need God's perspective because marriage today seems to be more troubled than triumphant in most cases.

First, it seems many people bring unresolved baggage from a previous marriage or relationship into the new one, creating a difficult atmosphere. Other marriages fail simply because one or both spouses don't know the difference between love and infatuation, or lust.

In other cases, marriage partners lack common relational and social skills, which dooms good communication. Financial burdens can also weigh down an otherwise healthy marriage very quickly with devastating results.

But above all of these problems, I see the greatest reason for marriage failure in our culture to be the lack of good and accurate models. Very few marriages are good examples of what God intended when He created marriage in the book of Genesis.

God's desire for marriage is far greater than we could ever imagine. So if you are married, take time today to talk and pray with your spouse. And spend time in His Word so you can build your marriage on His principles for a strong and vibrant marriage.

After all, it's His creation!

GOD'S DESIRE FOR MARRIAGE IS FAR GREATER THAN WE COULD EVER IMAGINE—SO LET'S FOLLOW HIS EXAMPLE.

Day 264

Then the man said, "This at last is bone of my bones and flesh of my flesh; she shall be called Woman, because she was taken out of Man."

—Genesis 2:23

Marriage is not some humanly devised idea that someone came up with one day. God Himself ordained man and woman to join together in complete union of body and spirit. The Bible teaches that man and woman were made for one another right from the start!

God's ideal for marriage is one man and one woman together for a lifetime. Anything else is a perversion and an alteration to His original plan. But despite the clarity of Scripture on this issue, the world continually tries to change and amend the concept of marriage to accommodate it to the latest cultural trends and ideas.

We human beings have a strong need for companionship. God put that desire and need in us, and He created marriage for the fulfillment of that desire. Man and woman were designed to share their lives together.

Marriage at its best is a companionship on many levels. It is a spiritual companionship in which the partners grow and support one another. Marriage is also a psychological union in which each partner knows and loves the other. And marriage is also a physical companionship, for the pleasure and enjoyment of one another.

Isn't it interesting that in Genesis God pronounced each day of His creation as "good"? The only part that was "not good" was the aloneness of the man. Marriage is God's idea and God's plan to fill that emptiness. Don't let anyone else tell you what marriage should be. Go back to the Word of God for your marriage instructions.

MARRIAGE IS DIVINE IN ORIGIN, SUPREME IN HUMAN RELATIONSHIPS, AND PERMANENT IN COMMITMENT.

Day 265

Therefore a man shall leave his father and his mother and hold fast to his wife, and they shall become one flesh.

—Genesis 2:24

Eve is described as a "helper" in the book of Genesis. Now, to many this word may seem like a derogatory term, but the complete opposite is true. This is a very positive term; it means an ally, a friend, and a rescuer.

I know it won't surprise you, but men aren't quite perfect by themselves! God knew this, and so He created women to meet the needs of men, which are abundant at times. A man needs a woman to help him maximize his strengths and minimize his weaknesses.

We are told that unmarried men don't live as long as married men. This is one of the facts that show how much men need the love and companionship of a woman to share life with.

The woman is designed to be a completer and a complement to the man. When God brings a man and a woman together in marriage, He is giving that man someone who can meet very specific needs in his life.

Of course, the caring and helping in marriage flows both ways, because in Ephesians 5, a man is commanded to love his wife the way Christ loves the Church. God knows what it takes to fulfill both partners in a marriage.

Man and woman were perfectly made and designed to share life together. Thank God today for the infinite wisdom of His plan.

MAN AND WOMAN ARE DESIGNED TO COMPLEMENT AND COMPLETE ONE ANOTHER. HOW WELL ARE YOU FULFILLING HIS DESIGN?

Day 266

However, let each one of you love his wife as himself, and let the wife see that she respects her husband.

—Ephesians 5:33

Perhaps the best way for Christian couples to have a strong testimony to the rest of the world is to have a strong, holy marriage. Marriage is meant to be a picture of what our relationship should be with Jesus Christ.

Christians are called the bride of Christ, and He is the head, or the groom, of this relationship. That's why the Bible tells husbands to love their wives with every fiber of their being—even with their lives if necessary. That's exactly how Christ loves us as His bride on earth!

We need to be reminded often that one major purpose of Christian marriage is to be a vibrant testimony to the outside world of the difference that Christ can make. Nothing shows the love of Jesus Christ to this world better than a committed Christian couple sacrificing for each other and lifting each other up.

Unfortunately, that's also why a Christian marriage that fails is a disaster on many levels. When Christian marriages fall prey to various problems and fall apart, the world wonders if Christ really makes any difference. This is on top of the damaged and destroyed lives that divorce causes among couples and families.

It's easy to get discouraged by the fact that Christian marriages are failing just as frequently as secular ones. But there is something positive you and I can do about that. We can make sure our own marriages are Christ-honoring, and we can pray for and encourage the married couples in our families, churches, and neighborhoods.

THERE IS NO BETTER TESTIMONY OF CHRIST'S LOVE THAN A HEALTHY MARRIAGE. TODAY, PRAY FOR A MARRIED COUPLE YOU KNOW, THAT THEY WILL FOLLOW THE LORD.

Day 267

And the rain fell, and the floods came, and the winds blew and beat on that house, but it did not fall, because it had been founded on the rock.

—Matthew 7:25

When you build your marriage upon the Rock of Christ, the winds and the rains of life will not shake you from your foundation. Make no mistake, whether you are married or single, you will be tested in this world. But if your life is anchored on the Rock, you will weather life's storms.

But what many couples don't understand is that a rock-solid marriage is built through a love that grows over time. It is like a beautiful flower that must be nurtured and grown. And love can only grow when fed with time, care, and commitment. That's why Christ meant marriage to be a lifetime commitment, because He knew that it takes a lifetime to get it just right.

When you spend a lot of time with someone, your reactions and communication become more natural and more meaningful. Friendship and love between two people require cultivation, and sooner or later your lives will be joined together as one.

The good news is that when we follow the instructions for marriage given to us by God in His Word, we can build a love relationship that continues to grow and will last as long as the marriage. If we keep our vows and understand the incredible gift that the Lord has given us in our marriage partner, we can live a great marriage testimony for Him.

So take time each day to nurture the love God has given you for your spouse. As you do, you will build a rock-solid marriage that will stand the test of time.

A LOVE THAT WILL STAND THE STORMS OF LIFE MUST BE FED WITH TIME, CARE, AND COMMITMENT.

Day 268

Therefore its name was called Babel, because there the Lord confused the language of all the earth. And from there the Lord dispersed them over the face of all the earth.

—Genesis 11:9

What a scene it must have been when the survivors of Noah's flood began to build the Tower of Babel. They were determined to build a monument to their pride and as their way of trying to approach God on their own terms.

It's hard to imagine the arrogance of that act, or the confusion that must have reigned in Babel as mighty and intelligent men began speaking different languages for the first time.

The Tower of Babel is a real historical event, but it is also an illustration of society even today. Men and women in our day are just like the proud people of Babel...believing they know everything there is to know and therefore can approach God on their own terms.

The Lord states many times in the Scripture that He detests arrogance and pride. "Haughty eyes" (Proverbs 6:17), or a proud look, is first on the list of things that God hates. People today are building towers to try and reach heaven; not physical structures, but towers of pride and self-sufficiency.

God honors a humble heart. So don't let the world fool you into thinking you need to be self-sufficient. Rather, reach up to God with with an open hand and heart to receive His grace each day.

GOD HATES PRIDE...BUT HONORS HUMILITY!

Day 269

Cush fathered Nimrod; he was the first on earth to be a mighty man. He was a mighty hunter before the LORD. Therefore it is said, "Like Nimrod a mighty hunter before the LORD."

—Genesis 10:8-9

In our previous devotional, we looked at the place known as Babel...a place that was ruled by an evil and powerful king named Nimrod. He was, in effect, the first great world ruler.

The very name Nimrod means "the rebellious one," and this guy certainly didn't disappoint. He was strong and powerful physically as well as politically. The translation of the text seems to imply that Nimrod thought he was mighty in God's sight—that even God was impressed with him!

King Nimrod is a perfect illustration of another person Jesus warns us about...the Antichrist. Nimrod was strong and arrogant, and he ruled over the world, then known as Babylon. The Antichrist will also rise up in the last world system, and lead arrogantly against Christ, including hunting down God's people.

More and more we see the spirit of Antichrist—those who oppose Christ and anything Christian—at work in our world today. But just as God has always protected His people, so will He protect you and me even in these unstable and somewhat scary times in which we live.

Our calling is to stand firm and continue being lights to a world that is slipping deeper into darkness. My prayer for you is that you won't give into the fear that so easily pervades our world today, but instead, be a strong and mighty witness of the power of God to change a life!

STAND FIRM IN GOD'S PROTECTION SO THAT YOU CAN BE A LIGHT IN OUR DARK WORLD.

Day 270

Jesus said to him, "I am the way, and the truth, and the life. No one comes to the Father except through me."

—John 14:6

It seems like more and more you hear people talking about how all the religions of the world are really leading to the same God. They want everyone to just get along, put aside our differences, and make this world a giant, hug-filled place of peace.

This kind of thinking has been especially prevalent since 9/11, when it became clear that religion can be not only divisive, but deadly.

If we're not careful, we as Christians can fall into this peaceful-sounding trap. While you and I as believers are certainly to be characterized by peace and love, we are not to give up or give in on our convictions...and give credibility to another false religion.

The truth of Christ divides people. Christ certainly preached a message of love and forgiveness, but He made it clear that not all gods are equal, and there is only one path to God. He is the ONLY way!

People of this world don't like the Gospel of Christ; they see it as narrow-minded and divisive. The world praises the idea of one religion that unifies everyone—which in fact is coming. But the problem is that it will be the religion of evil in the end times.

Don't surrender the truth of the Gospel for the sake of peace. We know that Christ is the only answer to the world's need, so be ready with that answer for people who are desperately searching for something real to believe in.

NEVER COMPROMISE ON THE GOSPEL BECAUSE CHRIST IS THE ONLY WAY TO GOD—AND NOTHING ELSE IS!

Day 271

Then they said, "Come, let us build ourselves a city and a tower with its top in the heavens, and let us make a name for ourselves, lest we be dispersed over the face of the whole earth."

—Genesis 11:4

The society that built the Tower of Babel was rebellious and defiant. Even the king, Nimrod, stood and defied God publicly.

I think it's safe to say that we see a similar situation in our own times.

For example, today there are more pornography outlets than McDonald's restaurants in America...the U.S.A. aborts 4,000 babies a day...and a teenager commits suicide in this country every 78 seconds. In addition, there's been a 400% increase in the number of child abuse cases, and almost two out of every three kids has used illegal drugs by the time they have finished high school.

My friend, we have just about finished building our own Tower of Babel in this country! America is trying to build its society without God, and that breeds evil, trouble, and rebellion. Babel became ancient Babylon, the symbol of a godless society that the Lord will judge and destroy.

If we're not careful, this same spirit of evil could overtake America as well. But as Christians, we can help turn back the tide of evil that is sweeping across America. I challenge you today to be awake and alert, faithful in prayer and in your witness for Christ, so that the evil invading America does not overtake it without a fight of faith!

DETERMINE TODAY...AND EVERY DAY...TO FIGHT THE FIGHT OF FAITH.

Day 272

"Enter by the narrow gate. For the gate is wide and the way is easy that leads to destruction, and those who enter by it are many."

—Matthew 7:13

When it comes to a person's eternal destiny, they have two choices in life: They can live by the tolerance of society or by the truth of Jesus Christ.

I believe that it's more important than ever that we make the choice clear because there are countless thousands of people who believe there are many ways to the same heaven.

But Jesus was not just some broadminded guru who gave people options to get to heaven. He stated that there are only two roads for us to choose. We can either choose the broad, popular path to destruction, or the narrow road to everlasting life.

The Tower of Babel in Genesis 11 is a perfect example of the broad road that leads to destruction. It was built in order to give mankind a new and better way to get to God.

And just like the people who were building the Tower of Babel, many people think that salvation is like a modern-day expressway you can get on or off whenever you want, and pick the lane you want. But Jesus said that the road to heaven is the narrow road of faith in Him, not a five-lane expressway.

The deception that was alive and well in ancient Babel is still alive and well in America today. But the road to heaven is still the narrow way, so let's be sure we are helping the people around us find it.

THE ROAD IS NARROW THAT LEADS TO HEAVEN, AND WE NEED TO HELP OTHERS FIND IT!

Day 273

There is a way that seems right to a man, but its end is the way to death.

—Proverbs 14:12

Proverbs 14:12 is such a humbling verse for me because as humans, we often think we have such great knowledge and wisdom. But God says that human wisdom leads to death.

That's what makes living the Christian life so difficult sometimes. There are so many choices out there that look good and seem to make sense, but they do not lead us to the narrow way that is the only road to eternal glory in heaven.

To the human way of thinking, it seems common sense that if you try hard to be good and don't kill anyone or commit any other horrifying crime, then you're one of the better candidates for citizenship in heaven. This may seem right to many people, but this kind of thinking leads to destruction, because the only way to heaven is to abandon our efforts at good works and trust Christ alone for salvation.

We don't get voted into heaven, nor will we make it because we come out looking pretty good in comparison to others. Only the blood of Christ shed on the cross to forgive sin can qualify us for heaven.

Take time today to thank God for His great gift of salvation through the blood of Jesus Christ...and make sure you aren't traveling the road that the world thinks is right.

TAKE TIME TODAY TO CHECK THE "ROAD" YOU'RE TRAVELING—AND MAKE SURE YOU ARE HEADING TOWARD CHRIST.

Day 274

But if [salvation] is by grace, it is no longer on the basis of works; otherwise grace would no longer be grace.

—Romans 11:6

I have always wondered about people who believe they can enter the kingdom of heaven by doing good works and being nice. I want to ask them, "How do you know when you've done enough or been good enough?"

The problem with human goodness is that it is not good enough to earn us a place in heaven. The Bible clearly states that none of us deserves heaven, because even the greatest person on earth is sinful in God's sight. The Bible is clear...all have sinned and come short of the glory of God (Romans 3:23).

You can achieve great things down here on earth...you can do good...and you can even be a truly nice person...but that just doesn't translate into eternal life.

As you share Christ with others, let them know that there's nothing wrong with achieving great things in life. But if they ever want to enter heaven, there is only one way, and that is to place their faith in Jesus Christ.

If they are playing the "good enough" game with God, they need to know that it will never work, because nobody is good enough to stand before a holy God. But the good news is that God has made a way through His Son!

Take time today to make that good news known...and praise God for His great gift to you of His Son!

THERE'S NOTHING WRONG WITH ACHIEVEMENT, BUT IT WILL NEVER GET ANYONE INTO HEAVEN.

Day 275

He is great in power; justice and abundant righteousness he will not violate. Therefore men fear him; he does not regard any who are wise in their own conceit.

—Job 37:23-24

When I'm in a large city, I often find myself staring at and admiring great skyscrapers. They are so huge and powerful, looming over me as I stand beneath them on the sidewalk.

But when I fly in a plane over a large city full of skyscrapers, I get an entirely different view. Although these buildings tower over us and make us feel small when we are standing next to them, they look like tiny grains of sand when we see them from 30,000 feet.

God views all human efforts to impress Him as tiny grains of sand…even though we may think that we are pretty great. A good example is the Tower of Babel in Genesis 11. It may have impressed its builders in their vain attempt to reach up to God, but it was just a tiny speck to Him.

Our wisdom is considered pretty foolish to God. God is never impressed with even our best efforts to please Him in our own strength.

Instead, God wants us to put our faith in Him, not ourselves or our own works. We need to take a "God's eye" view when it comes to our efforts to reach up to Him, because anything we do on our own falls short of His standards.

If you are living your life trying to impress God, stop. Make it your purpose instead to submit to His great power, justice, and righteousness.

GOD IS NEVER IMPRESSED WITH EVEN OUR BEST EFFORTS TO PLEASE HIM IN OUR OWN STRENGTH.

Day 276

By faith Abraham obeyed when he was called to go out to a place that he was to receive as an inheritance. And he went out, not knowing where he was going.

—Hebrews 11:8

A braham stands apart from everyone else in human history. His faith stands as an incredible example to us even today.

Think about how deeply he trusted God. When God revealed Himself to Abraham, Abraham was living a life of ease and comfort in Ur, an ancient center of commerce and idolatrous religion. But when the true God called him, Abraham left that life to go to a land that he didn't even know!

Abraham is such a great example of true faith…putting actions behind our words. Demonstrating true faith is one of the most difficult things a person can do, but Abraham did it.

And even though Abraham stands alone in the pages of history, we are like him in that we too are called to step out from the world in a dark and faithless time.

While God doesn't speak to us as He spoke to Abraham, He is still calling us to follow Him and demonstrate the reality of true faith to the world.

Because Abraham was faithful, and openly demonstrated his faith in God, thousands of lives have been influenced over the centuries to follow his example. I challenge you today to let your faith shine brightly, so that others may see it and be encouraged to trust God.

LIKE ABRAHAM, WE ARE CALLED TO DEMONSTRATE OUR FAITH TO THE WORLD SO THAT OTHERS WILL BE ENCOURAGED TO TRUST GOD.

Day 277

Blessed is the man who walks not in the counsel of the wicked, nor stands in the way of sinners, nor sits in the seat of scoffers; but his delight is in the law of the LORD, and on his law he meditates day and night. He is like a tree planted by streams of water that yields its fruit in its season, and its leaf does not wither. In all that he does, he prospers. The wicked are not so, but are like chaff that the wind drives away.

—Psalm 1:1-4

We all have one basic choice that we must make every day: To live for Christ or to live for ourselves. And the result of that choice will be either good fruit or useless chaff.

That word *chaff* may not mean a lot in our 21st century world, but it was a powerful picture in an agricultural society. Chaff was the husks that needed to be separated from the grain of wheat if the wheat was to be used. So the farmer would throw the grain into the air and the lighter, useless chaff would be blown away by the wind.

That's the picture of a life lived for self. A life that is blown around by the winds of life. Unstable and unsure.

But Psalm 1:1-3 gives us the other side of the story. It says that a person who walks with the Lord, who does not seek the counsel of or confide in sinners, but who trusts in God, will stand strong like a tree with deep roots that cannot be blown about.

On our own...living for ourselves...we are weak and get tossed about by all the winds of life. But living for God, in His strength, we can stand strong and tall against the strongest gales of life.

So the choice you have is clear. You can either stand in faith or fall in failure. Which will you choose today?

IF YOU LIVE FOR CHRIST, YOU WON'T BE BLOWN AROUND BY THE WINDS OF THE WORLD.

Day 278

[God] has said, "I will never leave you nor forsake you."

—Hebrews 13:5

It's great to have really close friends you can trust with just about anything, isn't it? I'm blessed enough to have quite a few, and I know these true friends love me unconditionally.

But the most amazing "friend" you and I have is God Himself. In John 15:15, Jesus makes an incredible statement when He says, "No longer do I call you servants, for the servant does not know what his master is doing; but I have called you friends, for all that I have heard from my Father I have made known to you."

Now, one of the best definitions of the word friend I've ever heard is, "a person who comes in when the world goes out." And that's a pretty good summary of today's verse.

God is the truest of all friends...One who is always there and, no matter the circumstance, will NEVER forsake you. He will support you and love you absolutely unconditionally. He is the Friend "who sticks closer than a brother" (Proverbs 18:24).

Jesus Christ is indeed your greatest and dearest Friend. And like any friend, I trust you speak with Him daily and love Him completely.

JESUS CHRIST IS THE TRUEST OF ALL FRIENDS!

Day 279

"The God of glory appeared to our father Abraham when he was in Mesopotamia."

—Acts 7:2

This world is such a self-centered place, especially here in America where so many people's universe begins and ends with themselves. Most people have such short-sighted vision that they can't see past their own concerns.

But as Christians, you and I are called to see something far greater, something that is invisible except to the eyes of faith. Christ wants us to "see"…to set our hearts, minds, and eyes on…Him and His kingdom. Just like Abraham did.

Hebrews 11:8-10 tells us, "By faith Abraham obeyed when he was called to go out to a place that he was to receive as an inheritance. And he went out, not knowing where he was going. By faith he went to live in the land of promise, as in a foreign land, living in tents with Isaac and Jacob, heirs with him of the same promise. For he was looking forward to the city that has foundations, whose designer and builder is God."

Abraham got up and left Mesopotamia because he "saw" a city that God had promised, and he acted on what he saw through the eyes of faith.

As a completely sold-out Christian, you should see a different reality. A reality that can only be seen through the eyes of faith as you trust God at His Word.

Ask yourself today, "Am I sold out to Christ? Do I have a vision that allows me to see what God sees?" If you're having trouble seeing the invisible today, ask the Lord to help you get your spiritual sight in focus.

AS CHRISTIANS, WE ARE CALLED TO SEE AND LIVE BY SPIRITUAL REALITIES THAT ARE INVISIBLE TO OUR WORLD.

Day 280

But as he who called you is holy, you also be holy in all your conduct, since it is written, "You shall be holy, for I am holy." And if you call on him as Father who judges impartially according to each one's deeds, conduct yourselves with fear throughout the time of your exile, knowing that you were ransomed from the futile ways inherited from your forefathers, not with perishable things such as silver or gold, but with the precious blood of Christ, like that of a lamb without blemish or spot.

—1 Peter 1:15-19

I want to focus your attention on the phrase "throughout the time of your exile" in today's passage. It's an important insight that can directly impact how you live your life here on earth as a follower of Christ.

The Bible calls us strangers or "aliens" in this world because our affections and ambitions are to be focused on things beyond this life. Like Abraham, who lived in tents and kept on moving through the Promised Land, we are merely travelers through this life.

As believers today, we need to live in spiritual "tents," not getting too attached to the stuff of this world. This world is not our home. We're only here temporarily!

We are in exile from heaven, which is our true home. And since our true citizenship is in heaven and not on earth, we must detach ourselves from the things of this world, and attach ourselves to eternal things.

If you live like an alien and stranger who is in exile here on earth, other people may wonder about you a little bit. But that's fine. Just be ready to fold your spiritual "tent," because you're moving onward and upward one day!

LIVE YOUR LIFE AS A CITIZEN OF HEAVEN WHO IS TEMPORARILY EXILED HERE ON EARTH.

Day 281

"All things are lawful for me," but not all things are helpful. "All things are lawful for me," but I will not be enslaved by anything.

—1 Corinthians 6:12

I've noticed something every time we have moved to a new home. We wind up getting rid of things we didn't need and were just cluttering up the house.

Some people are keepers and some are throwers—and they usually marry one another! The keepers hang on to things because of the comfort of the known and the emotional attachment to these items. The throwers toss stuff away because they know it isn't needed and will slow them down.

I want to propose to you today that we all need to be spiritual throwers. When God wants us to move on to another place in our spiritual lives, we should throw out all of the clutter we have accumulated—old ideas, attitudes, and habits from the past that just weigh us down. Let's get rid of anything that isn't necessary to keep living and moving forward for Christ. To not be enslaved to anything.

When a tall building is built, there's usually scaffolding that goes all the way to the top. But when the building is finished, the scaffolding isn't needed. It would be silly and unnecessary to keep scaffolding up around a finished building, but that's what a lot of believers are doing in their spiritual lives.

Don't be attached to or dependent upon unnecessary things. When God wants you to move on, drop everything that holds you back and go forward in faith and obedience!

BE A SPIRITUAL "THROWER," RIDDING YOUR LIFE OF ANYTHING THAT KEEPS YOU FROM MOVING FORWARD WITH CHRIST.

Day 282

Count it all joy, my brothers, when you meet trials of various kinds, for you know that the testing of your faith produces steadfastness.

—James 1:2-3

I'm not sure about you, but most people probably wouldn't welcome an intruder as a good friend. But as crazy and backwards as that sounds, it's exactly what James asks us to do when it comes to welcoming the problems and trials that come into our lives.

Today's verses tell us that problems and troubles are going to come. James said "when" we encounter trials, not "if." Everybody has problems.

What makes Christians different is the way we handle these challenges. We can joyfully accept hardships and trials because we know that God is going to use them to deepen our faith and strengthen our endurance.

I've always said that a faith that can't be tested is a faith that can't be trusted when the chips are down. The Christian life is a series of new beginnings, and more often than not those new beginnings begin with a trial or crisis of some sort. Those times are an opportunity to demonstrate our faith in God.

So don't be surprised "when you meet trials of various kinds." Remember, God has promised you His presence in the midst of your trials.

YOU CAN'T AVOID PROBLEMS, BUT YOU CAN OVERCOME THEM IN THE POWER OF CHRIST.

Day 283

And I am sure of this, that he who began a good work in you will bring it to completion at the day of Jesus Christ.

—Philippians 1:6

Sometimes problems are like a big truck you're following on the highway. It's so big that you can't see around it...and you're not sure you can get around it because you don't know what's ahead of you.

A problem can sometimes seem so big and overwhelming that you simply don't know if you're ever going to get around it.

The good news is that even though you can't always see on the other side of a problem, there's something good there—the anticipation that comes from knowing that when you wrestle through a problem, God is there on the other side with the promise of a brighter and hopeful future.

As a follower of Christ, you have the promise of God that He will finish what He started in you and not leave you stranded in the middle of a problem. And let me remind you that God permits trials in your life to strengthen your faith...and that should give you the anticipation of knowing that He is doing something wonderful through you and for you, even when the testing is hard.

So if you're going through a hard trial today, don't let go of the hopeful anticipation of what Christ is doing in your life.

REGARDLESS OF THE TRIAL, YOU CAN LIVE IN HOPEFUL ANTICIPATION BECAUSE OF GOD'S PROMISE TO FINISH WHAT HE STARTED IN YOUR LIFE.

Day 284

I am not ashamed, for I know whom I have believed, and I am convinced that he is able to guard until that Day what has been entrusted to me.

—2 Timothy 1:12

A Christian always lives for two days, this day and "that" day. Obviously, believers are to live for this day…the current day…the time God has given us here on earth to worship and serve Him.

But we are also headed for an even bigger day: "that" day! Paul was using this term to refer to the time when Jesus Christ will come for us and we finally get to see Him face to face in all of His glory! What a glorious day that will be, the day when Christ returns for us and we get to be with Him for all eternity.

So even though as Christians we live for this day, everything we do should be in preparation for that day when we will be with Christ. Our calling as believers is to obey God and live fully for Christ until the glorious day of His return.

Are you preparing for Christ's return? If not, you can start today by living this day in light of that day.

LIVE THIS DAY IN PREPARATION FOR THAT DAY—THE DAY OF CHRIST'S RETURN WHEN WE WILL SEE HIM IN ALL OF HIS GLORY.

Day 285

If anyone's will is to do God's will, he will know whether the teaching is from God or whether I am speaking on my own authority.

—John 7:17

We live in a multiple choice society. There are so many options when it comes to making everyday decisions that the average person can become overwhelmed.

Of course, some decisions such as which color shirt to wear or what to put on your hamburger aren't really that important in the larger scheme of things. But there are other choices we are called upon to make that can be life-shaping and life-changing: the choice to be true to our mates, or the decision to be honest in business, for example.

Making the right choices is vital to our Christian walk. Some people, such as Adam and Eve, made poor choices. And in their case, the human race will always be paying for their poor choice. Still others, such as Moses and Daniel, made good choices that proved them to be people of great faith.

Making the right choice is important because our lives are shaped by decisions. We first make our decisions, but then our decisions turn around and make us. We are free to choose our actions, but not free to choose the consequences of those actions.

The person you are right now is the sum of all of the decisions that you've made in the past. And Jesus said if you want to know and do God's will, He will reveal the truth to you. So if you are facing a tough decision today, go to God's Word and ask Him to give you the guidance you need…and He will!

WE FIRST MAKE OUR DECISIONS, BUT THEN OUR DECISIONS TURN AROUND AND MAKE US.

Day 286

So Lot chose for himself all the Jordan Valley, and Lot journeyed east. Thus they separated from each other. Abram settled in the land of Canaan, while Lot settled among the cities of the valley and moved his tent as far as Sodom.

—Genesis 13:11-12

There is a huge difference between firsthand and secondhand faith. You don't have to read far between the lines of today's text to see that difference illustrated in the lives of Abraham and his nephew, Lot.

Secondhand faith is a faith that is lived on the coattails of someone else's faith. And it's dangerous because it's not really faith at all.

That was the problem between Abraham and Lot. Lot had inherited many blessings by being in Abraham's family, and there is no doubt that Abraham was an incredible spiritual example and mentor to Lot. But all of that didn't add up to a godly lifestyle for Lot, a fact that we see in Genesis 13. Lot greedily chose the best land for himself when given the chance, and happily moved right on in to Sodom.

Hanging out with Abraham had made Lot successful and wealthy, but it didn't make him wise and godly. Although the Bible says Lot was a fair man, he ended up making a very bad decision that eventually cost him dearly. Lot's secondhand faith caused him firsthand trouble!

Which "hand" describes your faith?

NEVER LET YOUR FAITH BECOME A "SECONDHAND" FAITH.

Day 287

By faith Moses, when he was grown up, refused to be called the son of Pharaoh's daughter, choosing rather to be mistreated with the people of God than to enjoy the fleeting pleasures of sin.

—Hebrews 11:24-25

It breaks my heart when I see young people who were raised in the Church decide to search for something else. It's always sad when they think they have missed something by being in a home with conservative Christian convictions and values.

The truth is they find out they haven't missed anything—except a lot of heartache and trouble.

The Bible forthrightly acknowledges that there may be a "fleeting" pleasure to sin. Because sin does seem to offer pleasure, it takes strong convictions and rock-solid values to live for Christ.

Moses had those convictions, so he chose to follow the Lord even though, as the son of Pharaoh, he could have had all the pleasures that the world had to offer.

But notice that Moses' decision to live for God involved a willingness to be mistreated. There's a lesson here for us: There is no shortcut or quick fix when it comes to living a Christ-like life.

Holding to your convictions is not always the easy choice, even though it is always the right choice.

When you try to hold on to the world and to Christ at the same time, you'll get the worst of both worlds and the best of none. Being true to Christ is a decision you have to make every day. My prayer is that it will be the decision you make!

LIVING FOR CHRIST IS NOT ALWAYS THE EASY CHOICE, BUT IT IS ALWAYS THE RIGHT CHOICE.

Day 288

Can a man carry fire next to his chest and his clothes not be burned?

—Proverbs 6:27

It amazes me that many Christians want to see how close they can get to sin and still be what they consider a "good Christian." But that is absolutely contrary to what the Bible teaches.

We are to hate sin in every form and run from it as fast as we can. If we don't…if we try and get close so that we can have some kind of secondhand enjoyment of the sin…there will be consequences.

The Bible says in Genesis 13 that Abraham's nephew Lot pitched his tent just outside the evil city of Sodom—and before too long, he owned a house right in the middle of town! Many times we camp closer than we ought to the gates of evil. From there, all it takes is time and a foothold or two, and Satan can work his awful magic as he did with Lot, whose family was torn apart when God destroyed Sodom.

Many times when a Christian is caught in some scandal we think, "How could this person have fallen so far so quickly?" Truth is, it probably wasn't very quick at all. Most spiritual implosions are caused by a slow, steady leak in the heart or in the mind. Eventually, cracks begin to appear on the surface and everything caves in.

We must not only avoid evil, but all appearances of evil. Don't camp out next to sin and hope to still be a "good Christian." It won't work. Take down your tent and get out of there as fast as you can!

DON'T CAMP OUT NEXT TO THE GATES OF EVIL, BECAUSE EVENTUALLY YOU'LL MOVE IN!

Day 289

She took of its fruit and ate, and she also gave some to her husband who was with her, and he ate.

—Genesis 3:6

Our world is certainly not a perfect world. You don't have to go very far or listen very long to be reminded of the evil and sin all around us.

The secular humanist has no real answer to the philosophical question of the existence of evil. Humanists believe falsely that humans are basically good in spite of all evidence to the contrary.

One chilling example is a study done by the late professor Allen Bloom, who asked his college students, "How do you identify an evil person?" His question was met with silence. Not one student could give him a determining factor of evil!

While our society can't recognize evil or wrongdoing, the Scripture gives us a clear answer to the problem of evil. It all goes back to Genesis 3 and our first parents, who yielded to temptation. Sin came into our world at that point, and it's something we've had to deal with since.

But, according to the Bible, we do have hope...and that hope is in Christ. Through Christ we are freed from the power of sin and evil. And because of Christ, we can live as people of purity in a twisted world.

My challenge to you today is to reflect that purity in how you live so that a world that is in the grips of evil will see the only hope...the hope of Jesus Christ.

LIVE IN SUCH A WAY THAT OUR WORLD WILL SEE THERE IS AN ANTIDOTE TO EVIL—JESUS CHRIST!

Day 290

Now the serpent was more crafty than any other beast of the field that the LORD God had made. He said to the woman, "Did God actually say, 'You shall not eat of any tree in the garden'?"

—Genesis 3:1

In order for us to understand what happened when sin entered the Garden of Eden, we must understand that there was someone else there besides Adam and Eve—Satan, the tempting serpent.

A lot of people wonder where Satan came from. He was part of the angelic hosts that God created before He created humans. Originally, Satan was named Lucifer (Isaiah 14:12, KJV), and he was a great and mighty angel. Unfortunately, he wanted the power and worship that belongs to God alone, and rebelled against God. God judged Satan's pride by expelling him from heaven and dooming him to hell, which Jesus said was made for the devil and his angels.

There are two common mistakes we make concerning the devil: we either overestimate or underestimate his power. Both of these extremes are dangerous, because the devil is subtle and cunning.

At the very moment you think you don't have to worry about him, he is smiling because that's where he wants you.

But you also need to remember that the devil isn't more powerful than God. You can resist his attempts to get you to fall.

My encouragement to you today is to stand firm, and don't give in to Satan's temptation. Resist the devil and flee from him, and God will give you the strength to resist him.

REMEMBER THAT SATAN IS NOT MORE POWERFUL THAN HE WHO IS IN YOU!

Day 291

Be sober-minded; be watchful. Your adversary the devil prowls around like a roaring lion, seeking someone to devour.

—1 Peter 5:8

Make no mistake, Satan is real and he's out to destroy you and your faith. In fact, Satan is the ultimate terrorist...the terrorist of your soul!

I find it fascinating that many people blame God when tragedies occur. They say, "Why would God allow this to happen to us," or "Where was God when this happened? Doesn't He care?" But these questions omit the fact that Satan and his evil work are real. And that he is still active today deceiving and destroying.

Evil is real, and Satan is the author of every bit of it. That's why he shows up when he sees an opportunity to trip you up. Have you ever noticed that many temptations seem to just come out of nowhere? Everything is going well, and suddenly you're faced with an incredibly tough temptation to sin.

That's because Satan is an opportunist. He knows your strengths and weaknesses, and knows exactly where to hit you...and the kind of evil suggestions that will tempt you most.

So be careful not to blame God for your struggles, because they come from our adversary, the devil. Instead of blaming God for the temptation, you need to turn to Him for the strength to resist the devil.

Our world wants to blame God for evil—but we know who is really to blame. Your calling as a believer is to stand in Christ's strength against the devil's temptations and not allow him the victory in your life today.

SATAN KNOWS YOUR STRENGTHS AND WEAKNESSES. DO YOU?

Day 292

You are of your father the devil, and your will is to do your father's desires. He was a murderer from the beginning, and has nothing to do with the truth, because there is no truth in him. When he lies, he speaks out of his own character, for he is a liar and the father of lies.

—John 8:44

In this exchange with the religious leaders of the day, Jesus unfolds for us the true nature of the devil. He is a liar. In fact, lying is at the very core of his nature.

One of the areas he lies about is doubt. He loves to place little deposits of doubt and questions into our minds. Now, doubt isn't necessarily wrong in itself, but there is good doubt and bad doubt.

For instance, having questions about what it means to truly believe in Christ is fine, as long as we bring these doubts to the Lord and seek the truth. But the enemy will try to rob you of your faith by causing you to mistrust God and His Word…and when you allow him that victory, that is "bad doubt." Because this is exactly what Satan wants you to do.

Let me remind you that Satan is just the same today as he was in Genesis. He puts questions in your mind, and tries to get you to reject what God has said.

So here's what I want you to do today. I want you to commit to spending time in God's Word every day, grounding yourself in His truth. When you do, you will build a hedge around you heart and mind, and be able to stand against the doubts the devil will put in your mind.

DON'T GIVE SATAN A FOOTHOLD IN YOUR MIND BY QUESTIONING WHAT YOU KNOW TO BE UNQUESTIONABLY TRUE.

Day 293

God is faithful, and he will not let you be tempted beyond your ability, but with the temptation he will also provide the way of escape, that you may be able to endure it.

—1 Corinthians 10:13

Over the years, as I have read Genesis 3, I have often asked myself a very obvious question. Why was Eve just hanging around and talking to the serpent? I'm not really sure why she was there, but hanging out by the forbidden tree was not the place to be that day!

When Satan tempts you and me, the Bible is very clear as to what we are supposed to do: Run! The Bible says to flee the devil and his temptations. We shouldn't try to debate him. We just need to get out of there!

Getting into a debate or discussion with Satan is a losing proposition. We aren't smart enough or powerful enough to outwit him. And Eve learned that the hard way!

It really comes down to personal choice. The devil will always come at us with the same lies. And God knows that we are weaker than Satan, and that's why He gives us a "back door" of escape in every temptation. It's our choice whether we resist him or engage him.

But unfortunately, we can sometimes let our pride get the better of us and we end up doing things our way. I encourage you today, when Satan throws temptation your way, turn to God and ask Him to show you that way of escape. And when He does, take it and run as fast as you can from that enemy of your soul!

DON'T TRY TO OUTWIT SATAN BECAUSE THAT'S A LOSING BATTLE.

Day 294

Therefore, just as sin came into the world through one man, and death through sin, and so death spread to all men because all sinned.

—Romans 5:12

Tragedy can strike without warning. When it does, it often leaves people devastated...and even ruined.

The first tragedy in history occurred the day both Adam and Eve ate the fruit God had forbidden. At that moment, the tragedy of sin struck with full force bringing evil and destruction into the world.

And the impact of that tragedy is still being felt today as their sin is passed from generation to generation, to every human being.

As I look at this greatest of all tragedies, it reminds me that when someone sins, it usually impacts others. It's almost impossible to think of a sin or anything evil that affects only the person involved. Unfortunately, the tragedy of sin is that it is often felt from generation to generation.

There is a word of hope, though, that is given to us by the apostle Paul. He tells us in Romans 5 that Jesus conquered sin by His obedient life and atoning death. If you are in Christ, you don't have to allow sin to get an iron-clad grip on you. Even though your life is continually impacted by the devastation of Adam and Eve's sin, you can stand victorious over it and be a beacon of life and hope to others who have felt the tragic effects of sin in their lives.

So take time today to thank God for His gift of salvation from sin through His Son, Jesus Christ. And determine...through the power of the Holy Spirit...to live in the victory that God has given you!

ASK GOD TO HELP YOU LIVE IN VICTORY OVER SIN AND SHINE HIS LIGHT INTO YOUR WORLD TODAY.

Day 295

For I know the plans I have for you, declares the LORD, plans for wholeness and not for evil, to give you a future and a hope.

—Jeremiah 29:11

God has a good plan for you, and He has had it right from the beginning! That's right. Even before He laid the foundation of the world, God wanted your life to accomplish something wonderful for Him.

God believed in the plans He had for you so much that He sent His Son to die on a cross, so that you would be able to succeed for eternity. Because of that sacrificial gift of love, you can live your life according to the great hope and joy that He has planned for you.

None of us are perfect, and we will fall short from time to time. But we can always get back on the road that the Lord wants us to be on.

God has a wonderful plan for you…and a wonderful destination. But you must choose if you want to fulfill those plans. Make the choice today to live for Christ and walk down whatever path He takes you. And when you run off the path, stop, look to God for guidance, and get back on the right path.

God has great and unimaginable plans for you. Plans for a future and a hope!

THANK GOD TODAY THAT HE HAS A PLAN FOR YOUR LIFE.

Day 296

Then the eyes of both were opened, and they knew that they were naked. And they sewed fig leaves together and made themselves loincloths.

—Genesis 3:7

One of the results of sin entering the world was shame. Before Adam and Eve sinned, they lived in purity and innocence and there was no shame. But when they sinned, they lost their innocence.

They felt shame when they all of a sudden realized their state.

We all are born with that sense of innocence. But unfortunately, children today lose that innocence far too quickly. As a result, children grow up too fast these days, in part because inappropriate things are being thrust upon them every day.

And even though we may want to protect our children as long as possible, we can only do so much. The loss of that sense of innocence early in life seems to be inevitable in our fallen world.

But there is still a lot you can do to help your children stay true to the Lord. One way is to be honest with them about the real results of sin. Help your children see that sin produces shame. Teach them that sin will cost them more than they would ever want to pay, take them places they don't want to go, and keep them there longer than they want to stay.

Sin brings guilt, shame, and grief. Sin promises pleasures, but produces pain. Sin promises life, but delivers death.

You may feel as if you're fighting a losing battle at times as you fight for the protection of innocence. But that's not true. Don't give up! Do what you can to protect your children, but more importantly, teach them the horrific consequences of sin.

TEACH YOUR CHILDREN THAT SIN PRODUCES SHAME, GUILT, AND GRIEF...AND WILL COST MUCH MORE THAN THEY WILL WANT TO PAY.

Day 297

I heard the sound of you in the garden, and I was afraid . . . and I hid myself.
—Genesis 3:10

Perhaps one of the most damaging effects of sin is that it separates us from God and others. In fact, Satan loves nothing more than to try and cut you off from God.

Now, one of the ways he tries to do that is to make you afraid to face God. While you are certainly supposed to fear the Lord, that is not the kind of fear God intends.

But Satan tries to tell us we need to be afraid of God...and that we should run from Him, much like when Adam and Eve hid in the garden.

Putting the wrong kind of fear of God in your heart is part of Satan's plan to trick you into separating yourself from God. But that's a dangerous position to put yourself in, because you end up running from the protection and love of God and open yourself up to the devil's attacks.

Have you ever thought about how impossible it is to hide from God? In fact, if you think about it, there's really no rational reason for running from God. He can see you no matter where you are. And more importantly, He can see your heart.

Instead of running from God, let me encourage you to run to Him! Don't separate yourself from the protection and love of the One who knows you and loves you intimately. Fear the Lord, but don't be afraid of Him.

LEARN TO LIVE IN THE REVERENTIAL FEAR OF GOD, BUT DON'T FALL INTO SATAN'S TRAP OF BEING AFRAID OF GOD.

Day 298

The Lord God called to the man and said to him, "Where are you?"

—Genesis 3:9

In Genesis 3:9 we find a very fascinating verse…when God called out to Adam and Eve, "Where are you?"

Obviously, God wasn't ignorant of where they were or what they were doing. Instead, I believe He wanted Adam and Eve to realize what they had done and come to grips with it

I also believe God is asking you the same question today: "Where are you?" He is asking, "How are you doing spiritually?" …not for His own sake, but for yours. He wants you to realize where you are and what you're doing. And He is asking this question because He loves you too much to let you stay put in your faith and become either sinful or stagnant.

Too many times we go through our day or week and don't take a spiritual assessment. And when we do stop and assess where we are…and we're honest with ourselves…we must answer, "I'm not where I'm supposed to be."

Let me encourage you today to listen carefully to the voice of the Holy Spirit within you. He is gently probing and asking you the important questions to jar you back into reality.

So, "Where are you?"

GOD IS ASKING, "WHERE ARE YOU?" WHAT WILL YOUR ANSWER BE TODAY?

Day 299

The LORD God said to the serpent, "Because you have done this, cursed are you above all livestock and above all beasts of the field; on your belly you shall go, and dust you shall eat all the days of your life. I will put enmity between you and the woman, and between your offspring and her offspring; he shall bruise your head, and you shall bruise his heel."

—Genesis 3:14-15

With the entrance of sin into the world, there also came the need for salvation.

And with the verse above, we get the first words of eternal hope written in the pages of Scripture. In them, God Himself promises that His sacrifice for sin would one day crush Satan. And this promise was fulfilled when Jesus' body was bruised, when He was beaten beyond recognition, and His blood poured out for us.

While Satan thought He had fully crushed Jesus when Jesus died on the cross, Jesus did not stay crushed! He rose from the dead in triumph, and as we are told in Romans 16:20, Christ will ultimately crush Satan in the end. When that happens, the devil will stay crushed for all eternity!

What a hope Christ gives us. And our hope is sure because our salvation comes through the blood sacrifice of Jesus Christ, the very Son of God!

This is why the chorus rings throughout heaven, "Worthy is the Lamb of God who takes away the sin of the world!"

So today, take time to thank God for His gift of salvation. Thank Him that Jesus was crushed for your sins…and that Satan will be crushed for eternity!

PRAISE GOD FOR THE HOPE YOU HAVE OF ETERNAL LIFE BECAUSE JESUS WAS CRUSHED FOR YOUR SINS.

Day 300

Blessed be the God and Father of our Lord Jesus Christ! According to his great mercy, he has caused us to be born again to a living hope through the resurrection of Jesus Christ from the dead.

—1 Peter 1:3

So many people are looking for hope and for peace. And how I praise God that we have the answer!

There is hope and there is peace for this world. But that hope and peace is found only in Jesus Christ.

This living hope means we can persevere through trials, rough spots, and even pain. This living hope means we may stumble and fall, but we will not falter completely because we are in Jesus Christ. And this living hope means we have a future that is sure and that we aren't alone today.

The peace God gives us when we accept Jesus is a peace that the world could never know. It means that we can enjoy serenity of heart no matter what happens to us. Why? Well, Jesus said it best in John 16:33, "I have said these things to you, that in me you may have peace. In the world you will have tribulation. But take heart; I have overcome the world."

Where is the hope? Where is the peace? In Christ! My prayer is that you will experience that hope and peace in your heart today…and every day.

IN CHRIST, YOU HAVE THE HOPE AND PEACE THAT CAN ENDURE ANY STORM.

Day 301

We have this as a sure and steadfast anchor of the soul, a hope that enters into the inner place behind the curtain.

—Hebrews 6:19

I think Hebrews 6:19 is one of the grandest statements in the Bible. I love the picture of hope as the anchor of our souls. A ship's anchor holds it steady even when the winds are blowing hard and waves are crashing all around.

This kind of hope is what helps us cope with the reality of disappointment. Mary Magdalene in Scripture is a good example of this truth. The Bible tells us that Mary was possessed by seven demons when Jesus first met her. After He cast them out, Jesus continued to love Mary despite her sin and failures.

So she was understandably very disappointed and distraught when Jesus was crucified and then buried in the tomb (John 20). He had done so much for her, and now all she could do was weep bitter tears for Him. But then the resurrected Christ appeared to Mary, and her hope was instantly restored.

That's what true hope…the hope found only in the resurrected Christ…can do for anyone who is overcome by disappointment and tragedy. No matter how devastating the circumstances, the hope found in Christ can overcome the pain.

Is your soul anchored in the hope of Jesus Christ? If so, you have an anchor that can hold you fast despite any storm!

HOPE IN CHRIST IS AN ANCHOR FOR THE SOUL. IS YOUR HOPE ANCHORED IN HIM TODAY?

Day 302

No, in all these things we are more than conquerors through him who loved us. For I am sure that neither death nor life, nor angels nor rulers, nor things present nor things to come, nor powers, nor height nor depth, nor anything else in all creation, will be able to separate us from the love of God in Christ Jesus our Lord.

—Romans 8:37-39

Many people wonder what the difference is between Jesus Christ and other religious leaders. Why should anyone believe that Christ is superior to Mohammed, Buddha, or some other religious figure?

Someone once put the difference this way: Most religious leaders want to take living men and move them toward death, but Christ wants to take dead people and move them toward life.

The difference between Christ and every other religious leader of history is rather profound! Only Christ has conquered death and has the power to give eternal life to all who believe in Him.

That's why in a chapter in which Paul spoke of all the trials that can come our way, he used the language of victory. Only the One who took demon-possessed people and turned them into Spirit-possessed people can give us eternal hope like this.

And Christ is still living and working...unlike the religious leaders of history. There is no other leader from the past who is still alive, leading and loving His followers...and giving them victory over the grave.

Praise God today that you are not following a dead prophet but a living Savior. And take time to share that good news with someone you know!

PRAISE GOD YOU ARE FOLLOWING A LIVING SAVIOR WHO GIVES YOU VICTORY OVER DEATH AND THE PROMISE OF ETERNAL LIFE WITH HIM!

Day 303

And he said to them, "Do not be alarmed. You seek Jesus of Nazareth, who was crucified. He has risen; he is not here. See the place where they laid him. But go, tell his disciples and Peter that he is going before you to Galilee. There you will see him, just as he told you."

—Mark 16:6-7

I absolutely love sports. And perhaps the most exciting part of a big game is the comeback. I just love it when my favorite team is losing and as the game is nearing the end they make a furious comeback to pull out an exciting victory! Now that's fun!

God loves comebacks, too. He loves to give us the chance to pull off our own big comeback when we are at the point of defeat. Sure, we all get defeated from time to time, but God always gives us the chance to stage a comeback and claim victory in His name!

One of the best examples of a spiritual comeback is the apostle Peter. He became one of the strongest and most vocal Christians in the time of Jesus. But you'll remember that before Peter became that leader, he denied the Lord three times in rapid succession even though he had loudly proclaimed his undying faithfulness to Jesus.

But Jesus didn't allow Peter to remain in defeat and failure. After His resurrection, Jesus met with Peter in Galilee, and there, Jesus restored him. And days later Peter went out and on the Day of Pentecost (Acts 2), boldly declared the name of Jesus to a large crowd. And from that day on Peter continued on the comeback trail, preaching the name of Jesus until his death.

Perhaps you are living in defeat today. Maybe you've failed in your job…or your marriage is in trouble. But with Christ, I want you to remember that a comeback is always possible! Ask God to help you renew your faith and boldness today, and start turning that seeming defeat into victory.

WE ALL EXPERIENCE DEFEAT, BUT WE DON'T HAVE TO STAY THERE. THROUGH CHRIST, YOU CAN PULL OFF AN AMAZING COMEBACK!

Day 304

Then {Jesus} said to Thomas, "Put your finger here, and see my hands; and put out your hand, and place it in my side. Do not disbelieve, but believe."

—John 20:27

Doubt is a natural disease of the human condition. And perhaps the person who epitomizes doubt most is Thomas.

Poor doubting Thomas has been stuck with his nickname because he said he would not believe that Jesus had been raised from the dead unless he personally saw Christ…and put his hands in the scars in Jesus' hands and side.

Thomas was convinced this was something he would never do! But good thing for Thomas, he got what he asked for!

Unfortunately, there are millions of doubters just like him in the world today who think they can never be sure about Jesus because they weren't there to see and touch Him. Yet, there is just as much proof for the resurrection of Christ as there is for any other event in history.

While we might not be able to physically sit by Jesus' side and touch His nailed-scarred hands and His wounded side, we can know with certainty that Jesus rose from the dead, just as God's Word said He did. My friend, Jesus is alive today! That is something you can bank on!

Many of the people who doubt Him today only do so because of misconceptions about the nature of faith, or because doubt is all they've ever known. But Jesus Christ can make even the strongest cynic fall on their face and confess with Thomas, "My Lord and my God!"

THANK GOD TODAY FOR THE REALITY OF CHRIST'S RESURRECTION…AND PROCLAIM TO HIM TODAY, "MY LORD AND MY GOD!"

Day 305

It is appointed for man to die once, and after that comes judgment.

—Hebrews 9:27

The saying is true...the only two things that are certain in life are death and taxes! Every human is destined to die, and that includes you and me.

We are reminded of the frailty of life almost every day. Death can find us no matter where we are.

But here's the good news. We don't have to fear death as believers because Christ's complete victory over death is our hope and assurance for eternity!

I can't tell you the number of times I have stood at a graveside and tried to comfort the family of the deceased. But I can tell you this...it makes all the difference if that family has the eternal hope of Christ in their hearts!

Thinking about death can cause us to reevaluate our lives— which is not a bad thing. So as you think about your life...and the fact that some day you will indeed die...let me ask you, are you living with the hope and certainty of heaven? I pray that you are. And I pray that you help others find this peace and security in Jesus Christ today.

BECAUSE CHRIST KEPT HIS APPOINTMENT WITH DEATH...AND THE RESURRECTION...YOU CAN LIVE WITH CERTAINTY AND HOPE!

Day 306

In the course of time Cain brought to the LORD an offering of the fruit of the ground, and Abel also brought of the firstborn of his flock and of their fat portions. And the LORD had regard for Abel and his offering, but for Cain and his offering he had no regard. So Cain was very angry, and his face fell.

—Genesis 4:3-5

Have you ever wondered why there is so much terrorism and violence in the world today? And that it seems only to be growing? I think the answer is simple: Violence is evidence of a sinful nature...a nature that came through the fall of Adam and Eve.

This impact of sin even showed itself in the first set of siblings when Cain so violently killed Abel. And after all the millennia of history, we are still dealing with the same violence and sin.

The reason nothing has changed is that the real problem resides deep in the human heart. All of us have inherited a sinful nature from Adam and we all have the propensity to commit violent acts...even if it is only with the tongue.

Salvation from sin and its impact on life can only come from a personal relationship with the one true God through Jesus Christ—a relationship that involves a radical change of the heart.

Sin is the same problem today that it was for Adam and Eve and their children. And there is only one cure—a complete change of heart that comes through forgiveness and salvation in Jesus Christ.

So don't be surprised by all the violence in the world today. It's the natural expression of the sinful human heart...just as it was for Cain and Abel.

THE HEART OF OUR SIN PROBLEM IS THE PROBLEM OF THE SINFUL HUMAN HEART.

Day 307

This people honors me with their lips, but their heart is far from me.

—Mark 7:6

When Jesus spoke the words of today's verse, He was talking about a religious system that had lost its way and was trying to please God by keeping rules and regulations. People thought they could earn their way to God even though their heart was far from Him.

That's why there are so many different religious groups out there today. People want to make up their own rules in the hope that they can earn their way to heaven.

But that's also what separates Christianity from other religious systems. Every other religion you can name is based to some degree on working hard to please God and earning your way into the highest possible place in heaven. What a sad and hopeless system.

But what a great hope we have in Christ! Instead of trying to work our way to Him with "lip service," He just wants us to come to Him and say, "I know I'm not worthy of heaven, so I ask for your forgiveness and admit that I'm totally dependent upon You." It's a transaction of a broken and needy heart.

But as you continue to live out your Christian life, it is so easy to fall back into works…and for your heart to grow cold. Today, is your heart far from God? Do you find yourself in a legalistic relationship with a heart that is cold?

Give up the works system of "religion," because it will only let you down! Instead, draw close to God in your heart and confess to Him once again that you are totally dependent on Him…and He will draw close to you!

DRAW CLOSE TO GOD TODAY…AND HE WILL DRAW CLOSE TO YOU.

Day 308

By faith Abel offered to God a more acceptable sacrifice than Cain, through which he was commended as righteous, God commending him by accepting his gifts.

—Hebrews 11:4

I have often wondered about Cain and Abel. It's such an interesting story, with an unexpected twist. God accepted and blessed the offering of Abel, but refused to accept Cain's offering.

Now, the two offerings were probably about equal in amount, perhaps even more so on the side of Cain. So why did the Lord reject Cain's offering? The answer has to do with Cain's attitude. Cain made his offering with an attitude of unfaith and duty. Abel came with an attitude of faith and reverence.

But before we come down too hard on Cain, we need to be careful about how we might be bringing unacceptable sacrifices to God today. For instance, every time we sing a praise song when God Himself is the furthest thing from our mind, we bring false worship and a wrong attitude. Leftover worship and sacrifice is not what God desires. He desires authentic worship given with all that we have.

But I'm afraid many of us give God the leftovers far too often, whether it is our money, our prayers, or some other form of our worship. If we're too tired to pray at night, we'll just go to bed and pray later. If we just have to have that new car…even though we really don't need it…we'll just give less and deal with the issue of our tithe later.

But it's in the seemingly small decisions like these that our attitude toward God is revealed.

What is your attitude toward giving of yourself and what you have to the Lord? Does He have it all…or just the leftovers?

GOD DESIRES YOUR VERY BEST…NOT JUST THE LEFTOVERS!

Day 309

Hear my prayer, O LORD; give ear to my pleas for mercy! In your faithfulness answer me, in your righteousness! Enter not into judgment with your servant, for no one living is righteous before you.

—Psalm 143:1-2

The last part of this passage is a powerful statement! Its meaning is clear: Our attempts at goodness can never be enough to meet God's holy and righteous standard. The Bible clearly states that we are an imperfect people who cannot stand before a holy God on our own merits.

So how do we become acceptable to God? By standing before Him clothed in the righteousness of Jesus Christ, Who has covered us with His blood. Christ started and finished the work of salvation that we could never have even begun, let alone finish, ourselves.

So let me ask you a question today: Are you seeking to be religious or righteous? You see, our human effort and works don't add up to anything in God's sight. Being religious by itself isn't enough because all religion can do is try to get us to clean up our act thinking that in doing so God will accept us.

We need to understand that what God desires is for us to be righteous, not religious. Which is why He sent His Son to die on the cross for you and me. Through Christ we have been made righteous in the eyes of God. We are fully accepted in Him.

So if you find yourself trying to please God by being religious, I encourage you to stop. Instead, embrace the truth that God made you righteous when you accepted Jesus Christ as your Savior. Live in the power of that truth today…and every day!

WHEN YOU ACCEPTED THE GIFT OF SALVATON IN CHRIST, YOU WERE MADE RIGHTEOUS AND ACCEPTABLE TO GOD!

Day 310

By faith Enoch was taken up so that he should not see death, and he was not found, because God had taken him.

—Hebrews 11:5

Perhaps you are struggling with giving in to the temptations of our world. If so, I want to give you a word of hope today by reminding you of a man named Enoch.

Enoch wasn't a great missionary, a powerful preacher, or a leader of the people. But he stood out in a depraved generation. Specifically, the Bible says that Enoch walked with God.

Now that's interesting because the Christian life is often described as a walk. It's about taking small steps, one at a time. And as we take these steps, God sometimes places an event in our path that becomes a turning point for us.

For Enoch, there was a turning point, a time in his life where he went from normal to extraordinary. I believe this turning point came when Enoch had a child at the age of 65. This experience pushed him to be a better child of God and walk in true faith.

Many times, even though we're Christians, we are pushed to live holier lives by some turning point or experience.

It's not only possible to walk with God in the midst of a perverse generation, it's what God expects from us. If there is something that is keeping you from walking as closely as possible with Christ, ask the Holy Spirit to show it to you and help you deal with it.

Perhaps today will be a turning point in your life...when your life will go from normal to extraordinary!

GOD WANTS YOU TO WALK CLOSELY WITH HIM AND TO LIVE A LIFE THAT IS EXTRAORDINARY.

Day 311

This Book of the Law shall not depart from your mouth, but you shall meditate on it day and night, so that you may be careful to do according to all that is written in it. For then you will make your way prosperous, and then you will have good success.

—Joshua 1:8

Most of us use calendars, day timers, organizers, and BlackBerrys to order our hours and days. In fact, we wouldn't dream of going through life without these handy appointment reminders!

But too many times we fail to keep our most important appointment of the day—our time with the Lord in prayer, Bible study, and meditation on His Word.

But like all of our other appointments, this daily meeting with the Lord does not just happen; it needs to be a habit and a daily decision to choose God over other matters.

I want you to take a moment to think about your daily routines. You had to decide at some point to do the things you do every day. And once you started doing them, you had to keep doing them until they became second nature to you. And it's really no different when it comes to our daily time with God!

Spending time with the Lord each day requires us to agree that it's important to meet Him. That's why we call Christianity a daily walk; it requires us to take daily steps of growth in Christ.

Just like children, we should walk humbly and take the hand of God, following Him no matter where He wants us to go that day.

My prayer for you today is that you will make it a habit to meet with God each and every day. And as you do, to learn to walk closely, hand-in-hand with Him!

WALKING WITH THE LORD MEANS MAKING A DAILY APPOINTMENT WITH HIM.

Day 312

As soon as his master heard the words that his wife spoke to him, "This is the way your servant treated me," his anger was kindled. And Joseph's master took him and put him into the prison, the place where the king's prisoners were confined, and he was there in prison.

—Genesis 39:19-20

We have an acute sense of justice and fairness, don't we? We have the idea that when someone does the right thing, they'll be rewarded. We also have the idea that when someone does something wrong, they'll be punished.

But it doesn't always work that way, does it?

It certainly didn't work that way in the life of Joseph. He was treated unfairly so many times and he even ended up in prison—not for doing the wrong thing, but for doing the right thing!

Joseph is the classic example of someone who responded with faithfulness to God in spite of the circumstances of his life. And as far as we are told in the Scripture, he did it without complaining or compromising and with great contentment!

So what about you? Are you experiencing a time of adversity right now…whether your fault or not?

If so, what's your reaction to God look like? Have you been complaining and anxious and upset? Or have you, like Joseph, remained content despite your circumstances?

Remember, God can give you peace and contentment no matter what you may be going through. So lean on Him today!

BE FAITHFUL TO GOD REGARDLESS OF YOUR CIRCUMSTANCES.

Day 313

Only remember me, when it is well with you, and please do me the kindness to mention me to Pharaoh, and so get me out of this house. Yet the chief cupbearer did not remember Joseph, but forgot him.

—Genesis 40:14, 23

In today's verse, we read one of the saddest sentences in the entire Bible.

Joseph had asked the chief cupbearer to remember him when he was released from prison. But when the cupbearer was set free, he forgot about Joseph altogether!

Joseph had to languish in prison for two more years after this point. Yet through it all, Joseph trusted in God's timing. And God used those two years to fashion Joseph into an incredible leader...right there in prison!

Have you ever faced adversity or pain or pressure...a "prison" of some kind that you couldn't understand? Have you ever faced trials, tests, tribulations in your life?

Sure you have! And why? It's called life.

As followers of Christ, you and I are never promised an easy road or an exemption from problems and stress. Despite what you may hear some preachers say! What's important to remember is that how we handle our problems and pressures and adversities make all the difference in the world.

Rarely can we change our circumstances...but we can always respond to our circumstances God's way. Just like Joseph did there in that jail cell!

Because...just like Joseph...God can use adversity in your life to move you forward as long as you live in obedience to Him and trust in His perfect timing!

YOU WILL ALWAYS HAVE PROBLEMS...IT'S HOW YOU HANDLE THEM THAT MAKES ALL THE DIFFERENCE IN THE WORLD.

Day 314

I want you to know, brothers, that what has happened to me has really served to advance the gospel, so that it has become known throughout the whole imperial guard and to all the rest that my imprisonment is for Christ.

—Philippians 1:12-13

Problems, pressures, and pain really can produce possibilities and opportunities in our lives. While we often can't see it at the time, God is always creatively and constructively at work in the life of the believer.

For example, Paul wrote two-thirds of the New Testament in a jail cell! Paul was a proactive missionary...one who traveled throughout the ancient world proclaiming the Good News. Yet God allowed him to go to prison.

And there in prison, Paul heard from God and recorded these great passages of Scripture that describe the Christian life and the Christian faith.

God's light shines so brightly in the darkness! And I dare say, if you surveyed your circle of friends, most of them would say the most defining moments in their lives would be times of adversity, times of trouble, and tests of character.

Because it's during these times that you experience the presence of God and the reality of His love!

Today, I challenge you to start thinking about your troubles in a new light. Instead of seeing them as negatives, thank God that He's working in your life!

GOD IS ALWAYS CREATIVELY AND CONSTRUCTIVELY AT WORK IN THE LIFE OF THE BELIEVER.

Day 315

But they who wait for the LORD shall renew their strength; they shall mount up with wings like eagles; they shall run and not be weary; they shall walk and not faint.

—Isaiah 40:31

Today's verse is a promise from God that I've put my trust in for many, many years. Because so often when we're in a "wait" mode in life, it's tempting to push Providence. Let me explain what I mean.

The word *Providence* isn't a word we use much today, but you can think of it like "pro-video"…that God can see the future and what will happen in our lives. But not only can He see what's going to happen, He's leading us and working all things together for His glory and our good!

Perhaps today…

> …You feel like you've been treated unfairly.
> …That business deal you just knew would go through disappeared.
> …That promotion you were expecting didn't happen.
> …Someone made a promise to you in marriage and didn't keep that promise.
> …You've prayed for your health or the health of someone you love and you've been given nothing but sickness.
> …All the doors you desire to be open seem to have been shut!

If God has you in some "wait" training today, remember that He puts a premium on patience and perseverance. And know that adversity can produce possibilities that you could never imagine in your life! Wait on God and trust in Him today (James 1:12).

ADVERSITY CAN PRODUCE POSSIBILITIES IN YOUR LIFE THAT YOU COULD NEVER IMAGINE!

Day 316

Count it all joy, my brothers, when you meet trials of various kinds, for you know that the testing of your faith produces steadfastness. And let steadfastness have its full effect, that you may be perfect and complete, lacking in nothing.

—James 1:2-4

One of the great preachers of all time was a man by the name of Charles Spurgeon. Spurgeon was a British preacher in the late 19th century who led a church in London that was reputed to be the largest church in the world during its day.

Spurgeon was such a powerful preacher. Yet by his own admission, he battled a deep, dark depression his entire life.

He even wrote a chapter called "The Minister and His Faithing Fits" in his book, *Lectures to My Students*. In this chapter, Spurgeon spoke about how a servant of God should respond to dark days in life.

From Spurgeon's point of view, he knew that whenever he experienced a time of darkness or depression, God was preparing him for a greater season of service than he had ever known before. He knew that God used depression in his life like a "John the Baptist"…as a forerunner of greater things to come.

Maybe today, you need to see your dark hour…your dark day…as a "John the Baptist."

Perhaps this dark hole in your life is just a forerunner of something better to come as you look to God and listen to Him in spite of how you may be feeling on the inside! Give your dark hour to God…wait patiently on Him…and see what He can do!

SEE YOUR DARK HOUR AS A FORERUNNER OF GOOD THINGS TO COME.

Day 317

Beloved, do not be surprised at the fiery trial when it comes upon you to test you, as though something strange were happening to you. But rejoice insofar as you share Christ's sufferings, that you may also rejoice and be glad when his glory is revealed.

—1 Peter 4:12-13

Why does God allow Christians to experience adversity and endure suffering in life? This is a question we've all asked at different times in our lives.

And while I can't definitively explain why you may be going through a particularly difficult season in life right now, I do know that the Scripture gives us several reasons why God allows us to have adversity in life.

One reason we suffer and have adversity is simply because we're Christians.

Jesus Himself said, "Blessed are you when people hate you and when they exclude you and revile you and spurn your name as evil, on account of the Son of Man! Rejoice in that day, and leap for joy, for behold, your reward is great in heaven...."

Now, I know that it's not a natural reaction to "leap for joy" when you're mistreated because of your faith in Christ! But I want to encourage you to know that God sees and hears what others say and do to you because of your faith. And He will reward you because of it!

So stand strong today...and remember the promise in James 1:12, which says, "Blessed is the man who remains steadfast under trial, for when he has stood the test he will receive the crown of life, which God has promised to those who love him."

GOD WILL REWARD YOU FOR ANY ADVERSITY YOU ENDURE ON HIS ACCOUNT!

Day 318

For the moment all discipline seems painful rather than pleasant, but later it yields the peaceful fruit of righteousness to those who have been trained by it.

—Hebrews 12:11

When you face adversity, you have two choices. You can choose bitterness or you can choose happiness. But you can't choose both.

In Psalm 105:18, the Darby Translation says of Joseph, "They afflicted his feet with fetters; his soul came into irons." I love that! Joseph was being developed as God was putting iron in his soul.

God knew difficult days would lie ahead for Egypt, and that it would require Joseph to have a durable and doable faith. There in prison, God steeled Joseph's soul without Joseph hardening his heart. And as a result, Joseph became a veritable velvet-covered brick—soft on the outside, but strong on the inside.

I know there are some who teach that life is a dream if you're a Christian. That all you need to do is name it and claim it and you'll be happy. But that kind of teaching isn't biblical teaching. And it produces wimps instead of warriors for God.

In these uncertain days, we need Christians who have steel and iron in their souls!

As today's verse says, you are trained into righteousness...and problems and pressure and adversities and trials are God's gifts to you to make you stronger...to make you better in your faith and your walk with Him!

GOD IS LOOKING FOR SOME STRONG AND STEELY SAINTS TODAY. WILL YOU RESPOND TO HIS CALL?

Day 319

For the wages of sin is death, but the free gift of God is eternal life in Christ Jesus our Lord.

—Romans 6:23

When we share our faith with others, we love telling the Good News part, don't we?

We love to talk about the love, the grace, the power of God to save, and the forgiveness of God. That's the wonderful good news of the Good News. We love to talk about heaven and we should!

But then there's that troubling other side, the difficult side that Jesus talked about: hell. In fact, Jesus talked about hell more than He talked about heaven. He talked about judgment. And the Bible talks about how people without Christ are spiritually dead. And we are told that the wages of sin is death.

While most people don't like to talk about that too much, integrity demands that we tell the Good News and the bad news. Because it's the bad news that makes the Good News the Good News!

Now, let me ask you a simple question today: Do you want someone to tell you the truth or do you just want them to tell you something to make you feel better?

If we're going to have integrity with our message and our mission in our witness for Christ, all of us must be willing to tell people the truth!

If God is going to use you, you must be a person with integrity…which means telling people the Good News and the bad news! Which will make the Good News truly…GOOD NEWS!

IT'S THE BAD NEWS THAT MAKES THE GOOD NEWS THE GOOD NEWS!

Day 320

And Joseph's master took him and put him into the prison, the place where the king's prisoners were confined, and he was there in prison. But the LORD was with Joseph and showed him steadfast love and gave him favor in the sight of the keeper of the prison.

—Genesis 39:20-21

There's a phrase in today's passage I want you to go back and reread: the LORD was with Joseph. Over and over again, we see this kind of phrase. The Lord was with Joseph. Everywhere Joseph went, the presence of God was with him!

In the very same way, no situation or circumstance can separate you as a believer from the presence of God. Joseph knew God was with him and was conscious of the presence of God in his life. In fact, that, my friend, was the secret to his life! He always knew…he always believed…that God was with him.

Whenever we experience times of adversity, we'll only advance and mature by trusting in God instead of ourselves. We'll succeed only when we're dependent on Him rather than running to the latest self-help craze.

Today, I encourage you to commit this verse to memory: "It is the LORD who goes before you. He will be with you; he will not leave you or forsake you. Do not fear or be dismayed" (Deuteronomy 31:8).

You can lose your job, you can lose your career, you can lose your mate, you can lose your home…you can even lose your youthful beauty! But if you're a believer in the Lord Jesus Christ, you cannot lose Him!

AS A BELIEVER, THE LORD IS ALWAYS WITH YOU!

Day 321

When Joseph came to them in the morning, he saw that they were troubled. So he asked Pharaoh's officers who were with him in custody in his master's house, "Why are your faces downcast today?"

—Genesis 40:6-7

Don't you just love the buoyant optimism and biblical hope of Joseph?

In today's passage, we see him showing concern about the cupbearer and the baker who shared a prison cell with him. They must have been thinking, "Joseph, have you forgotten, we're in prison?!"

Rather than wallowing in self-pity and whining about his circumstances, Joseph cared for others. Why? Because his trials had taught Joseph to use his thorns and his tests as a ministry to others.

After all, how can we help dry wet eyes if we've never shed a tear? How can we comfort those who are grieving if we've never experienced great grief?

That's why God rarely, if ever, uses people until they've come to a place in their lives where their own struggles and trials have made it possible for them to minister effectively.

In 2 Corinthians 1:3-5, Paul says, "Blessed be the God and Father of our Lord Jesus Christ, the Father of mercies and God of all comfort, who comforts us in all our affliction, so that we may be able to comfort those who are in any affliction, with the comfort with which we ourselves are comforted by God."

Because you and I have experienced God's grace and comfort in the midst of our pain and struggles, we are able to serve others. That's the blessing of adversity!

PRAISE GOD TODAY THAT HE CAN USE YOUR HURTS TO HELP HEAL THE HURTS OF OTHERS.

Day 322

On God rests my salvation and my glory; my mighty rock, my refuge is God.

—Psalm 62:7

Through the years, I've read a number of wonderful books on personal development, motivation, and success.

And of course, there are many definitions about what success really is. My friend, Christian author and speaker John Maxwell, gives one of the best definitions I have ever read. He says, "Success is knowing your purpose in life, growing to reach your maximum potential, and sowing seeds that benefit others."

So according to Maxwell, success is knowing and growing and sowing.

Bible teacher and author Charles Stanley writes, "Success is the continuing achievement of becoming the person God wants you to be and accomplishing the goals God has helped you to set." Stanley says that success is becoming the person God made you to be…the person God designed you to become in Him.

In our success-crazed culture, it's important to remember that real success isn't found in the label of your clothes, the brand of the car you drive, or even your title at work. True success is found in your character and in your commitment to what really matters.

It's not fame or fortune, but the fulfillment of God's purpose and God's plan for your life that really counts!

TRUE SUCCESS IS BECOMING THE PERSON GOD HAS MADE YOU TO BE.

Day 323

Beloved, I pray that all may go well with you and that you may be in good health, as it goes well with your soul.

—3 John 2

In yesterday's devotional, we talked about the true meaning of success. Because that's such a vital issue to our day and culture, I want to give you some additional insight on this important subject.

In addition to the definitions by Maxwell and Stanley (that I quoted yesterday), one of my favorite definitions of success was given by the famed pastor of the First Baptist Church of Dallas, Dr. George W. Truett. He said, "Success is knowing and doing the will of God in our lives."

I would add that success is the progressive realization and then actualization of the will of God in our lives. It is the providential hand of God working behind the scenes and our cooperation with God's work in our lives.

It is God's will that we prosper according to His plan. This doesn't mean that everybody's going to be rich. I'm not speaking of a prosperity theology here. But the fact is, God has promised to give us success…but that success is success God's way, which is the only way to live.

So what about you? Is the goal of your life to have success God's way…or to have success the world's way?

It's my prayer that you will come to fully understand the true measure of success according to God's economy…and that you won't be sucked into believing the world's definition of success any longer!

SEEKING SUCCESS GOD'S WAY IS THE ONLY WAY TO LIVE!

Day 324

Not that I am speaking of being in need, for I have learned in whatever situation I am to be content. I know how to be brought low, and I know how to abound. In any and every circumstance, I have learned the secret of facing plenty and hunger, abundance and need.

—Philippians 4:11-12

God is committed to your success as a Christian. And one of the ways He prepares you for godly success is…believe it or not…through tests of prosperity.

Now, usually you hear preachers talk a lot about tests of adversity…which we've spent a lot of time on over the past several days. But I'd argue that perhaps the most difficult test in life is not the test of adversity but rather the test of prosperity.

Most of us are able to handle adversity in Christ. But many of us have more difficulty in handling our prosperity when we have been so blessed in Christ.

Paul was able to handle both adversity and prosperity…as we note in today's passage. But what about you? How do you respond when God blesses you? Do you find yourself depending less on God when times are good? Do you ever find yourself spending less time in God's Word and in prayer when your needs aren't so pressing?

As you grow in your relationship with Christ, it's my hope that you'll fall so much in love with Jesus that your desire to spend time with Him won't hinge on how stressed out you are. That you will learn, as Paul did, to be content in both adversity and prosperity.

GODLY SUCCESS COMES THROUGH THE TESTS OF PROSPERITY.

Day 325

But the Lord GOD helps me; therefore I have not been disgraced; therefore I have set my face like a flint, and I know that I shall not be put to shame.

—Isaiah 50:7

What does a life of success God's way produce? It produces a life of significance. A life of godly success is a life of true significance.

At the young age of 17, Joseph knew where he was going. God had given him a purpose in life...a purpose he pursued with all his heart. And so it is with the man or woman who lives a significant life. They have a purpose and a reason to get up every day. They are enthusiastic about life!

As children of God, we have such a life as we're on a mission for Him! This is what a life of significance is all about. And this sense of calling, this sense of compelling, this sense of purpose makes our lives worth living.

Is your life driven by a sense of direction every day? Is your life one that is filled with a reason to get up in the morning?

It's my prayer today that you will attack the opportunities that God has put before you this day. Squeeze every moment out of the life that God has promised you! If you do, you will live a life that is truly successful...and significant.

A LIFE OF SUCCESS IS A LIFE OF SIGNIFICANCE!

Day 326

And Pharaoh said to his servants, "Can we find a man like this, in whom is the Spirit of God?"

—Genesis 41:38

A life of significance is marked by an overriding sense of direction, as we looked at yesterday. But it's also marked by a new dynamic.

As we see in today's verse, Pharaoh noticed that there was a different spirit in Joseph. In fact, everyone noticed it! This man—Joseph—had a different spirit about him because the Spirit of God was living in him...giving him a different, high-energy spirit about life.

Have you ever noticed that successful people typically have very high energy levels? Rather than being slow or lazy or just trudging through life, they are motivated, trekking purposefully through life.

People who have high emotional and spiritual energy levels often have a physical response that is positive. They are generally healthier. And they live at a God-directed pace...not a frantic, hurried, or stressed-out pace.

Which makes me wonder, does this kind of person describe you today? Are you worn out, stressed out, and put out? If so, ask the Holy Spirit living in you to revitalize your heart and mind today.

You may work long hours and you may get weary. But that hard work can be done with joy and purpose and enthusiasm when it is empowered by the Holy Spirit Who lives in you!

A life of significance is marked by this kind of dynamic. And I pray you will know it today!

THE HOLY SPIRIT HAS THE POWER TO GIVE YOU A NEW DYNAMIC.

Day 327

Not that I have already obtained this or am already perfect, but I press on to make it my own, because Christ Jesus has made me his own. Brothers, I do not consider that I have made it my own. But one thing I do: forgetting what lies behind and straining forward to what lies ahead, I press on toward the goal for the prize of the upward call of God in Christ Jesus.

—Philippians 3:12-14

Over the last few days we have been talking about a life of significance...and how it is marked by a direction and a dynamic. But that kind of life is also marked by a dedication.

What I mean by this is that success in the Christian life isn't a point...it's a process. Just think about Joseph for a moment. No matter what he endured, we never find him harping or complaining.

But rather, he was faithful to God as he disciplined himself in body, mind, and soul to fulfill God's call for his life. There wasn't any bitterness in him, even though his brothers betrayed him and his friends forgot him. God was with him and he knew it. And throughout his journey of life, Joseph fulfilled James 4:10: "Humble yourselves before the Lord, and he will exalt you."

Like Joseph, we are on a life journey. And this journey you and I have with Christ is a process through which He is growing us day by day.

As the apostle Paul reminds us in today's passage, we must press on toward the goal...the life of significance that God promises us as His children.

So keep dreaming, keep hearing the call, and keep responding to God in faith and trust, knowing that He will exalt you as you dedicate yourself to learning and growing in Him!

SUCCESS IN THE CHRISTIAN LIFE ISN'T A POINT, IT'S A PROCESS.

Day 328

Do not lay up for yourselves treasures on earth, where moth and rust destroy and where thieves break in and steal, but lay up for yourselves treasures in heaven, where neither moth nor rust destroys and where thieves do not break in and steal.

—Matthew 6:19-20

Over the past few days, we have been looking at what a life of success or significance looks like. We've seen that it's marked by a direction, a dynamic, and a dedication. And today, we'll see that a life of success is one that prepares for the future.

Joseph is a great example of this as he prepared for the future. He stored up in advance for lean and difficult times. And because he did, he saved people from death.

Just like Joseph, we are to so live and to so give...to so prepare for the future...that we can be used by God to help save others from eternal death! Isn't that our mission? Isn't that our ministry?

It is a fatal flaw, a mistake, to assume that God's goal for your life is material success or prosperity. God looks at your life not based upon your net worth, but upon your real worth. And your real worth is based upon who you are in Christ!

There are two kinds of people in the world. There are those who are building their own kingdom...and there are those who are building the Kingdom of God. So which one are you? Is your life wrapped up in building a kingdom for yourself...of material success and "prosperity"? Or is your life wrapped up in building for the future...building the Kingdom of God?

Because you're either building your own personal kingdom or you're partnering with God in building His Kingdom...the only thing that will last forever!

ARE YOU BUILDING GOD'S KINGDOM...OR ARE YOU BUILDING YOUR OWN?

Day 329

Trust in the LORD with all your heart, and do not lean on your own understanding. In all your ways acknowledge him, and he will make straight your paths.

—Proverbs 3:5-6

Our closest friends and associates are usually those people we get along with best and agree with on most issues.

That's not a bad thing! Whether it's a marriage or a business partnership, or just a close friendship, it's important that these relationships be built around common commitments and values...with a sense of unity and agreement. As Amos 3:3 reminds us, it's impossible for two people to walk together unless they are in agreement.

The same principle applies to your Christian life. In order to have a strong and vibrant relationship with Jesus Christ, you must not only walk with Him, you must be in agreement with Him.

The difference, however, is in your relationship with Christ. You aren't His equal. He is God Almighty, and you are dependent upon Him for your very life and breath! And as your loving Father, He knows what is best for you. So the best thing you can do is agree with what Christ says in His Word and follow His leading for your life.

Which begs the question: Do you and Christ agree on how you're living your life? Be honest! And if your answer is "no," then you need to change your direction so that your life will line up with His will. Trust in the Lord, and walk in daily agreement with Him, and He will direct your paths.

MAKE SURE YOUR LIFE AGREES WITH HOW GOD WOULD WANT YOU TO LIVE!

Day 330

Therefore, since we are surrounded by so great a cloud of witnesses, let us also lay aside every weight, and sin which clings so closely, and let us run with endurance the race that is set before us.

—Hebrews 12:1

One of the most important phrases in today's verse is "let us run with endurance." Now, that's a constant challenge of the Christian life!

Physically speaking, running is one of the healthiest activities that we can do. Running is great for the cardiovascular system and helps promote health in a variety of ways. The problem is that many people, when they start jogging, try to run too hard and end up burning out in just a short period of time.

Unfortunately, the same can be true of our spiritual lives. Many of us run hard and fast for Christ, but quickly lose energy and heart and find ourselves out of strength. Why? Because we haven't laid aside the things that hold us down. It's like trying to run with weights tied to your ankles!

The Christian life is a marathon, not a sprint. And the only way you will be able to run with endurance is to do what the verse today says…to lay aside the sin in your life that weighs you down.

Are you struggling today in your walk with Christ? If so, take an honest look at your life and see if there is any sin that is unconfessed. If there is, confess it and cast it aside. When you do, you will find you will once again be able to run…and do so with endurance.

CAST ASIDE ANY SIN THAT IS WEIGHING YOU DOWN, SO YOU CAN RUN WITH ENDURANCE.

Day 331

Then we who are alive, who are left, will be caught up together with them in the clouds to meet the Lord in the air, and so we will always be with the Lord.

—1 Thessalonians 4:17

I don't know if these are the final days or not, but I do know that I want to be found walking faithfully with the Lord when He comes back. Just like Enoch in Scripture, I want to be well-pleasing to God and be a witness for Him.

A few years ago, there was a movie entitled *A Walk to Remember,* a beautiful and uplifting story of life and love. I want to talk with you today about a walk that's really worth remembering, because it's an eternal walk of life and love with Jesus Christ.

First, let me remind you that the Christian life is a life of faith from beginning to end. You became a child of God by faith… trusting in Christ for your salvation. And each day you must continue to live by faith in the One who loves you and died for you.

But as you walk by faith with Christ through life, I want to encourage you to look down the corridors of time and realize that you can know with certainty that one day you'll be with Him in heaven forever! Like our verse today promises, you have an eternity of life with God to look forward to!

So don't let the concerns and pressures of today rob you of the joy of knowing you will one day be living with God…FOREVER! As you take this eternal walk with Christ, you can be as certain of heaven today as if you're already there. Take time today to meditate on that truth…and thank God for this incredible hope!

AS A CHILD OF GOD, YOU HAVE AN ETERNITY WITH GOD TO LOOK FORWARD TO!

Day 332

But concerning that day and hour no one knows, not even the angels of heaven, nor the Son, but the Father only. Therefore, stay awake, for you do not know on what day your Lord is coming.

—Matthew 24:36, 42

Many godly leaders today believe that this world is ripe for judgment. The nations, including America, can't keep going down an evil and sinful road without expecting God to call them to account for their deeds.

And if you read your Bible alongside the newspaper, you'll notice that there are things happening today that seem to indicate we are fast approaching the last days.

My friend, God will eventually say, "Enough is enough," and He will judge the wicked in the world, just as He did in biblical times. But our response should not be one of fear, rather a determination to live godly lives in a world in desperate need of our Savior!

God has given you and me clear warning of what is to come. I pray it will inspire you to go out and share with others the message of God's grace and justice—to see many people come to faith in Jesus Christ as Savior.

GOD HAS GIVEN US A WARNING OF THE WRATH THAT IS TO COME. PRAY GOD WILL USE YOU TO REACH MANY FOR HIM AS THAT DAY FAST APPROACHES.

Day 333

Then the Lord said to Noah, "Go into the ark, you and all your household, for I have seen that you are righteous before me in this generation.

—Genesis 7:1

Sometimes it's tough to be a man or woman who walks with God. But imagine how hard it must have been for Noah. The Bible tells us that except for Noah and his family, the hearts and minds of everyone in his generation were so evil that sin is all they could think about.

Noah was a man who stood against the prevailing tide of society. He stood alone—and he stood out like a sore thumb when the evil people around him laughed and taunted him as he lived righteously and built the ark in his front yard.

Since our generation is much like Noah's, the question of the day is this: Are you going to stand against the tide of society? I realize the powerful presence of evil in our society; I know that it's very difficult some days to live godly in the midst of such a perverse generation. But we must wade into the water and stand strong against the heavy tide of society.

Noah proclaimed to the people around him that it would rain soon. Since rain had never touched the earth before this time, people thought this was ridiculous and laughed all the more. And just like Noah, we're doing the same thing today: proclaiming the wrath of God that is to come…and the hope that is found in Jesus Christ.

People may laugh or ignore us, but we know something that Noah also knew: God is faithful to deliver on His Word. So let me encourage you today to keep standing firm as you live for Christ, and keep sharing His Word with those around you. Some will hear and believe!

DETERMINE TO STAND FIRM AGAINST THE EVIL TIDE OF OUR WORLD.

Day 334

By faith Noah, being warned by God concerning events as yet unseen, in reverent fear constructed an ark for the saving of his household.

—Hebrews 11:7

The story of Noah and the flood is a wonderful illustration of how Christ has saved us.

First, the Bible tells us in 2 Peter 2:5 that God saved Noah and his family from the judgment of the flood by means of the ark. The ark was a type of Christ, who is the ark of our salvation, saving us from the flood waters of sin and death.

Second, just as Noah's ark preserved him and his family in safety, so Christ keeps us in safety when our trust is in Him.

Third, the ark was both divine and earthly. It was divine because the Lord commanded Noah to build it, but it was also made of earthly substance. This is a picture of Jesus Christ, who was divine and yet man.

Fourth, the ark was sufficient for Noah and his family, all of the animals, and all of the food and supplies necessary to meet their needs. This is a picture of how the Lord is sufficient for everything we need.

Finally, the ark was kept safe during the 40-day storm. No matter how hard the waves tossed and battered it, the ark remained intact and strong. This is a wonderful picture of our security in Christ, once we have accepted Him as Savior. No matter how we may be battered by the storms of life, we are safe and sound in Christ.

You may know the story of Noah and the ark, but I hope you see it in a new light today as a beautiful picture of what we have in Christ. And that you will take time to thank God for all He has given you in Christ!

THE ARK IS A BEAUTIFUL PICTURE OF THE SALVATION WE HAVE IN CHRIST.

Day 335

Therefore, stay awake, for you do not know on what day your Lord is coming.
—Matthew 24:42

Sodom and Gomorrah were terribly sinful places that were so full of sin and evil that the Lord chose to remove them from the earth. Most people know the story of how God destroyed those two cities…a story which I believe has an important lesson to teach us.

Many people today believe that America is basically no different than these two famously sinful cities. If you believe that's true, then that begs the question, "Why would God destroy Sodom and Gomorrah, but let a place of equal sin continue unpunished?" That's a very good question, and one we need to consider carefully.

One conclusion could be that God is trying to get our attention! Between all of the natural and manmade disasters that have occurred in recent years, I believe God is trying to get through to us. Unfortunately, too many times we don't listen until our very foundation gets rocked to the core, which has happened to us over the last several years.

So what can we do? I strongly believe the only hope for America is a true revival among the Christians in this nation. And that revival can start with one person!

Today, why not ask God to start a personal revival in your heart and let it spread to everyone around you. Start a spiritual fire around you that will burn brightly and draw others to its light and warmth.

ASK GOD TO BEGIN A REVIVAL…AND THAT IT WOULD START WITH YOU!

Day 336

You also, be patient. Establish your hearts, for the coming of the Lord is at hand.

—James 5:8

Yesterday we talked about how the great story of Noah and the ark illustrates the truth that Christ is our ark of salvation and deliverance in whom we find safety and security.

Today I want us to look outside of the ark, so to speak, and see that just like Noah was delivered from the flood that beat upon the ark (which was God's judgment and wrath against an evil world), so will we be delivered from His wrath that will be poured out against sin in the last days.

Just as God spared Noah and his family in the ark, God will spare believers from the wrath of the end times. The Bible tells us that Christ will come like a thief in the night (1 Thessalonians 5:2). It also tells us that there will be no condemnation for those who are in Christ!

The Bible also reminds us that believers will be caught up and rescued from the judgment that is to come. Christ wants us to know that there is absolutely nothing in this world or below it that will stop Him from coming for His people.

But until that time comes, we are to live steadfastly and prepare for it by establishing our hearts firm in the Lord and His promises. Nobody but God the Father knows the exact hour when Christ will return, but we can be sure of the results!

I hope you will live today as if you know the end of the story...because you do!

THOSE WHO ARE IN CHRIST WILL BE SAFE IN HIM WHEN HE RETURNS TO JUDGE THIS WORLD.

Day 337

The end of all things is at hand; therefore be self-controlled and sober-minded for the sake of your prayers.

—1 Peter 4:7

Over the past few days, we have talked about the end times. As you look forward to the return of Christ, I want to give you four attributes that I believe are important for you to exhibit each day.

The first attribute is prayerfulness. Now is the time for sincere prayer. Pray for yourself, your family, and the work of Christ. Make prayer a part of your daily life.

The second attribute is faithfulness. We need to be faithful to Christ and to His church. Make it a habit to be fully engaged in a Bible-teaching church, being faithful to worship, to use your spiritual gifts to serve others, and to encourage other believers around you.

The third attribute is godliness. Don't be ashamed to live boldly and purely for Christ. Let your light shine each day so that your walk matches your talk.

The fourth attribute is readiness. Jesus Himself told us to be ready and watchful in these days. Lift your eyes up to the Lord daily. Live with the reality that He is coming again!

As long as you're still here, it's not too late to live for Christ. Measure your life against these four attributes, and make them a personal priority.

IN THESE CRITICAL DAYS, GOD WANTS US TO BE PRAYERFUL, FAITHFUL, GODLY, AND READY!

Day 338

And while they were going to buy, the bridegroom came, and those who were ready went in with him to the marriage feast, and the door was shut. Afterward the other virgins came also, saying, 'Lord, lord, open to us.' But he answered, 'Truly, I say to you, I do not know you.' Watch therefore, for you know neither the day nor the hour."

—Matthew 25:10-13

In the ancient world, a bridegroom might show up at the wedding unexpectedly, so the bridesmaids had to be ready. Of the ten bridesmaids in Jesus' parable, only five were ready when the bridegroom arrived. The other five were caught off guard and scurried around trying to get ready, but it was too late.

This is just like so many people today who want to put off the decision about their eternal destiny until some time in the future. But more often than not, that time never arrives—or when it does, it is truly not just later, but too late!

Christ doesn't want this to happen to anyone, which is why He told this parable. Like the wise bridesmaids, we need to be ready for Christ's soon return.

But we also need to share the message of Christ's return with those who have yet to know Christ. We live in an unbelieving and unsuspecting world that must hear the news that the bridegroom will return soon…and they need to be ready.

While many may not believe, some will! Remember, God is still in the business of saving people, and He will move mightily in the hearts of lost souls if you and I will be faithful to warn them to be ready.

WE NEED TO URGE PEOPLE TO DECIDE THEIR ETERNAL DESTINY BY ACCEPTING CHRIST NOW BEFORE IT'S TOO LATE.

Day 339

The LORD saw that the wickedness of man was great in the earth, and that every intention of the thoughts of his heart was only evil continually. And the LORD was sorry that he had made man on the earth, and it grieved him to his heart. So the LORD said, "I will blot out man whom I have created from the face of the land, man and animals and creeping things and birds of the heavens, for I am sorry that I have made them." But Noah found favor in the eyes of the LORD.

—Genesis 6:5-8

God has such a gracious memory when it comes to His people. God determined to destroy the earth because of its evil, but He remembered His servant named Noah. And God's gracious memory led Noah into the ark of safety!

God even remembers His people when they are unfaithful. I think of Samson in Judges 13–16. In this passage, we are told how Samson had disobeyed God and been led astray by evil, but he called out to God in a last gasp. God heard him and gave him one last great feat of strength to win a victory for the Lord.

There are countless other stories in the Bible of God sparing people because He remembers that there are those who still serve Him. Even as He destroyed the evil cities of Sodom and Gomorrah, God remembered to spare Lot.

And who can forget the thief on the cross next to Jesus? This was a lawless and convicted sinner, but he repented and the Lord remembered him…and he was brought into the Kingdom of heaven that very day. I know that man would join others, including me, in saying, "Praise be to God for His faithful and forgiving memory."

My friend, God remembers His own! He has promised to never leave you or forsake you. He will be faithful to lead you throughout your life and someday bring you home to be with Him.

THANK GOD TODAY FOR HIS GRACIOUS AND FAITHFUL MEMORY!

Day 340

Rejoice in the Lord always; again I will say, Rejoice. Let your reasonableness be known to everyone. The Lord is at hand; do not be anxious about anything, but in everything by prayer and supplication with thanksgiving let your requests be made known to God. And the peace of God, which surpasses all understanding, will guard your hearts and your minds in Christ Jesus.

—Philippians 4:4-7

God is peace. That is an old and simple statement that never loses its truth or power.

Peace is a soothing word that makes me think of the ability to remain calm even in the middle of a storm.

In fact, you may have seen the famous picture of a storm raging on the sea with the winds blowing and the waves crashing on a big rock that stands alone in the middle of the ocean. And when you look closer, you see a little bird nestled safely in that rock.

Now that's a picture of true peace! The kind of peace Paul writes about in today's verses.

This kind of peace is not an absence of problems or storms, but it is God's preserving presence in the midst of the storm! That's why Paul said this peace surpasses all human understanding.

I don't believe you can fully describe God's peace. You can sense it, you can own it, but it's almost impossible to articulate it. But it is that which God gives us just when we need it most. Just when you need a verse, He brings it to mind. Just when you need a friend, He brings one into your life. God will flood your heart with peace if you let Him.

Is your life characterized by peace? As a child of God, it should be. God knows you and loves you with an everlasting love. That's why He gives you His indescribable peace.

PEACE IS NOT THE ABSENCE OF STORMS, BUT GOD'S PRESENCE IN THE MIDST OF THE STORM!

Day 341

And God said, "This is the sign of the covenant that I make between me and you and every living creature that is with you, for all future generations: I have set my bow in the cloud, and it shall be a sign of the covenant between me and the earth. When I bring clouds over the earth and the bow is seen in the clouds, I will remember my covenant that is between me and you and every living creature of all flesh. And the waters shall never again become a flood to destroy all flesh."

—Genesis 9:12-15

Some days God seems so close to us that we practically feel Him right next to us. On other days, we don't have that sense that He's right next to us, and we ask, "Where are you, God?"

In reality, we know the answer even when we ask it. The answer is that God is always right there next to you, even when you don't sense His presence. I'm sure that Noah had this same feeling after about two weeks on that ark with all those animals—but he knew God was ever-present. And God came and revealed Himself to him.

One of my favorite songs is entitled *God of Wonders*. The title to this song is absolutely true and should be the anthem of our lives. Our God is a God of wonders and of miracles, large and small. Just when you think that perhaps He has left you, He is there with exactly what you need!

If it is raining or even pouring in your life today, ask God to make His love and presence real to you. He is always there with just what you need, just when you need it.

OUR GOD IS A GOD OF WONDERS AND MIRACLES. HE'LL GIVE YOU JUST WHAT YOU NEED, JUST WHEN YOU NEED IT!

Day 342

And I am sure of this, that he who began a good work in you will bring it to completion at the day of Jesus Christ.

—Philippians 1:6

When God put Adam and Eve in the Garden of Eden, He had a master plan for the earth and everything within it. And while sin distorted God's perfect creation, in His mercy and grace He is still working His glorious plan...not only for all of the universe, but for you and for me.

Noah and his family are a great example of this truth. Even though the world was corrupt in sin and God decided to judge it, He spared Noah and his family. In fact, God had a specific plan for them as they floated in safety on the ark while God judged the earth.

Noah's salvation reminds us that even where sin abounds, God's plans remain intact because His grace abounds even more.

There were probably a few times that Noah wanted to jump ship and give up, but he remembered God's promise and trusted God to finish the work that He had started on the earth. We should do the same and not become impatient or lose hope when it seems that God's plan is being frustrated in our lives.

God has a perfect plan for you. Don't be anxious or jump ship and try something else. Stay the course and allow God to fulfill His purpose in your life!

GOD HAS A PERFECT PURPOSE AND PLAN FOR YOU, SO BE PATIENT AS HE COMPLETES THAT PLAN.

Day 343

"This is the sign of the covenant that I make between me and you and every living creature that is with you, for all future generations: I have set my bow in the cloud."

—Genesis 9:12-13

There's something beautiful about a perfect rainbow stretching across the morning sky, greeting you with bright colors. But did you realize that it takes a storm as well as sunshine to bring about a rainbow?

That's why I think a rainbow is a perfect picture of our lives. In order for something beautiful and wonderful to happen, we must go through the storm before we can come out the other end into the sunshine!

The rainbow was a promise from God that the storms would never destroy His creation again. And He makes you the same promise personally! The rainbow is God's assurance to you of His goodness and faithfulness. And please notice that the rainbow is not a one-time promise, but a promise "for all future generations."

I hope that every time you see a rainbow you think of God's never-failing grace and forgiveness, and His constant presence with you.

In fact, the next time you see a rainbow, stop right there and thank God for His eternal faithfulness and goodness. And remember that you too can produce beautiful results if you look for God's sunshine through the storm!

THE RAINBOW IS A PROMISE OF GOD'S FAITHFULNESS AND ABIDING PRESENCE FOR EVERY GENERATION.

Day 344

Noah built an altar to the LORD and took some of every clean animal and some of every clean bird and offered burnt offerings on the altar.

—Genesis 8:20

The very first thing that Noah did after leaving the ark was to worship God. That's right; his first action on dry land was to give something back to the Lord! Noah offered sacrifices to God as he remembered to put first things first, which was to thank God for His deliverance.

This principle is one we should remember daily in our own lives. I hope you remember the Lord's goodness and faithfulness and seek to put Him first in your life. God deserves first place in your heart because He always remembers and provides for you.

I think there are too many times that we fail to thank God for His faithfulness to us. There is a very convicting and compelling story in Luke 17 of ten lepers who were healed by Jesus. After being miraculously healed and made complete for the first time in their lives, only one of the ten men came back to Jesus in thankfulness and remembrance.

Would you or I have been like the one who remembered, or like the many who forgot? I don't know the answer to that question, but I know what the answer should be. I want to be like the one man who remembered to come back and fall at Jesus' feet in praise and gratitude. And I believe you feel the same way.

So make it a point to put God first in everything you do today—and then do the same thing tomorrow and the day after that!

REMEMBER GOD'S GOODNESS AND FAITHFULNESS TO YOU EVERY DAY.

Day 345

For all the promises of God find their Yes in [Christ]. That is why it is through him that we utter our Amen to God for his glory.

—2 Corinthians 1:20

There was once a man named George Matheson, who lived in Scotland in the 19th century. He was a gifted man, but he had an eye disease that left him blind. Because of this disease, his fiancée broke off their engagement and his life was thrown into disarray.

On the day of his sister's wedding, he felt an urge from within to write a verse. One refrain he wrote that day was, "I trace the rainbow thru the rain, and feel the promise is not vain."

But history tells us that Matheson's original wording was, "I climb the rainbow thru the rain." What a wonderful picture for us as Christians! When we climb the rainbow that God gives us and take hold of His promise, we can make it through the rain.

In the course of our lives, we struggle with many things and we hope for many things. But whether in rain or sunshine, God's promise is right there for us. We just have to climb up and seize it.

The problem is not that God has forgotten His promise to us; it's that we have forgotten our promises to Him. When we commit our lives to Him, we promise to obey and seek Him, but often we forget the significance of this promise. It's time to remember the One Who remembers you!

Of course, the ultimate sign of God's promise is not a rainbow like the one He gave to Noah. It's the cross that Christ died upon. Because of Christ, all of God's promises are ours. There is no storm you cannot survive if you will cling to Him and His Word.

REMEMBER YOUR PROMISES TO THE ONE WHO REMEMBERS YOU.

Day 346

As were the days of Noah, so will be the coming of the Son of Man. For as in those days before the flood they were eating and drinking, marrying and giving in marriage, until the day when Noah entered the ark, and they were unaware until the flood came and swept them all away, so will be the coming of the Son of Man.

—Matthew 24:37-39

In the days of Noah, people were evil…pure and simple. They didn't obey or respect God, and sin saturated society until things became more and more corrupt and God finally said, "Enough!"

Many people wonder what our world today is coming to. Well, as believers in Christ, we don't have to wonder, because the Bible tells us that this world is coming to the end and ultimately to God's judgment.

Society is becoming so tolerant of sin and evil that it's become frightening. People live in fear, wondering whether rogue nations will use chemical or nuclear weapons to fulfill violent and evil intentions.

There doesn't seem to be a lot of hope as we look out at the world scene. But we need to remember Jesus said that just before He returns, the world will get worse and worse, as it did in the days of Noah. And that's our hope!

Jesus is coming back to set things right in this world and redeem those who are His own.

So don't be afraid of what may lie ahead for this world. God is in control, and nothing can remove His hand from His own!

AS THE WORLD GETS WORSE, WE HAVE THE HOPE OF JESUS' SOON RETURN.

Day 347

For by grace you have been saved through faith. And this is not your own doing; it is the gift of God, not a result of works, so that no one may boast.

—Ephesians 2:8-9

One of the great truths of Scripture is the unmerited favor of God. What the Bible calls "grace."

Today's verse reminds us that grace cannot be earned or deserved. It is an unmerited gift of God to those on whom He showers His love and mercy.

If you have ever shopped for a diamond, you know that the jeweler places it on a dark cloth so that the beauty and clarity of the diamond might be seen more easily. That's what God wants us to be, His diamonds shining and showing His grace in a dark and evil world.

As Christians, you and I aren't better than everyone else. We simply have accepted a gift that was given freely to us from God.

So my friend, as a person who has experienced the magnificent grace of God, take time today to thank God for showering you with that grace…His unmerited favor. And determine to let your life shine like the jewel on a dark cloth!

GRACE IS GOD'S UNMERITED GIFT THAT CANNOT BE EARNED OR DESERVED.

Day 348

Noah...did all that God commanded him.

—Genesis 6:22

Noah certainly lived a life of faith in the Lord. The earth had never seen rain before, so the idea of water falling from the sky was a ridiculous and silly notion in those days. But that didn't stop Noah from announcing the fact that God was going to send rain.

Noah believed God so much that he built an ark right in the middle in his own front yard. What would you or I do if God commanded us to do something like that? Maybe we would just laugh and say, "Lord, You must be joking."

But as our society moves further and further away from God, we as Christians may find ourselves being called by God to do things that seem pointless to others. That's when we need to remember that Christ has a bigger and better plan than we do.

In Luke 19:13, the Lord says to take care of His business until He comes back. God's business is establishing His Kingdom on earth, and it's our responsibility to be salt and light in this dark world. These are desperate times of sin and unfaithfulness, and you and I have a message of hope that we are to be spreading like wildfire!

The only way to leave a lasting impression for Christ and ultimately change the world is to live a life of complete faith and obedience. That's something you can do today. And as you are faithful each day, God will use you to do something world-changing!

GOD CALLS US TO LIVE A LIFE OF COMPLETE FAITH IN AND OBEDIENCE TO CHRIST.

Day 349

"Calling ten of his servants, he gave them ten minas, and said to them, 'Engage in business until I come.'"

—Luke 19:13

The great evangelist and preacher John Wesley once said, "Do all the good you can, to as many people as you can, for as long as you can." Now more than ever, we as Christians need to heed Wesley's words and do good to others as well as each other.

Believers in this generation should be in the business of encouraging and equipping one another for ministry to those in need. In light of that truth, I have a question for you today: What is God calling you to do?

I believe that Christ calls every believer to something great and something specific, which makes our assignment to discover what He has called and gifted us to do.

If you aren't sure what your gifts and calling are, start by serving Christ right where you are, and ask Him to make it clear what it is that you can do most effectively for His Kingdom. He will make it clear to you!

But getting started means you need to listen for God's call—which often comes as a quiet voice amid all of the loud distractions that the world throws your way.

God has given you talents and abilities to serve Him. Like the servants to whom the master entrusted his wealth, let's get on with the Lord's business until He returns!

GOD CALLS EVERY BELIEVER TO DO SOMETHING UNIQUE AND WONDERFUL FOR HIM.

Day 350

And Joseph said to his brothers, "I am Joseph! Is my father still alive?" But his brothers could not answer him, for they were dismayed at his presence. So Joseph said to his brothers, "Come near to me, please." And they came near. And he said, "I am your brother, Joseph, whom you sold into Egypt. And now do not be distressed or angry with yourselves because you sold me here, for God sent me before you to preserve life." And he kissed all his brothers and wept upon them. After that his brothers talked with him.

—Genesis 45:3-5, 15

In today's passage, we see a wonderful biblical picture about the power of forgiveness.

Imagine, if you will, that you were one of Joseph's brothers…one of the brothers who had sold him into slavery. If it were me, I'd think I was done for!

Joseph was now in an incredibly high position of power in Egypt. He could have done anything to these guys! He could have put them in jail or executed them on the spot.

But look at what Joseph says to his brothers: "Do not be distressed or angry with yourselves because you sold me here, for God sent me before you to preserve life" (v. 5). And then, look at what happens in verse 15: "And he kissed all his brothers and wept upon them. After that his brothers talked with him."

What a reunion! What a restoration! Joseph embraces these brothers who betrayed him and welcomes them into his presence. He gives them the kiss of love and the kiss of life. Joseph's example serves as a testimony to the power of God to forgive and the power that God gives us to enable us to forgive.

So I'd like to ask you, is there someone in your life who you need to extend forgiveness to today? Because if Joseph can forgive his brothers for what they did to him, you can also forgive…with God's help!

GOD WILL GIVE YOU THE POWER TO FORGIVE.

Day 351

See to it that no one fails to obtain the grace of God; that no "root of bitterness" springs up and causes trouble, and by it many become defiled.

—Hebrews 12:15

I've never claimed to be the world's best gardener. But I do know that if you let weeds go, they can take over an entire garden.

But to get rid of weeds, you have to do more than clip them off at the top. You have to dig them out by the root.

The same is true for the weed of bitterness.

Today's verse points us to the need to deal with bitterness. And for good reason. It's a root that can easily take hold in any one of our hearts.

What does a root of bitterness look like? It's holding on to an offense, either large or small. It's determining to hold hostility in your heart towards someone who's hurt you. It's anger towards another person that's not dealt with appropriately.

What happens is this offense, hostility, or anger festers and grows. And eventually, it can take over your life! It's like a cancer that metastasizes in the human soul.

Over the next several days, we're going to be taking a closer look at bitterness and why you shouldn't allow it to have any place in your heart or life. In preparation for that, I want to encourage you to ask the Lord Jesus to prepare your heart. Ask Him if there is any root of bitterness in your soul right now. And commit to digging up the weed of bitterness from the garden of your life!

IF LEFT TO FESTER, BITTERNESS WILL TAKE ROOT AND DESTROY YOUR LIFE.

Day 352

Let all bitterness and wrath and anger and clamor and slander be put away from you, along with all malice.

—Ephesians 4:31

One of God's clear commands is to put away any bitterness from our lives. Why is this so important?

Bitterness and resentment chain us to the past. Bitterness produces an emotional and spiritual bondage that will keep you from moving forward in your life. It's like carrying around excess baggage!

The emotional baggage of bitterness will slow you down and keep you from becoming the person God intends for you to be.

And yet so many people are chained to the past...they're slaves to something that happened many years ago. And as a result, they can't get past it and they can't get on with their lives.

Now, I'm not saying that we all don't have things in our past that still hurt...wounds that take a long time to heal. But what I am saying is that we don't have to let those dark spaces in the past determine how we act, think, and feel now and in the future!

As a believer, you can tap into God's power to leave what happened in your past...in the past. And through His power, you can cut those chains of bitterness that keep you in bondage.

If bitterness has a hold on your heart today, ask God to help you put it away...for good.

BITTERNESS IS EMOTIONAL BAGGAGE THAT WILL KEEP YOU FROM BECOMING THE PERSON GOD INTENDS YOU TO BE.

Day 353

Search me, O God, and know my heart! Try me and know my thoughts! And see if there be any grievous way in me, and lead me in the way everlasting!
—Psalm 139:23-24

Yesterday, we looked at one reason we should dig the root of bitterness out of our lives: Bitterness chains us to the past.

Another reason we should remove bitterness from our lives is because it contaminates our personalities. Bitterness will make you negative, hard, brittle, critical, and caustic. I don't know about you, but I never want those things to be used by people to describe me!

But bitterness isn't happy with just affecting you. It spills out onto others. So many families are torn apart because of bitterness, resentment, and unresolved conflict in the home.

It's why so many churches have been divided and destroyed…and why so many businesses have been soured and their effectiveness destroyed. Bitterness can't help but contaminate everyone and everything it touches!

If you're struggling with bitterness today…if you have yet to deal with it…then I urge you to do so just as quickly as possible.

It's time to take those feelings to the Lord Jesus. As you do, use today's verse as your prayer to ask God to show you the way forward.

BITTERNESS CAN'T HELP BUT CONTAMINATE EVERYONE AND EVERYTHING IT TOUCHES.

Day 354

Behold, the LORD's hand is not shortened, that it cannot save, or his ear dull, that it cannot hear; but your iniquities have made a separation between you and your God, and your sins have hidden his face from you so that he does not hear.

—Isaiah 59:1-2

When Leonardo da Vinci was painting the magnificent Lord's Supper, he got into a bitter argument with a fellow painter.

Feeling that he was mistreated, da Vinci was determined to get back at this coworker. So when it came time to paint the face of Judas Iscariot, da Vinci painted the face of that painter on the face of the betrayer.

Da Vinci was pretty proud of himself until it came time to paint the face of the Lord Jesus. Because when he tried to paint it, he had an artistic block. He couldn't draw the face of Jesus!

The great da Vinci was so consumed by his hatred and revenge that it wasn't until he erased the face of the painter in the face of Judas and asked God to forgive him that he was able to paint the face of Christ in the Last Supper.

This is such a vivid picture of what bitterness will do to your relationship with Christ. It will color and contaminate it!

You cannot have a growing relationship with Jesus Christ if you are in bondage spiritually to bitterness. It will be impossible to pray. It will be impossible to worship. It will be impossible to witness. And it will be impossible to serve God effectively.

So if you have resentment in your heart today or are holding on to your hostilities, let them go. If you do, you will find your relationship with Christ will become deeper and sweeter than you have ever experienced before.

BITTERNESS WILL COLOR AND CONTAMINATE YOUR RELATIONSHIP WITH CHRIST.

Day 355

Be angry and do not sin; do not let the sun go down on your anger, and give no opportunity to the devil.

—Ephesians 4:26-27

A few years ago, I read an article in the *USA Today* that talked about the devastating effects of anger. In fact, the article listed hostility and anger (especially in men) as dangerous to our physical health causing high cholesterol and obesity!

Not only will bitterness chain you to the past, contaminate your personality, and color your relationship with Christ, but it will choke your productivity. This includes your physical productivity, your emotional productivity, and your mental productivity.

When you live with bitterness and anger in your life, you can't be productive in anything you do. Your mind will be distorted and you'll make all kinds of bad decisions.

What's funny—and tragic—is that a lot of people call anger and bitterness something else entirely. They call it "righteous indignation" or their "sense of justice." But I call it something else: sin!

When we live with the unrepentant sin of bitterness, it rips us from the inside out. And ultimately, if we don't root it out of our lives, we become critical and cynical!

Take time today to look at your life and see if you are giving place to bitterness and anger. If so, ask God to help you root it out so that you can live fully for our Lord.

IF YOU LIVE WITH BITTERNESS AND ANGER IN YOUR LIFE, YOU WILL NEVER BE FULLY PRODUCTIVE FOR CHRIST.

Day 356

"Blessed are the merciful, for they shall receive mercy."

—Matthew 5:7

Yesterday we talked about bitterness and how it can have such a devastating impact on your life.

While bitterness can develop as a result of some big event, major abuse, or significant mistreatment in your life, too often, it comes from some small hurt that is nourished and nurtured until it grows to be a powerful force and factor in your life.

As a pastor, I can tell you—I've seen the effects of bitterness again and again and again. And the natural question is, why on earth do people do this to themselves?

Well, some people do it because it just feels good. They're sort of addicted to their anger. Others do it because they have a sense of self-righteous superiority or pride.

Whatever the reason, it's resulted in a lot of angry Christians who are long on mad and short on mercy! And those lives don't reflect our Savior's love, mercy, and grace, which is infinite.

That's why I encourage you to model Christ today by showing mercy to someone who doesn't deserve it. Cut someone some slack! Assume that their intentions are good! I think you'll be amazed how your life will change when you do this on a consistent basis.

MAKE IT YOUR GOAL TO BE A PERSON WHO IS SHORT ON MAD AND LONG ON MERCY!

Day 357

Love suffers long and is kind; love does not envy; love does not parade itself, is not puffed up; does not behave rudely, does not seek its own, is not provoked, thinks no evil; does not rejoice in iniquity, but rejoices in the truth; bears all things, believes all things, hopes all things, endures all things.

—1 Corinthians 13:4-7 (NKJV)

I'd like to draw your attention to the phrase *thinks no evil* in today's passage. What does it really mean when Paul says that love "thinks no evil"?

In the Greek of the New Testament, the word *thinks* is actually a bookkeeping term. It's a word that means "to take into account" or "to write down as a permanent record." Which is exactly what a good bookkeeper or accountant does. They write things down as a permanent record.

In accounting, keeping permanent records is vital. But in relationships, it's deadly! If we're going to know the love of Christ and live in the fullness of that love and grace, we need to delete those negative relational files we've collected over the years! Because after all, this is what Christ has done for us (Romans 5:13).

The Scripture says that God has not imputed sin to us. Aren't you glad? When it came to settling the score, Jesus took the sin that was written down against us upon the cross. He died and rose again on the third day and because of what Christ has done for us, God has forgiven and forgotten our sin. It is deleted…forever gone.

Yet how many of us are unwilling to delete the files? If you want to have strong, vibrant, healthy relationships, you must keep short accounts. Because love doesn't keep score and love doesn't settle the score. Love believes all things and hopes all things. Love thinks no evil…but thinks the best.

LOVE DOESN'T KEEP SCORE BUT INSTEAD KEEPS SHORT ACCOUNTS.

Day 358

Beloved, never avenge yourselves, but leave it to the wrath of God, for it is written, "Vengeance is mine, I will repay, says the Lord."

—Romans 12:19

So often, people want to be the judge, juror, and executioner of other's faults and failures and sins. Can you relate?

It's like getting older…when physically we get less flexible and our muscles can stiffen after exercise. The same thing that happens to us physically can happen to us mentally and emotionally too.

Our attitudes can stiffen and harden, and over time we become cynical, brittle, critical, and inflexible. Instead of just growing older, we grow colder because we're holding on to some things that we refuse to let go.

You know, Jesus had some very, very strong words to the unforgiving and the unrelenting…to those who tried to play God with others. In fact, Jesus rejected them, while at the same time He accepted the sinful, repentant woman who came to Him to begin anew.

Perhaps you're carrying around a judgmental attitude today. If so, do you know what the antidote for that problem is? It's the power of forgiveness given to us by Christ Himself!

If you have a critical spirit in your heart today, ask God to help you let it go. Don't let your attitude stiffen and harden as you grow older! Instead, let God be the judge!

AS YOU GROW OLDER, DON'T GROW COLDER.

Day 359

> "Pay attention to yourselves! If your brother sins, rebuke him, and if he repents, forgive him, and if he sins against you seven times in the day, and turns to you seven times, saying, 'I repent,' you must forgive him."
>
> —Luke 17:3-4

Over the last few days we have talked about dealing with anger and bitterness. If this is a problem in your life, the antidote is the power of forgiveness. So how do you discover this power?

First, you must admit the bitterness in your heart. Now, I know this is a problem for a lot of people. We call it everything else. We try to justify it. As I've mentioned before, Hebrews says this thing of bitterness is a root. And the problem with roots is that they're invisible. Roots of bitterness are deep down within, so you have to find the root and then dig it up.

Second, ask God to help you to freely and fully forgive others. You say, "But it's so hard, I just can't do it!" You know, I don't often feel like forgiving. That's why we need faith to forgive, to do it anyway in obedience.

Third, accept God's plan. In Genesis 50:20, Joseph says to his brothers, "As for you, you meant evil against me, but God meant it for good…." God uses the troubles, sorrows, heartache, and pains in our lives to shape us, to make us more like Him, and to grow our character.

I think the greatest definition of forgiveness I've ever heard is this: "Forgiveness is giving up my right to hate you for hurting me."

It's my prayer that you will give God room to make this happen in your life today!

FORGIVENESS IS GIVING UP YOUR RIGHT TO HATE SOMEONE FOR HURTING YOU.

Day 360

He [Jesus] said to him the third time, "Simon, son of John, do you love me?" Peter was grieved because he said to him the third time, "Do you love me?" and he said to him, "Lord, you know everything; you know that I love you."

—John 21:17

In Matthew 10:29, Jesus tells us that not even a sparrow falls to the ground apart from God's knowledge. And if God cares about a sparrow, don't you think He would also care about you as His child?

Well, He does. It's an amazing thought that the same God who made the stars and calls them all by name is the same God who knows the number of hairs on your head!

Not only does He know the number of hairs on your head, He knows your name. Your name is recorded in God's infinite mind and heart!

God knows you. He knows your past as well as your future. And the thing He knows better than anyone else is your heart.

Now, that might strike terror into your life at times when you realize that God sees the worst about you! But what's so wonderful is that even though God knows the worst about you...He loves you anyway!

Perhaps today, you feel a little like Simon Peter...you feel like somehow you've let God down. Perhaps you feel ashamed of something from your past...a failure that you can't seem to get past.

If so, remember that with Jesus, no failure is final. The Lord restored Peter...and He can restore you as well! God knows your heart. He knows all about you. He knows what you need...and He wants to meet you at the point of your need today. Will you let Him?

EVEN THOUGH GOD KNOWS THE WORST ABOUT YOU, HE LOVES YOU ANYWAY!

Day 361

In the year that King Uzziah died I saw the Lord sitting upon a throne, high and lifted up; and the train of his robe filled the temple.

—Isaiah 6:1

I'd like for you to think with me for a moment about the glorious position of our holy God.

In today's verse, Isaiah describes his vision of God when he saw the Lord sitting on the throne of the universe.

Now, Isaiah and the rest of the Israelites were deeply troubled because their earthly king, King Uzziah, was dead. They were grieved...and they were concerned about the future. Yet when Isaiah entered into the presence of the Lord, he realized that there was a greater One than any earthly king sitting upon the throne of the universe. His name is holy God, the Lord of Hosts!

Like the Israelites, it's easy to worry about the future...and wonder what's gone wrong and what will happen next in our world.

But as believers in the Lord Jesus, we don't have to wonder! We don't have to wring our hands worrying, because we know that our God is sitting on the throne of the universe. Remember that there is no panic in heaven...only plans. God never walks up and down the streets of heaven wringing His hands wondering about what He's going to do next.

So no matter what's going on in your world today...no matter how out of control things may seem...remember that God is still on His throne!

Today, it's my prayer that you will get your mind off the earthly and temporary, and fix your eye of faith on your Lord and Savior, Jesus Christ, who is gloriously reigning and ruling upon the throne of this universe!

THERE IS NO PANIC IN HEAVEN...ONLY PLANS.

Day 362

But while he was still a long way off, his father saw him and felt compassion, and ran and embraced him and kissed him.

—Luke 15:20

The parable of the prodigal son in Luke 15 is one of the most dramatic pictures of God's love in all the Scripture.

And today's verse is one of my favorites. What a picture of God Almighty! What a picture of God the Father! I like the way Phillips translates the last phrase of this verse. It says, "His father's heart went out to him while he was yet a long way off."

This is not a father who can't wait to punish his sinful son. This is not a father who has written that boy off as wasted and worthless. This is a loving, caring father who cannot wait to embrace his son and to welcome him home! That's why, when the father sees his son off in the distance, he leaves the house and runs down the road to meet him and to embrace him and bring him in.

What I hope you see here is a picture of the Father's love for you. God's love is an aggressive love...a love that's eager and excessive. His love is approachable. And His love is abundant.

The prodigal son's father didn't hold back his love from his child. And God will never withhold His love from you!

GOD IS A LOVING FATHER WHO CAN'T WAIT TO EMBRACE YOU AND WELCOME YOU HOME!

Day 363

The steadfast love of the LORD never ceases; his mercies never come to an end; they are new every morning; great is your faithfulness. "The LORD is my portion," says my soul, "therefore I will hope in him."

—Lamentations 3:22-24

God...is...faithful. Allow me to restate that again. God is faithful! He will do what He says He will do!

And not only is God faithful and reliable, but He is committed to your spiritual growth and maturity. First Thessalonians 5:23-24 says, "Now may the God of peace himself sanctify you completely, and may your whole spirit and soul and body be kept blameless at the coming of our Lord Jesus Christ. He who calls you is faithful; he will surely do it."

I love that! Because it promises you and me that God is constantly working on us...creatively, constructively, and continually. The Spirit of God is working in your body and in your soul. And His purpose is to make you more like Him!

But you need to remember that God is patient...and that God is persevering. And according to Philippians 1:6, "he who began a good work in you will bring it to completion at the day of Jesus Christ." When God gets through with you, you're going to stand complete, perfect in the glory of Jesus Christ. Someday you shall arise in His likeness. Someday you will be like Jesus!

That's God's goal in your life and mine...and He will be faithful to perform it!

GOD IS CONSTANTLY WORKING ON YOU, CREATIVELY, CONSTRUCTIVELY, AND CONTINUALLY.

Day 364

The heavens declare the glory of God, and the sky above proclaims his handiwork. Day to day pours out speech, and night to night reveals knowledge. There is no speech, nor are there words, whose voice is not heard. Their measuring line goes out through all the earth, and their words to the end of the world.

—Psalm 19:1-4

God speaks to us today in the skies…through His creation. We can know God…we can see the presence of God…by simply looking up at the sky.

The Greek word for *man* in the ancient world and in your New Testament is *anthropos,* which means "the upper-looking one." Animals look down, but God created man to look up into the heavens to see His glory and to experience His power in creation.

And when we do, God speaks to us in the starry skies!

Indeed, the heavens declare the glory of God. As the psalmist says, "Day to day pours out speech, and night to night reveals knowledge." Creation is constantly, continually, and eternally speaking. And when we look into the creation, we know that because there is a creation, there must be a creator!

Now, you may not be a morning person, but I'd encourage you…if you want to catch a glorious glimpse of your Creator…to get up early one morning this week to watch the sun rise. I can assure you, seeing His handiwork in creation will speak words of encouragement to your soul!

GOD IS CONSTANTLY, CONTINUALLY, AND ETERNALLY SPEAKING TO US THROUGH HIS CREATION.

Day 365

"Heaven and earth will pass away, but my words will not pass away."
—Luke 21:33

In today's verse, Jesus promises us that His words are eternal. This means not one jot, not one tittle, not one mark, not one word will pass away!

God's Word is infallible. In all that it teaches and all it affirms, it is correct and right and perfect. And the Word of God is inerrant. That is, there are no errors in the Scripture.

Now, when people deny the authority of Scripture, they deny the authority of God. It's as simple as that. In effect, when they deny or distort the authority of Scripture, they deny and blaspheme the work of the Holy Spirit in giving us the Scriptures.

They even defame the deity of Jesus Christ, who is described in the Bible as the incarnate Word of God. His very name is the Word of God! And while the Word of God and the God of the Word are not identical, they are inseparable. You cannot separate God from His Word. Even Jesus came believing and teaching and preaching the Word of God, affirming the Old Testament and proclaiming the new and the living way of salvation.

That's why you can trust the Bible through and through. From Genesis to Revelation, we have the Word of God…consistent, clear, and concise…telling us how to go to heaven, how to know Jesus Christ, how to experience eternal life, how to know and worship God.

This is the Word of God! And you can trust it as your ultimate authority of life and truth!

YOU CAN TRUST THE BIBLE THROUGH AND THROUGH AS IT IS THE VERY WORD OF GOD.

**Please call 1-800-795-4627 or visit jackgraham.org/store
to order the following products:**

ASK: Unleashing the Power of Prayer	$ 7.95
Dealing with Doubt	$ 2.95
Experiencing God's Peace in a Pressure Cooker World	$ 2.95
How to Raise Sexually Pure Kids	$ 2.95
Is the Bible Just Another Book?	$ 2.95
Kingdom First	$ 2.95
Marriage by the Book	$ 2.95
New Life in Christ	$ 2.95
Revealing the Fraud of the Da Vinci Code	$ 6.95
Rock Solid	$ 2.95
Stress Test	$ 2.95
Triumph! How You Can Overcome Death and Gain Eternal Life	$ 7.95
True Womanhood	$ 2.95
The Truth About Influence	$ 4.95

**These books by Jack Graham
are available at quantity discounts:**

Courageous Parenting	$17.99
A Hope and a Future	$12.99
Lessons from the Heart	$18.95
Life according to Jesus	$12.99
A Man of God	$17.99

1-800-414-7693 (1-800-414-POWER)
jgraham@powerpoint.org
jackgraham.org